The Bhopal Tragedy

Citizens Commission on Bhopal

The Commission, representing a broad spectrum of some 50 environmental, consumer, and church organizations, trade unions and workers' groups, medical, legal, and scientific organizations, and individuals, supports prompt and effective relief and redress for the victims of the Bhopal tragedy.

It is also encouraging the rigorous investigation of what really happened at Bhopal and the dissemination of independent research on issues raised by that disaster. It is working toward the adoption of more effective policies at the local, national, and international level to assure that workers and communities at risk throughout the world have the right to know and to act in protecting themselves from such man-made disasters.

This is one of a series of background reports prepared for the Commission. The views expressed in these reports are those of the authors and do not necessarily reflect the views of the Citizens Commission or its members.

Several persons active in the Commission made significant contributions to this report, including A. Karim Ahmed of the Natural Resources Defense Council, Clarence J. Dias of the International Center for Law in Development, and David Dembo of the Council on International and Public Affairs. Anthony Mazzocchi of the Workers' Policy Project and Les Leopold of the Labor Institute contributed the foreword. The two authors, however, remain solely responsible for the contents of the report.

Further information on the work of the Commission is available from Citizens Commission on Bhopal, 45th Floor, 122 East 42nd Street, New York, NY 10168 (212/949-0049).

The Bhopal Tragedy

What Really Happened and What it Means for American Workers and Communities at Risk

by
Ward Morehouse and M. Arun Subramaniam

A Preliminary Report for the Citizens Commission on Bhopal

...the struggle of man against power is the struggle of memory against forgetting.

Milan Kundera
The Book of Laughter and Forgetting
(translated by Michael Henry Heim)
New York: Alfred A. Knopf, 1981.

Income from the sale of this book, after meeting publication costs, will be used to seek justice for the Bhopal victims and to support efforts of communities and workers in both India and the United States exposed to high-risk technologies to assert their rights to know and to act in protecting themselves and their environment.

The views expressed in this book are solely those of the authors and do not necessarily reflect the views of the Citizens Commission on Bhopal or any of its members.

ISBN: 0-936876-47-6

Manufactured in the United States of America

For information on how to order additional copies of this book, write to:
Council on International and Public Affairs
777 United Nations Plaza
New York, NY 10017 USA

CONTENTS

FOREWORD

We are all saddened by the tragedy in Bhopal, India. It is a catastrophe which has no parallel in industrial history. 5,000 to 30,000 lives lost. 200,000 injured. 30,000 to 50,000 who are too ill to ever return to their jobs. This is the Hiroshima of the chemical industry.

We are fearful. Millions of citizens both here and abroad live near toxic facilities and waste sites. We do not know what chemicals surround us. Those of us whose livelihoods depend on these industries must also worry about our jobs and our communities' economic well-being. Our families' economic survival and physical health are held hostage by the production of toxics.

We are angry. We are angry with Union Carbide for its negligent policies and practices. We are angry with the chemical industry which plays roulette with our lives each day of the year through its mad rush to produce toxic after toxic. We are angry at governments for not protecting us. And we are angry at ourselves for not doing more to control the production of toxics.

But sadness, fear, and anger need to be transformed into a meaningful and lasting response to this tragedy. On March 20th and 21st, we began a process of action in Newark, New Jersey, a Third World city which is surrounded by one of the largest petro-chemical complexes in the world. Two hundred and fifty representatives of the medical, scientific, environmental, church, and labor communities came together to analyze, discuss, and debate the key questions surrounding the tragedy in Bhopal.

The conference featured representatives from Indian environmental, medical, and health and safety organizations who provided us with first-hand accounts of the events in Bhopal. They were joined by scientific, medical and environmental, and industrial experts from the U.S. who have had direct experience with the issues raised by Bhopal.

For the first time in the United States, details of the events leading up to the tragedy were shared. Comprehensive medical reports on the plight of the victims were revealed. Expert after expert confirmed our worst fears —-that we are all at risk, that such a tragedy can and will happen again, that this is not just a Third World problem of development but rather a world problem of toxic production. And we began the hard work of developing strategies for preventing future Bhopals both here and abroad.

Sagar Dhara, a speaker from India's health and safety movement captured the spirit and the message of the conference when he said: "We now should know we are not so different. Human blood pulses through all our veins. We are connected in this tragedy by our common frailties and our common risk. No one is immune."

These dedicated panelists from India and the U.S. gave their time, their energy, and their resources to catalyze a significant process of human chemistry. New knowledge was gained and shared. New energy and imagination was unleashed to bring attention to the immediate needs of the Bhopal victims as well as to the needs of all those exposed to toxic production.

A positive chain reaction in human chemistry has been unleashed. The work of the conference participants has already helped to form the Citizens Commission on Bhopal, a broad-based coalition of major enviromental, church, and labor groups to provide an independent, forceful, and coordinated voice to insure that the victims and the events of Bhopal will not be forgotten, or distorted.

This book, inspired by the Newark Conference, moves beyond the discussion there to bring up to date the Bhopal story and its implications for workers and communities at risk everywhere. But the chain reaction started in Newark, and we invite you to join that positive, human, caring reaction to this, the worst industrial disaster in history.

Les Leopold   Anthony Mazzocchi
Director, Labor Institute   Director, Workers' Policy Project

New York
December 1985

PREFACE

On the night of December 2/3 in Bhopal, the capital city of the state of Madhya Pradesh in India, there occurred the worst industrial disaster in history. An historic event is bound to inspire more than one book, and Bhopal is proving to be no exception. Why, then, this particular book?

There are two basic reasons. The first is our growing sense that the real story of what happened on that awful night in December 1984 and with what consequences for the people of Bhopal was not well understood, especially but not only in North America. We seek to tell that story simply and directly, based on the best available evidence now available.

The second reason for this book is our increasing uneasiness that Bhopal, even though an historic event, might slip into the obscure recesses of history with scarcely more than a ripple unless a determined effort were made to change the way in which we deal with hazardous industries and substances. Such industries and substances are fast becoming a ubiquitous feature of modern industrial society, and the time has long since come for us to develop more effective methods for dealing with them and to see that the risks they pose are more equitably distributed.

Some of the principal actors in the Bhopal affair have compelling motivation to settle the matter as quickly and quietly as possible, hoping that everything will return as much as possible to the *status quo ante*. If that were to happen, all of the agony, suffering, and death visited on the people of Bhopal by Union Carbide will have been in vain. Through this book, we hope to help empower citizens, including workers and people from surrounding communities whose lives are at risk from hazardous industries, to prevent that from happening, and instead, to work toward the objectives of seeing that justice is done to the victims of Bhopal and that the risks posed by hazardous industries and substances are minimized and much more fairly distributed than they are now.

Our book is directed in the first instance toward citizens in the United States—those who care about the safety and well-being of workers and communities exposed to risk, who are concerned about the poisoning of our environment by many of the products of modern industry, and who believe the U.S. economic system, for all of its vaunted productiveness, could be made much fairer in distribution of costs and benefits. Americans have a special relationship to the Bhopal disaster. If the parent Union Carbide corporation, a U.S. company whose worldwide operations are controlled and directed from its corporate headquarters in Danbury, Connecticut, bears major responsibility for what happened in Bhopal—and we believe there is not a scintilla of doubt this is so—then it was an instrument of U.S. industry that wreaked such terrible havoc on the poor people of Bhopal.

Americans, therefore, have a particular responsibility to see that the lessons of Bhopal are not forgotten. But we hope our book will be of interest to concerned citizens elsewhere as well, including India where a number of citizen groups have been at work for many months to see that justice is done to the victims and that the lessons of the worst industrial disaster in history are not forgotten.

While we have drawn on the best available evidence at the time of writing to tell the Bhopal story, we recognize that we have not presented the final word. There are numerous investigations still in progress, some of which will take months or even years—e.g., epidemiological studies on the long-term health effects—to complete. Furthermore, litigation is underway in both Indian and American courts, and one of the compelling arguments for urging that at least some of this litigation run its course is that we will get closer to the truth of what happened and who is responsible as facts become established in courts of law through the discovery process and rigorous rules of evidence.

Nor is the Bhopal story over. Events are occurring daily as the consequencesof this awful tragedy continue to unfold. We ourselves are actively involved in observing and analyzing these events, and even, in our boldest moments, trying in a small way to influence their outcome.

We ask our readers to remember these circumstances as they get into the book. They should approach it as an interim report on a complex and dynamic situation. It reflects the best distillation of our knowledge and understanding at the time of writing but almost certainly will have been overtaken by subsequent developments in at least some respects by the time of publication.

Given all of the foregoing circumstances, it has seemed to us only prudent that we label this book a ''preliminary report'' to the Citizens Commission on Bhopal.

This book was inspired by and is based in part on a conference held in Newark, New Jersey, on March 20-21 on the theme, ''After Bhopal: Implications for Developed and Developing Nations.'' The conference was organized by the Workers' Policy Project in New York City and co-sponsored by the following concerned organizations:

> Academy of Medicine of New Jersey
> American Public Health Association
> Council on International and Public Affairs
> Department of Preventative Medicine and Community Health,
>   New Jersey School of Medicine and Dentistry
> District 8 Council of Oil, Chemical, and Atomic Workers Union
> International Center for Law in Development
> The Labor Institute

While we have drawn heavily on presentations made to the confenrence, particularly in Chapters 5 and 6, which examine the implications of Bhopal for worker safety, public health, and environmental protection in the U.S., the book is not intended to be a proceedings of the conference. We have also used many other sources, especially in the chapters on the Bhopal tragedy in the first part of the book. Chapters 1 and 2 are based in considerable measure on the investigative reporting of one of the authors (MAS) who has been covering the Bhopal story for *BusinessIndia* since it happened.

These circumstances have dictated a rough division of labor between us. MAS has been largely responsible for preparing first drafts of the chapters on what happened in Bhopal and the impact of the disaster, while WM has concentrated on the subsequent chapters dealing with legal developments and implications for the U.S. However, each of us has had an opportunity to rework the other's initial drafts in order to try to produce a common end result.

This book would not have been possible without a lot of help from many different people, including but not limited to the following:

Tony Mazzocchi, Director of the Workers' Policy Project (and former Vice President of the Oil, Chemical, and Atomic Workers

Union), for contributing the foreword and for deciding in the first place to organize the Newark conference, and his colleague, Les Leopold of the Labor Institute, for his help with the Foreword, for providing us with tapes of the Newark conference, and for lending a hand in numerous other ways.

Clarence Dias of the International Center for Law in Development,

David Dembo of the Council on International and Public Affairs, Karim Ahmed of the Natural Resources Defense Council, and Kevan Cleary, public interest attorney in the Bhopal case (until his recent appointment as a U.S. Attorney in Brooklyn) for reading various parts of the manuscript and contributing to the end result in other ways too numerous to mention.

Judi Rizzi for struggling, first, to produce a transcript of the Newark conference, then to render in coherent form on a word processor the manuscript of the book, and finally, to cope with the seemingly endless drafts and revisions, all in record time.

The list of those who helped in various other ways is much longer. While it is not possible to name all who have played a part, we do need to mention several more persons. Corrin Ferber, an intern from Brandeis University at the Council on International and Public Affairs during the summer of 1985, helped to organize and catalog our growing Bhopal resource and documentation collection. Karen Flaherty and Sylvia Tognetti of the Christic Institute provided helpful support in preparation of drafts of Chapters 1 and 2. Ashok Bhagat, a chemical engineer, provided crucial technical advice. Paul Shrivastava of New York University, and himself a native of Bhopal, gave generously of his knowledge of the situation in Bhopal and provided numerous other valuable insights. So also did Claude Alvares, an Indian investigative journalist who has been following the Bhopal story. Martin Abraham of the International Organization of Consumers Unions helped in identifying citizen groups concerned with Bhopal and other industrial disasters. Mark Reynolds, as his contribution to this collective undertaking, made copies of all of the tapes from the Newark conference.

We would be remiss if we did not express appreciation as well to the speakers at and participants in the Newark conference for giving us insights into the implications of the Bhopal disaster for U.S. workers and communities at risk. Ashok Advani of *BusinessIndia* helped make it possible for one of us to come to the U.S. to take part in the Newark conference and participate in the writing of this book. Critical financial support for preparation of the book was also made available by the J. Roderick MacArthur Foundation.

None of the foregoing, needless to say, bears responsibility for what is written in the pages following. That responsibility is ours alone.

We are pleased that this book is being published as a report for the Citizens Commission on Bhopal. That body, a logical sequel to the Newark conference which in many ways inspired it, reflects the determination of a broad spectrum of consumer, environmental, church, worker, scientific, and other organizations to see that justice is done to the victims of the Bhopal tragedy, that those responsible are held accountable, and that the lessons of that tragedy are not forgotten.

New York and Bombay
January 1986

Ward Morehouse
M. Arun Subramaniam

Chapter 1

WHAT HAPPENED AT BHOPAL

A Critical Choice

On the night of December 2-3, 1984, a gas leak at a small pesticides plant in central India owned by a subsidiary of Union Carbide Corporation devastated a whole city. On the basis of what we know so far, it appears that Union Carbide was not only grossly negligent in the design, maintenance, and operation of the plant but equally callous in its response to the accident. The Bhopal disaster, which killed several thousand people and injured another 200,000 in the space of a few hours, constitutes a watershed in the history of the chemical industry. It revealed, perhaps for the first time, just how hazardous this industry really is and just how vulnerable we all are to its failures.

The disaster at Bhopal confronts us with a critical choice. If on the one hand, justice is done to the poor and hapless victims, even the minimum program of action we have set forth in Chapter 3 will require a substantial portion, if not all, of the company's assets. An unambiguous message will thus be delivered to hazardous industries the world over that they can no longer give the quest for profit priority over human life. If on the other hand, Union Carbide is allowed to settle the case for an amount that does not significantly diminish its assets, the opposite message will be conveyed: that these industries may continue business as usual, comfortable in the knowledge that any company in a similar situation can expect to survive the worst industrial catastrophe in history. The impact of litigation on Union Carbide will determine for years to come the standard of conduct for hazardous industries around the world.

The Origins of the Tragedy

Union Carbide's operations in India go back to the beginning of this century, when it began marketing its products there. In 1924, an assembly plant for batteries was opened in Calcutta. By 1983, Carbide had 14 plants in India manufacturing chemicals, pesticides, batteries, and other products. Union Carbide's operations in India were conducted through a subsidiary, Union Carbide India, Ltd.(UCIL). The parent U.S. company (UCC) held 50.9 per cent of UCIL stock; the balance of 49.1 per cent was owned by various Indian investors. Normally, foreign investors are limited to 40 per cent ownership of equity in Indian companies, but the Indian government waived this requirement in the case of Union Carbide because of the sophistication of its technology and the company's potential for export.

Managerial control of UCIL is exercised by Union Carbide through its Eastern Division, which is headquartered in Hong Kong. UCC has a reputation among observers of U.S. corporate management of having a relatively centralized decision-making style. The precise nature of the control exercised by the parent company over its Indian subsidiary will emerge during the discovery process in litigation now before the Federal District Court in New York, because it is a key legal issue. In the meantime, according to a delegation of international (including U.S.) and Indian trade union officials who made an on-the-spot investigation of the Bhopal tragedy in April 1985 (*The Trade Union Report on Bhopal*, published by the International Confederation of Free Trade Unions in Brussels and the International Federation of Chemical, Energy and General Worker's Union in Geneva in July), "Bhopal workers and national union officials maintain that even minor production and maintenance decisions were made by Hong Kong."

In 1969, Union Carbide set up a small plant in Bhopal, the capital of the state of Madhya Pradesh, to formulate a range of pesticides and herbicides derived from a carbaryl base. The process of carbaryl manufacture begins with the reaction of carbon monoxide with chlorine to yield the intermediate phosgene. Phosgene is in turn reacted with monomethylamine to produce methyl isocyanate (MIC), the principal gas (but not the only one, as is discussed in Chapter 2) involved in the Bhopal tragedy. In the final stage, MIC is reacted with alpha napthol to produce carbaryl, different concentrations of which are used to formulate the end product.

Until 1979, UCIL imported both MIC and alpha napthol from its parent. Only in that year did the company commission its own facility to manufacture MIC, using the process described above. The MIC facility was located in the existing Carbide plant to the north of the center of the city, adjacent to an existing residential neighborhood and barely two kilometers from the railway station. According to the 1975 Bhopal Development Plan, the MIC unit should have been located, along with other obnoxious and hazardous industries, in the northeast end of the city away from and downwind of heavily congested areas. Indeed, M.M. Buch, a former government official who was instrumental in preparing the 1975 Bhopal Development Plan, asserts that UCIL's initial application for a municipal permit for the MIC plant was rejected, but Carbide ultimately received approval from the central government authorities and proceeded with construction of the MIC unit within its existing plant.

It is certainly true that some squatter settlements grew up around the Carbide plant after it was opened in the late 1960s. The very poor have no place else to go, and vacant land in an urban setting operates as a powerful magnet. But some of the areas worst affected by the gas leak had been inhabited for many decades before the Carbide plant opened. The problem, therefore, was not that some people decided to live near the plant after it was built but rather that the plant was located very close to large pre-existing concentrations of people.

An explanation for the disaster of December 2-3 has to be sought not so much in Carbide's decision to manufacture MIC but in the manner in which it did so. At the design stage itself, a controversy arose regarding the question of whether substantial storage capacity for MIC was required (as at the Union Carbide MIC plant near Charleston, West Virginia), or whether nominal storage, determined solely by downstream process requirements, would suffice. The parent company, which provided the basic design of the plant, supervised its engineering, and defined operating procedures to run it, insisted on the former. UCIL, on the other hand, felt that the latter was preferable in that it was inherently safer.

According to the affidavit filed in the Federal District Court in Manhattan by Edward Munoz, a retired Vice President of the Union Carbide Corporation and Managing Director of Carbide's Indian subsidiary at the time this decision was made, the parent company insisted on large-scale storage.

Sketch Map of the City of Bhopal
With Location of Union Carbide Plant

As a result, three tanks 40 ft. long and 8 ft. in diameter, code numbered E610, E611, and E619, were built, each with a storage capacity of 15,000 gallons. One of these was a reserve tank to be kept empty and used for transfer of material in the event of an emergency involving either of the other tanks.

Hazardous Maintenance and Faulty Equipment

The plant had been shut down for a complete maintenance overhaul and to reduce inventories for over a month prior to the accident. The maintenance operation was almost complete and the plant ready to resume operations by early December. Around the 26th of November MIC plant operators were instructed by management to pressurize tank E610 containing approximately 42 tons of MIC in order to transfer some of it for processing. However, workmen found that despite feeding nitrogen into the tank they could not generate the required pressure to vent MIC. This suggested that one of the two pressure equalization valves of the nitrogen system, the outflow (or blowdown) valve was defective. Instead of attending to the defective valve, the management decided to switch over to tank E611 containing about 40 tons of MIC—a decision that was to prove so fatal in the light of subsequent events.

At about 9:30 p.m. on the 2nd of December workmen began washing out four lines downstream of the MIC storage area, all of which were connected to the relief valve vent header (RVVH). As its name suggests, the RVVH provides a relief line for toxic gases to be routed to the vent gas scrubber (VGS), in the event that a pressure buildup in any one of the tanks causes a large volume of gas to escape. The system is so designed that if the pressure within the tank exceeds 40 psig (pounds per square inch above atmospheric pressure), it causes a rupture disc fitted to the end of the RVVH line to give. The gas so released forces the relief valve to open which allows the gas to flow down the RVVH directly to the VGS.

A second line leads from the tanks to the VGS, called the process vent header (PVH). Connected to this line is the nitrogen pressurization system. MIC, a highly volatile compound, reacts violently with water. To ensure that MIC does not come in contact with moisture in the air, the chemical is stored under pressure and protected by a blanket of dry nitrogen. If the pressure in the tanks falls below the operating pressure of 2 psig, nitrogen is fed into the tank. Conversely, if the tank pressure exceeds 2 psig, some of that pressure can be reduced by venting nitrogen. These routine releases of gas are routed through the PVH to the VGS or the flare tower to be either neutralized or incinerated.

The VGS is a large, bottle-shaped steel vessel designed to neutralize toxic gas emissions. When the gas enters a scrubber, it reacts with caustic soda and is rendered harmless. A second safety device provided, the flare tower, is a tall steel structure that has a flame burning constantly on top. Gases from all over the plant can be routed to the flare to be incinerated at a safe distance from personnel and equipment. The line from the VGS to the flare tower allows gases that have not been completely neutralized to be burnt.

To return to the events of the 2nd and 3rd of December, workmen in the second shift were engaged in washing four downstream branches of the RVVH line. According to standard operating procedures, the maintenance crew had prepared the job (i.e., closed the isolation valve between these branches and the RVVH) and the operator concerned started pumping water under high pressure into the line. However, he noticed that the outflow of bleeder valves on these four lines were not

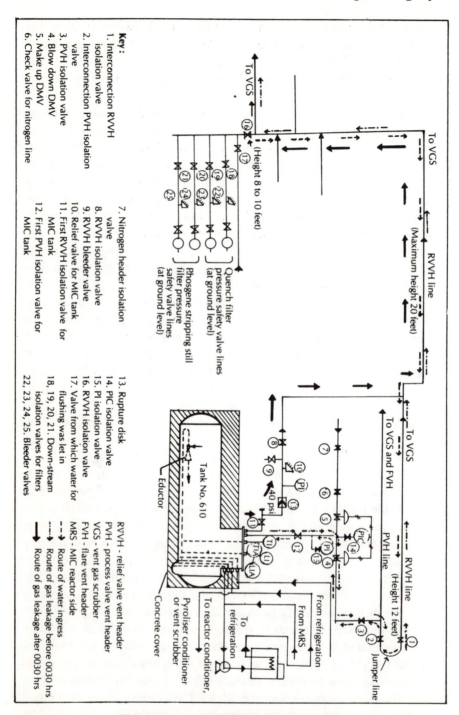

Key:

1. Interconnection RVVH isolation valve
2. Interconnection PVH isolation valve
3. PVH isolation valve
4. Blow down DMV
5. Make up DMV
6. Check valve for nitrogen line
7. Nitrogen header isolation valve
8. RVVH isolation valve
9. RVVH bleeder valve
10. Relief valve for MIC tank
11. First RVVH isolation valve for MIC tank
12. First PVH isolation valve for MIC tank
13. Rupture disk
14. PIC isolation valve
15. PI isolation valve
16. RVVH isolation valve
17. Valve from which water for flushing was let in
18, 19, 20, 21. Down-stream isolation valves for filters
22, 23, 24, 25. Bleeder valves

(Height 8 to 10 feet)

Quench filter pressure safety valve lines (at ground level)

Phosgene stripping still safety valve lines (at ground level)

To VCS

To VCS

RVVH line (Maximum height 20 feet)

To VCS

To VCS and FVH

RVVH line (Height 12 feet)

PVH line

From refrigeration

From MRS

To reactor conditioner, or vent scrubber

To refrigeration

Pyroliser conditioner or vent scrubber

Concrete cover

Eductor

Tank No. 610

40 psi

Jumper line

RVVH - relief valve vent header
PVH - process valve vent header
VCS - vent gas scrubber
FVH - flare vent header
MRS - MIC reactor side

→ Route of water ingress
-→ Route of gas leakage before 0030 hrs
➜ Route of gas leakage after 0030 hrs

Diagram of MIC Storage Tank

releasing water at the same rate at which it was being pumped in; two were completely clogged and the others were only partly clear. He stopped washing and reported the problem to the supervisor.

After a lapse of about 15 minutes, under instructions from the supervisor,the workman resumed washing the lines. But the bleeders remained obstructed and soon water accumulated in the pipes. In a matter of minutes water reached the RVVH isolation valve located about eight feet from the ground. As the isolation valve could not provide a complete seal on the line and in the absence of a slip bind to reinforce it, water soon passed the valve and entered the RVVH. The RVVH which runs mostly at ground level, reaches 20 feet at its highest point. Once water had accumulated to a height of 20 feet, it began draining by gravity flow back into the system.

The absence of the slipbind was a crucial factor leading to the gas leak. We now know that—again in contravention of established Carbide procedures—the written instructions which the workers were to follow in washing out these lines omitted the procedure that a slipbind be inserted, according to a report by the Union Resarch Group of Bombay, ''The Role of Management Practices in the Bhopal Gas Leak Disaster'' (June 1985). This report is based on extensive interviews with Carbide workers at the Bhopal plant.

How the Water Got in the MIC Tank

This in itself could not possibly have caused the accident. Water moving down the RVVH would still have to pass the relief valve and the rupture disk in order to find its way into the tank. But this was improbable for two reasons. First, the relief valve fitted on a relatively unused line would have been far less corroded than similar valves on the main process lines and would have effectively prevented water from getting past it. And second, the rupture disk was found to be intact when it was checked on the 30th of November and would, therefore, have effectively sealed off this route to the tank.

But in fact water did have an alternative route to the tank. This was through the ''jumper'' or shunt line connecting the relief valve vent header and the process vent header (see diagram of MIC storage tank). Until May 1984, hardly six months before the accident, these two lines had been unconnected and each performed a separate function. The plant's management, however, had long felt the need for a standby line in the event that either the PVH or the RVVH needed to be shut down for repair. The jumper line provided an easy solution:

if the need arose, routine emissions could now be routed through the RVVH or, alternatively, larger releases through the PVH.

As the parent company held sole responsibility for all design decisions relating to the Bhopal plant, the Indian subsidiary must have secured the parent company's approval for this process modification. According to the Indian Central Bureau of Investigation (India's FBI) inquiry into the disaster, this approval was given in May 1984 in order "to provide a route for toxic gases to the scrubber which neutralizes the gas in case any one of the vent headers was undergoing repairs." So the jumper was installed. And on the night of the accident, as a section of the PVH was under repair, the jumper line had been left open.

The Runaway Reaction

Thus water that had entered the RVVH now traveled down the jumper into the PVH past the nitrogen outflow valve and into tank E610. One estimate is that at least 200 liters (about 50 gallons or 450 pounds) of water entered the tank, setting off a rapid exothermic reaction. The amount of water entering the tank is in dispute. Union Carbide claims it was 120-240 gallons (1,000-2,000 pounds). Dr. S. Varadarajan, the Director General of the Indian Council for Scientific and Industrial Research, at one time asserted that it was a very much smaller quantity, perhaps as little as 3 or 4 pounds (about a pint), although his report, finally released in December 1985, backs away from that position, suggesting a figure of 1,100 pounds, which is within the Carbide range.

Another explanation has been advanced by various Indian investigative journalists covering the Bhopal story, including Radhika Ramaseshan in the *Sunday Observer*, Kannan Srinivasan in the *Indian Express,* and Ivan Fera in the *Illustrated Weekly of India*. This explanation (which in some versions assumes an intermediate quantity of water—some 750-1,200 pounds or around 90-140 gallons) argues that there were in fact two runaway reactions occurring in tank E610. The first, and the dominant one, was the reaction of MIC with itself, catalyzed by iron which was washed into the tank from the corroded walls of the process vent header line. (Contrary to Union Carbide's own design requirements, components of the PVH and RVVH pipelines were made not of stainless but of carbon steel. In the Federal District Court in New York, where all of the personal injury and wrongful death suits generated by the Bhopal disaster have been consolidated, evidence is said to have been secured that the decision to substitute carbon for stainless steel was made by the parent U.S. corporation.)

The second reaction was of MIC with water. But, as these journalists contend, Carbide's own manual indicates that a runaway reaction of MIC with water *by itself* occurs only after 23 hours at 20 degrees C (60 F). But such a reaction is greatly accelerated and can take place in just a few hours—as occurred in the Bhopal tragedy—when MIC is reacting with itself, catalyzed by iron. Whatever the amount of water and the type of reaction or reactions, all agree that the MIC in tank E610 got quickly out of control and triggered a runaway reaction.

The reaction of MIC with water produces 1,3-dimethyl urea and liberates large quantities of CO_2 and heat. Dimethyl urea in turn reacts with MIC to produce trimethylbiuret, liberating more CO_2 and heat. Under extremely high temperatures, MIC begins to react with itself and this chain reaction causes MIC to polymerize. Of the 42 tons of MIC in E610, approximately five tons had been polymerized when the rapid pressure buildup caused the rupture disk to give, releasing a torrent of heated gas comprising of unreacted MIC and a variety of reaction products down the relief valve vent header and into the vent gas scrubber.

But the VGS was not operational. Nor was the flare tower for that matter. Reports indicate that attempts to activate the VGS proved futile. While some have claimed that the scrubber was in operation but for some reason the caustic soda shower could not be activated, others have maintained that the caustic soda pump had been dismantled. What is beyond dispute, however, is that the VGS proved wholly inadequate to neutralize the large volume of gas that flowed into it.

As the valve in the pipeline leading to the flare tower was closed, while the one in the eight-inch pipeline leading to the atmosphere was left open, the gas flowed straight through the scrubber and out into the night. Indeed, the VGS very likely provided another escape route for the gas—via the caustic overflow loop. Unlike the scrubber installed in the Carbide MIC plant at Institute, West Virginia, the Bhopal scrubber had a provision for excess caustic soda to be drained into an overflow tank. As this tank is uncovered, gas under pressure forces the caustic soda out and thus finds a second route to enter the atmosphere untreated.

The estimated time of the leak is 12:30 a.m., shortly after the start of a tea break. By 2:00 a.m. most of the contents of storage tank E610 had escaped.

Union Carbide's Explanation

On March 20, 1984, Union Carbide held a press conference at its headquarters in Danbury, Connecticut, to release its own report on the Bhopal disaster. (The press conference was neatly timed to upstage the opening day of a conference in Newark, New Jersey, in which representatives of a number of consumer,environmental, public health, and trade union groups were taking a critical look at the Bhopal tragedy and its implications for hazardous industries and communities at risk in the U.S.) The Carbide report is based on the work of the Bhopal Methyl Isocyanate Incident Investigation Team. This team included seven engineers and scientists charged with assisting in the safe disposal of the remaining MIC at the Bhopal plant after the accident and with determining the probable cause of the accident.

According to the Carbide report released at the press conference, the team spent 24 days in India and continued its work for a period of more than two months thereafter. While the team was able to inspect "many relevant written documents" in India and to obtain core samples of the residue from tank E610, they were not permitted to interview UCIL employees directly involved by the Indian Central Bureau of Investigation, which has been conducting its own investigation under orders from the central government and which sealed the plant shortly after the accident.

There are substantial points of agreement between the Carbide report and independent accounts of the accident such as the foregoing. The Carbide team's "hypothesis" is that the runaway reaction in the tank occurred "when a substantial amount of water was introduced."

In a section of the Carbide report entitled "A Hypothesis for the Event," the Carbide team observed that "a single scenario" could not be advanced "with complete certainty" since "sufficient critical information" was lacking but that "a high probability" can be given to the scenario set forth in the report.

The scenario is based on a proposition that a substantial quantity of water—1,000 to 2,000 pounds (120 to 240 gallons)—entered the tank, triggering the runaway reaction that led to the accident. According to the Carbide report, "the exact source of the water is not known." The report goes on to state that"water could have been introduced *inadvertently or deliberately* directly into the tank through the process vent line, nitrogen line or other type of line." (Emphasis supplied.)

This is the key sentence in the report, underscored in oral statements by Carbide officials during the press conference. Carbide apparently believes—at least responsible officers of the company so stated at the March 20 press conference—that the Bhopal tragedy was caused by ''sabotage.''

In a carefully orchestrated performance bearing the heavy imprint of the company's legal counsel, these same officials sought to lay it on their Indian colleagues. As Warren M. Anderson, the Chairman of Carbide, self-righteously asserted in his opening statement, ''the investigation team has identified a number of independent operating events and circumstances which...were not in compliance with standard operating procedures. Compliance with these procedures is the responsibility of operating plant personnel.'' This posture stands in marked contrast with the Carbide position in the days immediately after the tragedy, as ''The Betrayal of Bhopal'' (a Grenada TV Production shown over British television) demonstrates all too vividly. Then Anderson and other senior Carbide officials were insisting that safety standards in design, maintenance, and operation were the same at Carbide facilities throughout the world.

At the time the report on the Bhopal gas leak was issued, the company's plant in Institute, West Virginia, near Charleston, where MIC is also made, was temporarily shut down. After the accident in India, Carbide officials have stated that they would not reopen the Institute plant until they determined the cause of the Bhopal disaster. Their report plainly did not accomplish that goal since, by its own admission, it did not have access to critical information and its conclusions were expressed as a ''hypothesis.''

Frustration with the unrevealing, if not misleading, character of the Carbide report led several participants at the Newark conference on Bhopal taking place simultaneously with the Carbide press conference to issue their own statement to the press, criticizing the report as mystifying, rather than clarifying, what caused the worst industrial disaster in history. The report, their statement concluded, ''appears to be aimed, not at discovering what really happened at Bhopal, but at justifying the reopening of the MIC plant in West Virginia and at shifting responsibility for the disaster from the U.S. company to its Indian subsidiary.''

That responsible officials of a major U.S. corporation would seriously propose such a fanciful and self-serving explanation as ''sabotage'' as the cause of a terrible human tragedy is dismaying. Indian journalists such as Radhika Ramaseshan, Kannan Srinivasan, and Ivan Fera mentioned above effectively destroy the sabotage theory. Not only would the accident have occurred 23 hours later if water were put directly in the MIC storage tank (instead of coming through the pipes being flushed out, which washed into the tank the iron that was necessary to start MIC reacting with itself and greatly accelerate the MIC-water reaction). Fera, for example, insists that there are no valves, vents, or bleeders on any of the lines leading into or out of the tank to which a hose could be put. He also points out that, even if all the valves leading into the tank were closed, as Carbide contends, these valves were leaking, thus making it impossible for tank E610 to be pressurized with nitrogen.

An even more authoritative source for debunking the sabotage theory that water was deliberately introduced into the tank comes from a senior Union Carbide official, Jackson Browning, Vice President for Health, Safety and Environmental Affairs. According to the *Chemical and Engineering News* (April 8, 1985), Browning told a Congressional committee investigating the Bhopal disaster and the possibility of such a catastrophic accident occurring in the U.S., "that the MIC tank line fittings are colored-coded and that the water line couplings are incompatible with the gas line couplings that go into the tank."

The Real Causes of the Bhopal Disaster

The courts will ultimately determine whether Carbide was guilty of negligent behavior but as the story of what really happened on that awful night in early December 1984 unfolds, there is compelling evidence that *both* the parent company and its Indian subsidiary were grossly negligent. At the most immediate and obvious level are three technical faults, at least one of which is clearly the responsibility of the parent company. First, had it not been for the jumper line, which—if standard Carbide procedures were followed—would not have been installed without the knowledge and approval of the parent company, water could not have entered the tank. The jumper line was first reported as the most probable route for the water to get into the tank by Arun Subramaniam and Bharat Bhushan in *BusinessIndia* (February 25-March 10, 1985). It was subsequently confirmed by the ICFTU-ICEF trade union delegation to Bhopal mentioned above through their extensive interviews with Carbide workers. While the results of what is often asserted to be the most complete and thorough

WHO COMMIITTED SABOTAGE?

The Union Carbide Story

Water could have been introduced inadvertently or deliberately directly into the tank through the process vent line, nitrogen line, or other piping . . . If someone had connected a tubing to the water line instead of the nitrogen line either deliberately or intending to introduce nitrogen into the tank, this could account for the presence of water in the tank.

•Ronald Van Mynen, Union Carbide's Corporate Director of Safety and Health, March 20, 1985, Press conference at UCC headquarters, Danbury, Connecticut.

We have all but ruled out everything but sabotage.

•Bud Holman, attorney for Union Carbide, *Wall Street Journal*, August 1, 1985.

What Carbide's Critics Say

I think that sabotage definitely was the cause of the Bhopal disaster. That the refrigeration unit at the Carbide plant was out of operation for a period of five months was clearly an act of sabotage by the Carbide management. It was also an act of sabotage to put all of the blame on its Indian subsidiary and claim that the accident was caused by sabotage.

•Bill Kane, United Auto Workers Staff Representative in the New Jersey Right to Know Coalition, Workers' Policy Project Conference on Bhopal, Newark, New Jersey, March 21, 1985.

Given what we heard from Union Carbide [at its press conference the day before] about the shut down of various safety equipment, perhaps the Bhopal disaster was caused by sabotage, and perhaps the Indian government had the saboteur briefly in custody after the event. His name is Warren Anderson, the Chief Executive Officer of Union Carbide.

•David Weir, Director, Center for Investigative Reporting in San Francisco, at the Workers' Policy Conference in Newark.

investigation of the accident (or at least, based on greatest access to relevant documents and other evidence)—namely, the Central Bureau of Investigation inquiry—has not yet been made public, a press account of the CBI investigation (appearing in an Indian magazine, *Sunday*, 7-13 April 1985), also indicated support for the jumper line explanation of how the water got into the tank.

Union Carbide's March 20 report is completely silent on this design modification, even omitting it from the company's diagram of the MIC storage tank. Carbide is silent for good reason: the jumper line establishes, clearly and unequivocally, the parent company's complicity in the disaster. (The subsequent assertion by a Carbide spokesman, Thomas Failla, to the *New York Times*, (July 31, 1985) that the jumper line theory was discussed at the March 20 UCC press conference at which its report of the disaster was presented appears disingenuous, to say the least. In his extensive opening statement to the press conference, Ronald Van Mynen, Carbide's Corporate Director of Safety and Health, observed only that "entry of water into tank 610 from this washing [of safety valve discharge piping to the relief valve vent header] in the MIC unit would have required simultaneous leaks through several reportedly closed valves, which is highly improbable." That route would have been highly improbable were it not for the alternative channel provided by the jumper line.)

There are other theories about how the water got in the tank, well summarized by Wil Lepkowski in a special report on Bhopal in the *Chemical and Engineering News* on the first anniversary of the disaster (December 2, 1985). Water could have entered at some point in the nitrogen line near the tank, through the refrigeration line, or directly through the process vent system. There are, however, serious problems with these other theories, and while some questions remain about the jumper line theory outlined here, we believe that it remains the most plausible explanation of how the water got into the MIC storage tank.

The second of the most obvious and immediate faults concerns water flushing. If the flushing was indeed stopped for 15 minutes, orders should not have been given to resume it without determining the cause of the blockage. To underscore how closely interconnected design and operation are in a complex event like this, assuming the explanation of two simultaneous reactions is correct, who decided to substitute carbon steel for stainless steel in components of the piping being washed during the construction of the plant? The answer appears to be, according to evidence generated by the discovery process in the Federal District Court in New York, the parent U.S. corporation.

That the discovery process should have established that this decision was made by the parent U.S. corporation is not surprising. Changes like that and the installation of the jumper line mentioned above required such approval. As Kamal Parekh, the Bhopal plant's former safety officer put it (in *BusinessIndia*, December 2-15, 1985):

> The MIC plant layout and equipment were based on their designs, their drawings; any design change made in India had to be approved by the U.S.; any change in the material of construction of various equipment had to be approved, because, you see, they

had experience in dealing with MIC, we didn't. We were dependent on them for recommendations.

The third technical fault involves pressurizing the MIC storage tank E610. If it could not be pressurized, the outflow valve should have been checked and replaced. But this is only a part of the story. The disaster also brought to light a number of design and safety shortcomings.

In the MIC storage area there were at least three instrumentation faults. For the MIC tanks, there is a temperature indicator alarm (TIA), a pressure indicator/control (PIC), and a level indicator (LI) on the control room panel. According to MIC plant operators, the TIA which is supposed to sound a high temperature alarm if the tank's temperature were to exceed a set limit (15 degrees C) had been faulty for the last few years. Thus, even when the temperature in E610 was rapidly rising in consequence of the MIC water reaction, there was no indication of it in the control room.

Similarly, both the PIC and the LI were known to have also been faulty. That is why, although the PIC indicated a tank pressure of 10 psig—five times the normal—around midnight, workmen chose to ignore it.

Beyond these three technical faults, there are still other shortcomings in both design and operation of the plant that contributed to the accident. Even if the TIA had gone off, there was precious little that could have been done to bring the temperature down. The freon-based 30-ton refrigeration system designed to keep stored MIC at a temperature of around 0 degrees C (32F), had been disconnected. In fact, it would seem that the plant management never intended to utilize the system: freon from the refrigeration unit had been drained off for use elsewhere in the plant about a year prior to the accident. Similarly, even if both the vent gas scrubber and the flare tower had been operational they could not have prevented the escape of MIC into the atmosphere.

The normal rate at which toxic gases are expected to enter the VGS for neutralization is about 180 kg/hour at a temperature of 35 degrees C (95F) and the VGS has a maximum allowable working pressure of 15 psig at 120 degrees C (248F), according to Carbide's Operating Manual for the Bhopal MIC unit. But MIC was flowing into the scrubber at a rate of more than 200 times this capacity. Furthermore, it reached a temperature of at least 200 degrees C (392F) as indicated in Union Carbide's own report of the accident, and perhaps as high as 400 degrees C (725F).

More significant, given that the rupture disk is set to burst at 40 psig, the minimum pressure at which MIC will escape the storage tank is 166 per cent higher than the VSG's 15 psig capacity. It follows that the VGS was not designed to neutralize a large-scale release of MIC from the storage tanks, but rather was intended to handle minor gas releases of a routine nature. If the VGS could not have coped with a massive release of MIC that night, the flare tower was even less capable of doing so. Even the UCIL management has admitted that not only was the flare tower incapable of burning all the gas that escaped but would in fact have caused an explosion had the flare been ignited.

Nor is that all to the shocking record of gross negligence and callous disregard for the inhabitants of the city that provided Carbide with its home for making the deadly gas that caused this terrible tragedy. The Bhopal plant had reportedly been losing money for some time and was operating at much less than its full capacity because of weak demand in India for the pesticide made with MIC at the plant, known by its trade name as Sevin. Along with poor and inadequate design, dangerous and irresponsible operating procedures, and lack of proper maintenance were sharp reductions in work crew sizes, worker training, and skilled supervision. According to the report of the trade union delegation to Bhopal, major personnel reductions were made in 1983 and 1984 in an effort to cut costs. A number of workers were encouraged to take early retirement, some 300 temporary workers were laid off, and another 150 permanent workers were put in a pool to be assigned to jobs as needed. Workers interviewed by the trade union delegation insisted that employees were often assigned to jobs for which they were not qualified—a practice also noted by the parent company in its 1982 inspection report of safety and maintenance at the Bhopal plant.

More specifically, staffing at the MIC facility had been reduced from 12 production staff (11 operators and one supervisor) to only six (five operators and one supervisor), while the maintenance crew was reduced from six to two. On November 26, less than a week before the accident, the maintenance supervisor position on the second and third shifts was also eliminated. When that position was eliminated, responsibility for maintenance apparently shifted to the production supervisor. But the production supervisor who was on duty the night of December 2-3, according to the Union Carbide workers, had been transferred from a Carbide battery plant only one month before and was very likely not fully familiar with operating or maintenance procedures.

If the claims of the Bhopal victims are in fact litigated, the extent to which the parent company was aware of these circumstances and gave them its tacit, if not explicit, approval will be more fully revealed through the discovery process in a court of law. But we already know from internal Carbide documents, such as the 1982 safety inspection report, that key officials in the parent company were well aware of the safety and maintenance problems of the Bhopal plant. Given the pattern of type of control and close monitoring of its subsidiaries that characterizes the Carbide management style, including the submission of detailed monthly operating reports by the Indian subsidiary, there is little doubt that many of these circumstances were fully reported to the parent company.

The intimate connection between the parent corporation in the U.S. and its Indian subsidiary has been summed up by *BusinessIndia* in its cover story on the first anniversary of the Bhopal tragedy (December 2-15, 1985) in these words:

> Just how close the relationship between the two companies actually was can be seen from the fact that four senior executives of UCC's regional division, Union Carbide Eastern (UCE), including its chairman, were members of UCIL's board of directors. UCIL's budgets, major capital expenditures, policy decisions and company reports had to be approved by UCC corporate headquarters. The Bhopal plant formed an integral part of UCC's agricultural products division (APD), and was directly under the control of the director, APD, at the UCE headquarters in Hong Kong. The director, APD, in turn occupied the position of executive vice president at UCC. Thus the chain of command stretched all the way from Bhopal to corporate headquarters in Danbury, Connecticut.

At a minimum, senior management officials in the parent corporation would have known of accidents that had occurred with dismaying frequency at the Bhopal plant, leading to one death (in 1981) and numerous injuries of Carbide workers, often serious. In the words of Union Carbide's own health and safety regulations, all accidents involving fatal or serious injuries "will be reviewed by the UCC chief executive officer."

Then there is the troublesome problem of double standards. In spite of the assertions by Warren Anderson, the Union Carbide Chairman, in the days immediately following the accident that safety standards were the same at Bhopal and its sister plant in Institute, West Virginia, evidence accumulates that there were in fact substantial differences in the way in which the plants were designed and operated.

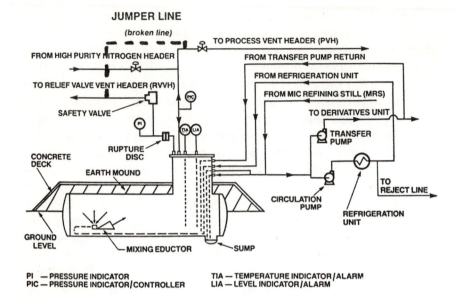

**Union Carbide Diagram of MIC Storage Tank
with Jumper Line Added**

These have been summarized by the Centre on Science and the Environment in its authoritative account of the Bhopal disaster in *The State of India's Environment, 1984-85: The Second Citizens' Report*. They point out that, among other things, Carbide never installed in the Bhopal plant the computerized pressure/temperature-sensing system which had been used for several years at the Institute plant as a warning device.

A second significant difference involves the community living near the plant. It had never been told of the significance of the public danger alarm. This alarm had sounded several times accidentally in the past but resembled another nearby factory's signal for change in shifts. In a similar manner, the surrounding community had never been informed about just how dangerous and toxic were the substances used in the plant. While comparable conditions in Institute were far from perfect, at least some effort was made there to do these things.

Safety conditons in the Carbide plant in Bhopal were very bad, certainly when compared with the West Virginia plant. The record of plant accidents was much worse in Bhopal than in Institute. There had been no deaths in the U.S. plant in 17 years of handling MIC, and while there were some accidents, none appeared to have been serious. By contrast, the Bhopal plant had been plagued with problems from the beginning, including the death of a worker in 1981.

As we have noted, there was little heed for safety and maintenance at the Bhopal plant. Control instruments were faulty. The refrigeration unit and other safety devices were out of commission. Lack of adequate spare parts meant vital devices like pressure gauges were not functioning. Underqualified people were running the plant at the time of the disaster. On and on, the sorry record of double standards goes.

As if to compound all of the foregoing sins of omission and comission, the Carbide management in 1984 proceeded to rewrite its own rules in order to get around the problem of being constantly confronted with breeching company safety regulations. The 1978 MIC operating manual clearly stated that MIC is best stored at a temperature of 0 degrees C (32 degrees F) and should never go above 5 degrees C (41 degrees F). The 1978 manual insisted that the scrubber be kept operational 24 hours a day as long as there was any hazardous material stored on the site. By contrast, the 1984 version permitted the scrubber to be shut off when the plant was not actually in operation. In a similar vein, it was now made permissible to shut off the MIC refrigeration unit, a logical corollary of allowing higher storage temperatures for MIC.

The web of evidence that the Union Carbide Corporation in the U.S. and its Indian subsidiary (the latter with both explicit and tacit approval from the former) put profit ahead of safety in Bhopal thus thickens. The case against Carbide at this juncture—with all of the evidence far from being in—can be summarized in the following ten decisions and actions:

1. Manufacturing Sevin with extremely toxic methyl isocyanate when less hazardous alternatives were known.
2. Storage of highly unstable MIC in large quantities.
3. Plant design that allowed MIC to reach the atmosphere untreated through the vent gas scrubber.
4. Woefully undersized safety systems to handle a runaway reaction.
5. Use of substandard materials in the MIC plant piping system known to be a source of contamination of MIC.
6. Modification of original plant design with installation of the jumper line between the process vent header and the relief valve vent header.
7. Endorsement of unsafe practices in the 1984 revision of the MIC plant operating manual.

8. Neglect of some of the key findings of Union Carbide's own safety audits of the Bhopal plant.
9. Preoccupation with cost-cutting over safety as manifested in the reduction of maintenance manning levels and shutdown of the refrigeration unit.
10. Failure to develop and communicate to competent local authorities and the surrounding community an emergency response plan, notwithstanding internal company recommendations to do so.

These multiple causes are in fact characteristic of large-scale industrial disasters like the one at Bhopal and underscore the inherent contradictions in the corporate infrastructure and organizational objectives of large companies like Union Carbide that make these disasters all but inevitable. This thesis, being examined by Professor Paul Shrivastava of the New York University School of Management (and himself a native of Bhopal), in a forthcoming book on the management implications of Bhopal, is shared in part by Charles Perrow, Professor of Sociology at Yale, whose new book, *Normal Accidents* (New York, Basic Books, 1984) appeared prophetically a few months before the Bhopal disaster. Their ideas are further discussed in Chapter 5 below, "Can It Happen Here?".

A City Is Vaporized

To return to the story of that grim night in December, attempts at starting the vent gas scrubber having failed, a workman sounded the toxic gas alarm at 12:50 a.m. When this alarm is activated, both a loud public siren and an internal alarm are set off. In accordance with the plant's emergency procedures, the control room operator immediately switched off the siren and made an announcement over the plant's public address system informing workmen of the leak. He then restarted only the internal alarm which is inaudible outside the plant.

In the original design of the plant's emergency warning system, the siren and the alarm operated simultaneously, i.e., one could not be operated independently of the other. This system insured that people living in the plant's vicinity would be alerted to every emergency involving the plant, even if it did not necessitate their evacuation. But minor leaks were so frequent at the Bhopal plant that the company, to save itself the embarrassment of having to explain its failures to the public, decided to change the system. Sometime in 1982, the plant's management delinked the siren from the alarm so that they could now warn just their workmen, without "unnecessarily" causing panic in the surrounding populace. Nothing perhaps expresses the company's total disregard for the community's safety more clearly than this one act.

Given the paucity of detailed meteorological data, the dispersion of the gas over the city cannot be accurately determined. However, what is known is that the plume initially travelled westward at a considerable height above the ground. Thus, although the residential areas that lay west of the plant like Tilla Jamalpura and Shahjahanabad were the first to be hit by the gas, they were spared its highest concentrations. But there appears to have been a change in wind direction at this point, which caused the gas cloud to drift southwards, toward the city, where it descended in a heavy mist upon the shantytowns that lay to the south and southeast of the plant. The chemical composition and movement of this cloud appears to be much more complex than originally thought and has much to do with explaining the different health and environmental impacts that are further discussed in the next chapter.

Sometime around 12:45 a.m., people living in Jayaprakash Nagar, which lies barely 100 yards south of the plant, woke up feeling asphyxiated, their eyes and throats stinging. They rushed out into the open but found the air outside even more unbreathable. Panic-stricken, they started running away from the factory—but in the same direction that the gas was moving. Soon there were thousands of people on the road, gasping for breath, unable to see for the terrible stinging in their eyes and the mist that surrounded them, fleeing southward on foot or by whatever means of transport they could find. Within minutes, people had started collapsing; some died instantly while others, overcome by nausea and fatigue, fell down unconcious. But even those who did not immediately succumb to the gas could not escape from it; for however far they fled, they remained within the gas cloud which had by now extended over an area of about 40 sq. km.

At about 1:15 a.m., the police control room was informed that there had been a major gas leak in the north of the city and that people were fleeing the area. The police contacted Union Carbide immediately but were informed by the works manager that he did not know of any leak and moreover that even if there had been one, it could not be from Carbide as the entire plant had been shut down. The police called Carbide several times in the course of the next hour, but were told the same thing. At 2:15 a.m., Carbide's public siren sounded and a little later, an engineer from the plant walked into the police control room to announce that the "leak has been plugged"—their first admission that there had been a leak at all, and an admission made only after almost the entire contents of E610 had been released upon the city.

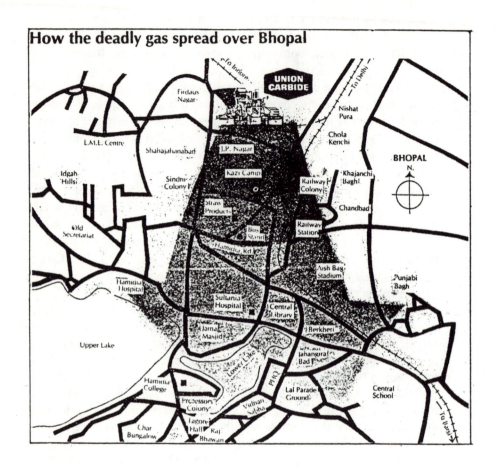

How the deadly gas spread over Bhopal

What is really quite incomprehensible is why Carbide failed to inform the authorities of the MIC leak. As early as 12:30 a.m., workmen were instructed to evacuate the plant; as the wind sock on the MIC plant structure indicated that the wind was blowing westward, they were instructed to move to a location east of the plant. But the company did not pass on this information to the police so that they could warn communities that lay in the path of the gas. In fact, until the leak was confirmed, the police advised everybody who contacted them not to panic and to stay indoors. It was only around 2:30 a.m. that they decided to evacuate the city. It is clear that if Carbide had only informed the police earlier and intimated both the direction of the wind and the extreme toxicity of the escaping gas, people could have been advised to move either east or west, advice that by any reckoning would have saved the lives of thousands.

Chapter 2

THE IMPACT OF BHOPAL

The Death Toll

It was around 3:00 a.m. when the first deaths due to the gas leak from the Carbide plant were reported to the police that the authorities realized the extreme gravity of the situation. But it was already too late. By morning, over a thousand people lay dead, their bodies strewn across the city.

Many of those who lived near the plant in slum areas such as Jayaprakash Nagar and Kazi Camp were exposed to some of the highest concentrations of the gas and died in their sleep. Others who fled the city in terror died in forests and fields around Bhopal; still others who managed to escape from the city but who had inhaled lethal doses of the gas, died in towns as far as 25 miles from Bhopal.

For these and other reasons, we will never know for certain just how many people died in Bhopal on that fateful night and in the days that followed. What is certain, however, is that the toll is far in excess of what the government authorities in India have estimated. We believe there is substantial evidence to support a figure of 5,000. This is two and a half times the government calculation (which is based only on recorded deaths for which certificates were given) and twice the number most frequently used by the U.S. media (typically reported as ''at least 2,000 deaths'' or ''more than 2,500 died'').

The government has based its estimates on the number of deaths registered at hospitals, crematoriums, and burial grounds. And these tended to vary considerably. For instance, on the 3rd of December, although only 574 deaths had been registered at hospitals, the number of corpses received by crematoriums and burial grounds exceeded 1,200.

A doctor in Hamidia Hospital described it in these words: "I was standing in the pediatric department. There was such a terrible crowd that there wasn't even place to keep the bodies on the floor. As soon as a patient was declared dead, his relatives would vanish with the body. I saw at least 50 babies taken away like this. I would estimate that anything between 500 and 1,000 bodies were taken away before their deaths could be registered."

In any case, not even half the dead were buried or cremated at official grounds. The authorities, confronted with a health crisis of catastrophic proportions, had first to clear the city of the dead. And that included over 4,000 head of cattle and several hundred dogs, cats, and birds. So it was only to be expected that the disposal of the dead would be conducted at a rapid pace, permitting of little ceremony, whether it meant identifying the dead or accurately estimating their numbers.

Indeed, as government authorities subsequently acknowledged, voluntary agencies played an important role in averting a health crisis by participating in the gigantic and urgent task of removing corpses from the city. The inevitable consequence of many hands working at this gruesome but essential task is that the government diminished still further its control over vital statistics. No one was bothering to count at that stage. They were just dealing with the problem of disposal of a serious menace to public health.

A number of estimates place the death toll closer to 10,000. These are based on the number of death shrouds sold in Bhopal in the days following the catastrophe (7,000 by one count) or by extrapolating the figures of smaller communities where it was possible to determine independently the extent of fatalities.

For instance, Jayaprakash Nagar, one of the worst affected areas right across the road from the Carbide plant, lost at least 25 per cent of its 7,000 inhabitants, according to the local volunteers from one of the political parties (Congress) who had conducted a voter registration campaign only a week before the incident. Similarly, the discovery of mass graves (in one case seven bodies were found buried, although only one death certificate had been issued) lends credence to these higher figures.

Even the government admits that many hundreds of homeless people who had taken shelter at the bus and railway stations vanished without a trace. As in the case of gypsies who had set up temporary dwellings in the affected areas, these people had no record of habitation in Bhopal and have therefore been excluded from the surveys that have been conducted to determine the numbers of the dead and injured. A senior UNICEF official, after spending a week investigating conditions in Bhopal shortly after the disaster, commented that many doctors and other health officials privately reported to him that they believed the death toll was around 10,000. Given the circumstances surrounding the disposal of the dead and other factors mentioned above, we consider 5,000 to be a conservative figure, although we recognize that the widespread use of a lesser number than 2,500 has given those numbers the status of conventional wisdom about the Bhopal tragedy. But we are not certain arguing over the number who died makes very much difference at this stage; the tragedy was awful enough, whether the fatalities totalled 2,500, 5,000, 10,000, or more.

That the state government had no effective control over recording deaths in the aftermath of the tragedy is clear from its own August 1985 report on efforts being made to deal with the tragedy. There the government notes that the "first contribution [of voluntary organizations] was the expeditious disposal of dead bodies and animal carcasses strewn all over the affected areas and inside houses and shanties. This forestalled the outbreak of an epidemic, which decomposing bodies may have caused."

Furthermore, all the numbers are not yet in. There are still people dying as a consequence of their exposure to toxic gases on that fateful night in early December 1984. Given the complex chemistry of the gas leak and the correspondingly complex nature of impacts on health which are further discussed below, it is clear that the death toll will continue inching upward for many months, probably years, to come. Compounding these circumstances is the vulnerable physical condition of many of the victims, almost all of whom, being very poor, enjoy less than ideal nutrition and continue to be exposed to unsanitary environments and drinking water.

If the death toll and the rapidity of its rise seemed dramatic, the manner in which people died was even more so. This description is from a doctor in the Railway Colony: "Several of them fainted, felt extremely weak and became unconscious. Others vomited, defecated and urinated involuntarily. Some died within a few minutes of exposure...Within one hour, at Bhopal railway station alone, 21 persons died, 200 lay unconscious and the whole station complex was littered with around 600 suffering people lying in their own excreta…Most dying persons were not noticed to have shouted or become violent. It appeared that their power of voice or limbs had greatly weakened. People had died quietly, in awkward positions, unable to protest.''

The Agony of the Survivors

By early morning, the city's hospitals were virtually overrun by the flood of victims. Thousands poured in, blinded, breathless, and giddy, carrying those who had collapsed along the way. In cases of acute exposure, victims had suffered extensive damage to their lungs. Post mortems revealed that tissues had been so badly necrosed that the lungs had turned grey. In some instances the chemical had so severely corroded the tissues as to cause perforations in the lungs.

Almost every case showed serious and extensive damage to mucous membranes and inflammation of the respiratory tract. The chemical action within the lung caused it to secrete fluids, creating severe oedema in the patient; in acute cases the entire lung was flooded, with the fluids so released causing asphyxiation and death in the patient. This was most apparent in the case of those who had run great distances in order to escape the gas. The exertion made them breathe deeply and therefore inhale larger quantities of the gas.

Those who did not succumb to their injuries are today increasingly falling victim to secondary infections of the lungs and the respiratory tract. The number of people reported to be suffering from bronchitis, pneumonia, and asthmatic complaints is increasing while tuberculosis patients are experiencing an exacerbation of their symptoms.

The Indian equivalent of *Time* or *Newsweek*, *India Today*, used these words in its February 15, 1985 issue to describe the agony of the survivors:

> The dead may not have been so unlucky after all. Their end came horribly, it is true, choking on air that had suddenly gone vile. But at least the nightmare was brief. And then it was over. For those who survived the poisonous methyl isocyanate leak from the Union Carbide plant, release will not come so quickly.
> Thousands of the seriously affected survivors have suffered such extensive lung damage that they can no longer apply themselves physically. Their vision often gets blurred, spells of dizziness overtake them, and walking briskly even for a few minutes sends them gasping to their knees, their chests aching. There are women who have peculiar gynecological problems. And there are oth-

ers—particularly children—who keep reliving those awful hours over and over again.

The human dimensions of the tragedy are writ large in the tales of individual survivors. Suresh, aged 13, lost his father, a construction worker, and his mother, and two of his younger brothers in the disaster. He now faces a bleak future, being housed for the time being in the Children's Relief Centre in Bhopal, suffering from severe and apparently irreversible damage to his lungs that makes it impossible for him to play with his contemporaries.

Three orphans come from the same family: Sunil, 16, a younger sister, 14, and a little brother, 2. They are the only survivors of a family of 10 who lived in one of the slum colonies right next to the Carbide factory. Sunil also suffers from serious lung damage and can no longer exert himself physically.

Not being able to work as they once did and earn money they sorely need is a pressing problem among many of the survivors. Most of those who did manage to find jobs before the disaster were manual workers. A good example is Sukhram, aged 50, one of the 200 porters working at the Bhopal railway station. He spends much of his time lying in his tiny room, able to work for only short periods and to carry half the load of baggage he once did. His earnings of some $50 a month have been more than halved.

Among the more horrifying experiences of the survivors is that of Kalabai, a woman in her mid-40s who lives in one of the residential colonies not far from the Carbide plant. During the awful morning of December 3, she became separated from her husband, fell unconscious, and was taken to the hospital. There she was given up for dead and sent to the mortuary, where she finally regained consciousness. So terrifying was this experience that even when her relatives found her several hours later, she would not at first let them come near her.

Great adversity brings out the best—and the worst—in human beings. Among the heroes of the Bhopal tragedy are three railway workers—B.B. Sharma, V.R. Dixit, and B.K. Sharma—who were on duty in the railway control room in Bhopal when disaster struck. As the railway station is quite close to the Carbide factory, all three were severely affected by the gas leak but remained on duty, trying to stop all trains approaching Bhopal. Another valiant performance was that of Dr. A.K. Sarkar, the division medical officer for the Indian Railways in Bhopal, who made his way through the gas to the control room, where he gave the order that no trains were to be allowed into Bhopal. All of these railway personnel were greatly exposed to the gas while continuing to perform their duties and their health has been badly affected as a result. Their actions almost certainly saved many lives and hundreds of passengers on trains approaching Bhopal from serious injury.

The Health Impact and the Medical Response

In the immediate wake of this disaster, the medical establishment and the health care facilities in Bhopal were overwhelmed and struggled as best they could against insuperable odds. Not only were equipment, supplies, and trained people hopelessly inadequate to meet the massive need. No one, especially in the first crucial few hours, knew what they were dealing with from a medical standpoint. Even when they did, there was scant information based on authoritative prior experience about what to do, and what little information there was often became surrounded with controversy.

Given all of these circumstances, it is remarkable that so much was done. Very much a part of the Bhopal disaster as an historic episode are the cases of individual doctors and other medical personnel working desperately around the clock to cope with an impossible situation. Within a few days, help began coming in from other parts of the country, including doctors volunteering their services to do what they could to assist the poor and hapless victims. But all of these well-intentioned efforts were plagued by lack of knowledge about how to treat victims of exposure to methyl isocyanate and other toxic substances that spewed forth from the Union Carbide plant on the morning of December 3.

Union Carbide knew as much as anyone else about what to do—or at least should have known what to do or it had no business playing around with something as dangerous and unstable as MIC. But it was less than forthcoming, especially in the early stages, when it insisted that MIC caused such intensive irritation to the eyes, even in small concentrations, that any person exposed to the gas would instinctively flee before any further harm could result. But if the medical establishment in Bhopal might be forgiven for accepting this contention at face value, the company certainly knew just how misleading it actually was.

Carbide's MIC plant operating manual clearly states: "Its obnoxious odor and tearing effect (watering of eyes) cannot be used to warn of dangerous concentration, since this concentration is approximately two parts per million (ppm), one hundred times greater than its threshold limit value—the maximum permissible exposure limit—of 0.02 ppm.'' And surely the company could not have been unaware that the U.S. Occupational Safety and Health Administration in 1984 revised the threshold limit value for isocyanates to five parts per *billion*!

It was only to be expected, then, that the lethal effects of the gas—which killed over a thousand people within 24 hours of its escape—would have taken doctors as much by surprise as the rest of the public. The initial medical response, fumbling and haphazard at its best, clearly reflected this situation. But once it was evident that the gas was highly toxic and that its effects would not be confined to just the eyes and lungs (the two organs most severely damaged), and its toxic by-products would percolate through the circulatory system to almost every organ of the body, it became imperative to devise lines of treatment that would deal not only with the symptoms but also provide effective anti-toxin therapy.

In the early stages, patients were administered large doses of the diuretic Lasix to relieve oedema, cortico steroids to contain inflammation of the lungs, as well as bronchodilators and oxygen inhalation in acute cases. While oxygen inhalation at worst proved ineffective, the ingestion of Lasix only made matters worse. Exposure to MIC generated such intense heat within the body so as to almost completely dehydrate the victim; the nausea and retching that it induced led to further fluid loss. Doctors report that most of the corpses were brought to them stark naked, suggesting that the victims had ripped off their clothing in a desperate effort to relieve the heat. The administration of Lasix in these circumstances only compounded the problem, proving fatal in several cases.

The other organ most seriously affected was the eyes. Exposure to the gas caused burns on the cornea, which initially appeared to be so severe that doctors feared that as many as 100,000 patients were in danger of completely losing their sight. Although the extent of corneal damage has proved to be far less severe than doctors anticipated, other eye afflictions have persisted even six to eight months after the accident. These include lacrimation (watering), blurred vision, photophobia (an acute sensitivity to light), and eye infections. These complaints have so far been treated with atropine and eye drops to relieve irritation.

There appears to be no evidence of damage to the optic nerve and so doctors expect little permanent damage to the eyes in most cases. But even so many as 2,000 people have have had their sight seriously affected as a result of exposure to MIC, according to a survey conducted by the government, and almost 10,000 others still face the possibility of permanent damage to their vision.

Besides the lungs and eyes, MIC exposure has damaged the liver, kidneys, and the gastrointestinal tract, as well as affected the immunological, reproductive, and central nervous sytems. Within barely two weeks of the accident, Bhopal faced a jaundice epidemic, which doctors suspected was chemically, rather than virally, induced. Other delayed effects reported include intestinal bleeding, pain in the kidneys, general debility, and paralysis in some cases. In fact, most of the deaths recorded after the third day involved a failure of the central nervous system. Patients suffered from convulsions or paralysis, then lapsed into a coma and died.

Even among the survivors, damage to the central nervous system is clearly evident and is reflected in symptoms such as mental deterioration, including memory loss, personality changes, lack of concentration, and insomnia and anorexia. As MIC was not then known to be neurotoxic, doctors attributed such damage principally to hypoxia. However, it is now known that there were other toxins involved in the gas leak, in addition to MIC, and it is possible that their presence in the blood stream may account for the persistence of these symptoms.

MIC is known to be an immuno-suppressant, as well as a cross-sensitizing agent. A study sponsored by the Indian Council of Medical Resarch and conducted by the K.E.M. Hospital and Cancer Research Institute of Bombay with assistance from the School of Environmental Health at the University of Pittsburgh found that MIC lowers the response of certain cells such as T and B cells and their subcells which are crucial to the body's immune mechanism for fighting disease. According to Praful Bidwai, one of a handful of Indian journalists giving sustained and critical scrutiny to the Bhopal story, in the *Times of India* (December 4, 1985):

> This means very simply that MIC has damaged the natural immune system, and hence that its victims are now both more vulnerable to all manner of infections and less likely to be cured of the ailments afflicting them, especially those of the lung.

These circumstances help to explain why the survivors are falling prey to a variety of secondary infections, as well as their acute sensitivity to air-borne irritants. For example, women are unable to cook as the inhalation of smoke from stoves, or even steam for that matter, induces violent asthmatic reactions.

At least as disturbing as the foregoing is evidence of serious, widespread, and persisting psychiatric problems of the victims. Some 22 per cent of those screened from among the victims reporting at various government health clinics in Bhopal were found to have mental disorders, ranging from neurotic depression to anxiety state and "adjustment reaction." If ever evidence were needed to convince an American jury that the victims of an accident experienced pain and suffering and endured emotional anguish, it exists in great abundance in Bhopal.

The devastating, multiple, and long-lasting health impacts of MIC and the other toxic substances to which the Bhopal victims were exposed cry out for serious, systematic long-term medical studies so that at least the suffering of these poor people will contribute to better understanding of what to do when people are accidentally exposed to such lethal substances in the future. In fact, of course, such studies should have been done *before* a disaster like Bhopal happened, and should be the explicit and legally enforceable responsibility of companies using such lethal chemicals before they are permitted to manufacture, store, transport, or market these chemicals.

In the case of methyl isocyanate, as we are now sadly aware, precious little was known before Bhopal about its health impacts, and not very much more about its chemical behavior or environmental impact. Indeed, present knowledge of chronic damage to human beings by isocyanates in general is based largely on two small but prolonged series of studies of 35 British firemen exposed to toluene diisocyanate (TDI), which were published in the *British Journal of Industrial Medicine* in 1976.

Given the remarkable, albeit tragic, opportunity thus presented to advance our knowledge about these important subjects, all too little has been thus far done. The Indian Council of Medical Research sent some medical and other specialists to Bhopal shortly after the disaster and developed a rather elaborate profile of studies in pathology, forensic toxicology, teratogenecity, carcinogenecity, ophthalmic and cardiovascular investigations, and other medical aspects of the tragedy. Some of the leading medical research institutions in India are involved in these investigations, and no doubt, something useful will emerge in time.

ICMR also reports that it has initiated "a large scale epidemiological study of the health effects of MIC exposure." Approximately 100,000 persons in the exposed area are being surveyed regularly, according to a recent ICMR report, "The Health Effects of Inhalation of Toxic Gas at Bhopal." This and other studies, according to ICMR, "will need to be continued over a long term as in the Hiroshima study."

In the meanwhile, one of the most substantial medical investigation has been undertaken by doctors and research workers associated with the Seth G.S. Medical College and K.E.M. Hospital in Bombay and the Central Railway Medical Services. Their report, based on detailed examination and tests of 82 victims brought from Bhopal to Bombay where more extensive equipment and facilities are available, is an arresting catalog of the devastating impact of the Bhopal incident on human health. Their report concluded:

> In the 82 subjects studied in Bombay [from 8 to 53 days after the accident], the main symptoms were dry cough (96 per cent), throat irritation (66 percent), dyspnoea [choking] on exertion (95 per cent), chest pain (68 percent), eye irritation (90 per cent), blurred vision (30 per cent), vomiting (42 per cent), diarrhea (23 per cent), muscular weakness (22 per cent), and altered consciousness (28 per cent). Forty-five of them had persistent rales in the lungs, with 24 per cent showing prolonged expiration; 21 percent had mild symptoms, 30 per cent had severe illness. Radiographically, five per cent had normal films but a majority showed punctate (50 per cent) and/or linear (68 per cent) deposits in the lower zones. A few (seven per cent) showed pneumonitis and four per cent showed pleural reaction.... [in the wake of the accident], several subjects were stricken by panic, depression, confusion, and apathy, and a few developed convulsions.

Similar, although less detailed, findings about the diverse impacts of MIC and other toxic substances on the victims were reported by an independent survey team of doctors associated with an Indian voluntary health organization, Medico Friends Circle. They also expressed concern about efforts by government to restrict access to medical and pathological information and urged that such information ''be made available to the public and to the medical community, including clinical findings, laboratory investigations, treatment records, autopsy reports, and any further clues as to the nature of the toxic substances involved in the tragedy.'' The survey team also urged that duplicate health records be maintained for all gas-affected patients, with one copy being given to the patient and that there be careful monitoring of vital statistics in the affected areas on a long-term basis in order to detect trends in mortality and morbidity of the exposed population for at least two generations.

The legal significance of these recommendations for Union Carbide is very great. Long-term epidemiological studies, conducted with scientific rigor, are a critical form of evidence in American courts in determining damage to human health through exposure to toxic substances. One of the classic studies, which opened up a whole new era in bringing justice to those whose health was ruined by such exposure, was the study by Dr. Irving Selikoff and his colleagues at the Mt. Sinai School of Medicine on workers exposed to asbestos in New Jersey. Thus, Union Carbide has a clear and direct legal interest in seeing that such studies are not done, and that the kinds of careful medical records essential for such studies are not kept (or at least, if they are kept, not made accessible).

Thus, some of the voluntary agencies providing medical services have begun themselves to maintain medical repords on their patients. When the Peoples' Health Centre set up by the Jan Swasthya Samiti in the Union Carbide plant was closed down by the police in late June in a confrontation with some of the voluntary agencies working with the victims in Bhopal (further discussed below), and the records of the center siezed, some interpreted this as yet another manifestation of a Union Carbide conspiracy with key figures in the local medical establishment and a further attempt by government to control, if not supress, vital information essential for the litigation now proceeding in the Federal District Court in New York.

It seems unlikely that such efforts would be successful, certainly not in any comprehensive way, given the substantial number of studies and surveys now underway, as reported in the Indian Council of Medical Research report mentioned above, not to mention those already published or otherwise available. Many of the latter are included in the citations in the section of Appendix 4 on the health effects of gas-affected persons in Bhopal. Nonetheless, attempts to inhibit the collection, preservation, and analysis of data on health effects can certainly diminish the significance of such evidence in the litigation generated by the Bhopal tragedy. Certainly the stakes are high enough, as our discussion of levels of compensation of the victims in the next chapter makes abundantly clear, to stimulate such attempts.

Impact on Women

In mid-July 1985 the government of India Health Minister stated that 36 pregnant women had spontaneously aborted, 21 babies were born with deformities, and there were 27 stillbirths, all suspected to have been caused by the poison gas leak in Bhopal the preceding December. Very much earlier, however, evidence had begun to surface about the particularly adverse impact of exposure to MIC and other toxic substances from the Carbide plant by women.

An examination of 114 women in the field clinics in two of the gas-affected slums in Bhopal three months after the disaster revealed that an extremely high proportion of these women had developed gynecological diseases such as leucorrhoea (90 per cent), pelvic inflammatory disease (79 per cent), cervical erosion and/or endocervicities (75 per cent), excessive menstrual bleeding since exposure to the gas (31 per cent), and supression of lactation (59 per cent). An ICMR-sponsored survey of 2,500 women known to be pregnant at the time of the gas leak found that the rate of spontaneous abortion in the first 20 weeks of pregnancy was 14.8 per cent, more than twice the normal rate of seven per cent recorded elsewhere in India.

There were several thousand pregnant women in the communities that were among the worst affected by the gas. Respiratory complications and the resulting hypoxyia were bound to affect the fetuses as much as it did the mothers, if not more so. Yet no effort was made to warn these women of the possible birth defects that could result, nor were they given the option of medically terminating their pregnancies. Considering that many of these women were in their first trimester of pregnancy, it is likely that they would have opted for termination if they had been alerted to the risk.

The Cyanide Controversy

As early as 12:00 noon on December 3, post mortems conducted at Gandhi Medical College produced strong evidence that some deaths had been due to cyanide poisoning. Several cases showed cyanide traces in blood and body tissue, while others indicated the presence of monomethylamine or MIC. But even where traces of cyanide could not be detected, overwhelming empirical evidence pointed to its presence.

The victims had died of respiratory arrest even in cases where neither pulmonary oedema or the perforation of lung tissues was evident. Nor was there any evidence of cyanosis—blue discoloration of the body due to the presence of de-oxygenated blood, which would normally accompany asphyxiation. In fact, the body retained a reddish-pink color which was generalized over all organs, indicating the presence of highly oxygenated blood. It was also significant that corpses showed little sign of decomposition even after three days of unrefrigerated storage in the forensic laboratory, suggesting that the toxin had killed all the bacteria.

These symptoms strongly suggested the involvement of cyanide and this diagnosis was communicated to doctors in charge of treatment by Dr. Heeresh Chandra, head of Forensic Medicine at Gandhi Medical College in Bhopal. He suggested that in the circumstances, sodium thiosulphate, a well-known antidote to cyanide, be administered. But the doctors rejected these findings and chose instead to accept Union Carbide's assertion that isocyanates are "unrelated" to cyanide and, moreover, that there is no known metabolic pathway that converts isocyanate into cyanide. Carbide also claimed that as MIC rapidly hydrolyzes in the presence of water, the gas would be neutralized by moisture in the lungs and could, therefore, not possibly penetrate any further than the lungs. As a result, doctors discounted the need to administer antidotes and, instead, concentrated on symptomatic treatment.

But even if there were no known metabolic route for the conversion of isocyanate into cyanide, Carbide could hardly claim that the two were unrelated. As the company's Material Safety Data on MIC clearly states in Section 5, "thermal decomposition may produce hydrogen cyanide, nitrogen oxides, carbon monoxide and/or carbon dioxide." Given the high temperatures generated by the MIC-water reaction and other chemical changes in tank E610, it is more than likely that a considerable amount of MIC did, in fact, thermally decompose to yield a host of decomposition products.

Union Carbide has admitted in its March 20 report on the causes of the accident that 26,000 pounds of the decomposition reaction products—some 30 per cent of the total contents of the tank—were released from the tank in the course of the leak. And even more surprising, Carbide claims not to know what these reaction products are. It is also interesting that the very first communication received by doctors in Bhopal from Carbide headquarters in Danbury, Connecticut, states that "if cyanide is suspected, use amyl nitrate. If no effect, use sodium nitrite 0.3 grams and sodium thiosulphate 12.5 grams." The company however, later claimed that this advice had been given inadvertently.

As Paul Shrivastava notes in his mid-June report on the situation in Bhopal, "medical relief is plagued by the cyanide posioning controversy." In February 1985 the Indian Council of Medical Research, after a study of 500 patients, found that treatment by a cyanide antidote—sodium thiosulphate—produced "amelioration of symptoms in a good proportion of cases" and recommended to the Bhopal medical community use of this drug under carefully supervised conditions with complete documentation and monitoring of patients. However, except for the Peoples' Health Centre, no other clinic in Bhopal has as yet vigorously pursued the use of this drug. "Part of the medical establishment (allegedly pro-Union Carbide doctors) outright rejected the

ICMR recommendation, claiming that in their experience victims showed no cyanide poisoning,'' Shrivastava notes. "Given the special care it needs for administering the drug and lack of government enthusiasm, very few victims are getting this drug which is the *only* toxin antidote being used in treating victims of the gas leak. All other medicines are being used for symptomatic treatment."

This issue also has important legal significance for Union Carbide. Although scientific opinion on this point is divided, some toxicologists believe only that the presence of a fast-acting toxin like hydrogen cyanide would explain the large number of deaths that occurred in the first few hours after the gas leak. And we now know—from a study by two chemists at University College, Cardiff, Wales, in Britain published in 1982—that hydrogen cyanide is one of the major decomposition products of methyl isocyanate at high temperatures in the range of 427-548 degrees C (800-1,018 degrees F) (P.G. Blake and S. Ijadi-Maghswoodi, "Kinetics and Mechanism of the Thermal Decomposition of Methyl Isocyanate," *International Journal of Chemical Kinetics*, 1982, Vol. 14, pp. 945-952).

This scientific evidence becomes all the more significant in determining whether Union Carbide should be governed by the doctrine of strict liability in the Bhopal disaster. For as Judge Fisher put it in instructing the jury in the landmark Borel case on asbestosis, "the manufacturer is bound to keep reasonably abreast of scientific knowledge and discoveries concerning his field, and, of course, is deemed to possess whatever knowledge is thereby imparted." This line of argument becomes more compelling when the confidential research mentioned below, which was sponsored by Union Carbide back in 1963 and 1970 on the toxicology of MIC, is taken into account. In contrast to Carbide's cautious observation in its Material Safety Data Sheet on MIC that thermal decomposition "may" produce hydrogen cyanide, this study asserts that such decomposition *does* produce hydrogen cyanide.

The Environmental Impact

Not very much is yet known about the environmental impacts of the gas leak from the Bhopal plant. The Indian Council of Agricultural Research has issued a preliminary report on damage to crops, vegetables, animals, and fish from the accident, but the investigations reported there were mostly in their early stages, with few conclusive findings.

The ICAR report does indicate that the impact of whatever toxic substances emerged from the plant were highly lethal on exposed animals. Many were reported to have died within three minutes of such exposure. Large numbers of cattle (estimates range as high as 4,000), as well as dogs, cats, and birds were killed.

Plant life was also severely damaged by exposure to the gas. Vegetable crops such as spinach, cauliflower, and tomatoes grown by small farmers on the outskirts of the city were destroyed. There was also widespread defoliation of trees, especially in low-lying areas, according to a report by two investigators from the Madhya Pradesh State Forest Research Institute published in the *MP Journal of Tropical Forestry* in March 1985.

Perhaps the most revealing finding comes from a report, as yet unpublished, of the government's Air Pollution Control Board, giving the chemical analysis of samples of air collected on the 5th and 6th of December, just two to three days after the accident. The report concluded that "the samples are negative for cyanide for four outside locations, but positive for two factory locations." A sample taken near the MIC storage tank had a concentration of cyanide of 4,533 mg/m (4.5 ppm). This is almost half the Maximum Allowed Concentration (MAC) and around 1/50th of the Lethal Concentration (LC) for hydrogen cyanide—*48 hours after the gas leak*. The cyanide level dropped to 2,533 mg/m some 50 yards away from the tank, and no cyanide was detectable in air samples from several nearby locations outside the factory.

The clear implication from this evidence is that cyanide was still leaking from the MIC storage tank even on the 5th and 6th of December. A June 1985 report issued by Medico Friends Circle on the use of sodium thiosulphate in the treatment of Bhopal victims concluded that:

> The most probable origin of the cyanide must have been the thermal decomposition of MIC stored in the ill-fated tank. When one ties up the above mentioned evidence with the reports that cyanide was detected by the German toxicologist, Dr. Max Daunderer, in the blood of the gas victims and also by the CBI team [Central Bureau of Investigation— India's FBI] in the ambient air using chemical spot-tests a few days after the tragedy, the case of sodium thiosulphate therapy for the surviving gas-affected population becomes almost irrefutable.

As in the case of the impact on human health, we know all too little about the impact on the environment, including plants and animals, of a large-scale release of toxic substances such as occurred at Bhopal. Such a situation can never be created experimentally. Hence, Bhopal provides an unparalleled opportunity, thus far little utilized, to advance our knowledge about the environmental impacts of MIC and other toxic substances so that we may better understand and cope with the environmental consequences of these substances in the future.

A More Complex Chemical Event

While there is little doubt that cyanide poisoning has afflicted some of the Bhopal victims, closer examination of the medical evidence suggests that it offers an incomplete explanation. This may well explain why the administrationof sodium thiosulphate, even on the limited scale that has been attempted, has produced such mixed results. The picture that emerges from a continuing analysis of accumulating evidence is of a much more complex chemical event than was originally thought to be the case.

Methyl isocyanate was certainly a major component of the leak from the Carbide plant on December 3, but equally clearly, it was not the only substance. Union Carbide's March 20 report on the disaster notes that some 54,000 pounds of unreacted MIC left the storage tank together with approximately 26,000 pounds of reaction products. Its report does not specify what this 26,000 pounds of reaction products consisted of, but they must certainly have included several, if not all, of the compounds found in the tank residues analyzed by the Carbide investigating team. The list is long, including MIC trimer, 1,3,5 trimethyl isocyanurate and 1,3 dimethyl isocyanurate, trimethylamine hydrochloride, dimethylamine hydrochloride, monomethylamine, and trimethyl biuret. It is also likely that these reaction products would have included some of the substances mentioned in Carbide's Material Data Safety Sheet on MIC, including hydrogen cyanide, oxides of nitrogen, and carbon monoxide.

Once it came in contact with the moisture in the atmosphere, MIC would react rapidly to yield monomethylamine (MMA) and more carbon dioxide. The vapor densities of carbon monoxide, carbon dioxide, and oxides of nitrogen are all considerably lower than that of air and that of hydrogen cyanide (HCN) slightly less. MMA has a higher vapor density than air while MIC is exactly twice as heavy as air.

In a controlled environment, each of these substances would find its own level. MIC would form the lowest layer, followed by MMA, then air and HCN, and finally, the oxides of nitrogen, carbon dioxide, and carbon monoxide. If such a cloud were released at ground level, the lighter elements would quickly rise, leaving only the heavier ones close to the ground. But there is strong evidence that the victims in Bhopal were exposed to some of the lighter elements, including HCN and carbon monoxide.

The answer to this apparent anomaly is that the gas escaped from two points in the Carbide plant. One was at ground level (from the caustic overflow tank) and a second was 100 feet above (from the atmospheric vent at the top of the MIC tower structure). The result is that even as the lighter elements in the gas released at ground level were beginning to rise, the heavier gases descending from the atmospheric vent trapped them and held them close to the ground.

Given these circumstances, people in the colonies lying directly in the path of the gas were more likely to have been exposed to a combination of all of the different gases released from the tank. The fatality rates for these colonies were, as a consequence, extremely high. Death was instantaneous but its causes were several, including the high concentration of HCN (270 ppm can kill instantly) and MIC (both through its direct toxic effect as well as by asphixiation).

The complex chemistry of the Bhopal disaster—further examined in Appendix 4 by Dr. A. Karim Ahmed, Research Scientist, and three of his colleagues at the Natural Resources Defense Council in New York—has important, but thus far little examined and even less understood, implications for the health and environmental impact of the tragedy—and, of course, what should be done in attempting to cope with the tragedy, particularly the course of medical treatment for the survivors. For one thing, the variety of chemical compounds involved helps to explain the diversity of symptoms manifested by the victims. Another important implication is the emergence of MMA as the chemical likely to have afflicted the largest number of people. (Not only does MIC, reacting with moisture in the air, generate MMA, along with carbon dioxide, but MMA being less heavy than MIC, would have moved farther faster.)

Monomethlyamine is, fortunately, much less toxic than MIC—about 500 times less, according to Union Carbide's *Unit Safety Procedures Manual*, which describes MMA as "a colorless flammable gas having a fishy odor in lower concentrations and strongly ammoniacal odor in higher concentrations." It has nonetheless been assigned a health hazard rating of 4 (the maximum) in the Carbide hazard rating system. But the fact remains that it is much less toxic than MIC. Thus if the cloud from the Carbide plant, which is estimated to have spread over 25 square miles and affected close to 50 per cent of Bhopal's population, remained primarily MIC, the death toll would very likely have been in excess of 100,000. The fact that the death toll was much lower suggests that MMA, and not MIC, was the predominant substance afflicting the largest number of people.

The longer term consequences are, however, far less reassuring. The UCC report on the disaster calculated that some 80,000 pounds of material were discharged from the plant—58,000 pounds of vapor and 22,000 pounds of solids and liquids. If these solids and liquids are relatively stable compounds, it is more than likely that they will have survived in the environment. Indeed they would by now have been widely distributed as a fine crystalline dust, and made their way into the bodies of a substantial proportion of Bhopal's population—either through inhalation directly or through indirect means such as consumption of water and food.

We can only guess at their health effects, but since most of these substances are members of the isocyanate group, there is good reason to assume that they are toxic in some degree. Thus it appears that over 500,000 residents of Bhopal have been exposed to varying concentrations of toxic substances. Many of these substances have not been adequately researched, particularly their toxicological properties. While the acute effects of some of these substances are beginning to be better known, the sub-acute and long-term effects of all of the various substances discharged from the Carbide plant on that fateful morning in December 1984 are virtually unknown.

The Carbide Strategy of Containment

Faced with a disaster of truly historic proportions by what appears, on the basis of evidence already available, to have been perpetrated by its own negligence, Union Carbide quickly adopted a carefully orchestrated strategy of containment. The objectives of the strategy are clear: downplay the seriousness of the situation, minimize the adverse impacts, especially on health, and seek to implicate others. Aside from a few inadvertent lapses in the first confused hours after the disaster happened—for example, a telex message from Carbide officials in the U.S., later disavowed, specifying treatment for cyanide poisoning (see discussion of the cyanide controversy above)—the strategy has been consistently followed, especially by the parent U.S. corporation which has seen fit to place as much of the blame as possible on their colleagues in their Indian subsidiary.

The goal of such a strategy is equally clear: protect the assets of the company at whatever cost. It also appears to be a typical, if not standard, industry response to situations in which industry actions have inflicted great personal injury, suffering, and even death on their own workers, users of their products, and residents of communities nearby their industrial installations. Anyone who questions this observation should read Paul Brodeur's meticulously documented story of 50 years of industry efforts to supress medical evidence and avoid the legal consequences of the adverse impact of asbestos on human health published in *The New Yorker* (June 10, 17, 24, and July 1, 1985).

The motivation for such a strategy is very real. At stake are millions—in the Bhopal case, more properly billions—of dollars in compensatory and punitive damages from the victims and their survivors. Thus Carbide had very real reasons for trying to downplay the toxicity of MIC or the existence of much more lethal hydrogen cyanide or other decomposition products from the runaway reaction that occurred in tank E610. Only the discovery process in a judicial proceeding will reveal fully just how much Carbide actually knew about these matters in relation to what it publicly stated in the immediate wake of the worst industrial disaster in history, but at least some elements of the picture, discussed below, have begun to emerge.

But even without discovery, it is becoming more and more apparent that Union Carbide knew a great deal more than they were admitting publicly about just how dangerous a substance methyl isocyanate is. Furthermore, Carbide knew this to be the case for a long time before the Bhopal tragedy—even before the Bhopal plant was built. As far back as 1963, confidential research was undertaken for Union Carbide at the Mellon Institute at the Carnegie Mellon University in Pittsburgh on the toxicity of methyl isocyanate. That research, described in a confidential special report to Carbide, concluded that "methyl isocyanate appears to be the most toxic member of the isocyanate family" and that it "is highly toxic by both the peroral and skin penetration routes and presents a definite hazard to life by by inhalation." A second piece of confidential research undertaken for Union Carbide at the Mellon Institute in 1970 reinforced the earlier findings with additional data. That confidential report stated that MIC "is highly toxic by inhalation, an irritant to humans at very low vapor concentrations, and a potent skin sensitizer."

Notwithstanding this kind of clear and compelling evidence, Union Carbide has repeatedly sought to downplay the very serious health effects of MIC since the Bhopal disaster. Even the choice of and terms of reference for the three doctors Union Carbide sent from the U.S. to Bhopal in the wake of the disaster fit the strategy of containment. Allegedly part of Union Carbide's effort to respond to the needs of the victims as set forth in the Carbide lawyers' May 8, 1985, letter to Judge John F. Keenan of the Federal District Court in New York, their role appears to have been at least as much a medical intelligence-gathering exercise for Carbide's legal defense.

One of the doctors, an eye specialist and chief of the glaucoma service at St. Vincents Hospital in New York, Dr. Peter Halberg, sought to underscore the transient effect of MIC on the eyes and minimize its permanent damage in his presentation to the March 1985 Newark Conference on Bhopal organized by the Workers' Policy Project and other labor, church, and environmental groups. He also sought to counter evidence from an Indian doctor at the conference who had been part of a medical survey team in Bhopal, about the long-term and irreversible damage to the lungs and other vital organs—matters way beyond his own medical specialty.

Another doctor sent to Bhopal by Carbide was Dr. Hans Weill, a pulmonary specialist from the Tulane University School of Medicine in New Orleans. According to Brodeur in his *New Yorker* series (June 10, 1985, p. 89), Weill, who had undertaken studies of asbestos workers for industry in the past, turned up as a witness for one of the defendant companies, Johns-Manville, in the landmark Borel asbestiosis case in Texas in the early 1970s. His testimony that the plaintiff, an asbestos worker named Borel, had never suffered from asbestiosis—based entirely on reviewing chest x-rays and no direct physical examination—was quickly demolished by Borel's attorney who forced Weill to admit that without ever having examined Borel's lung, he was trying to refute the diagnosis of asbestiosis made at first hand by Borel's internist, by the surgeon who had removed Borel's lung, and by the pathologist who had examined tissue from Borel's lung in the hospital laboratory.

Since Carbide claims the visits of these three doctors to Bhopal as part of their effort to render assistance to the Bhopal victims, we thought it would be useful to see reports of their findings and recommendations made on their return. In two of the three cases, we were told that their reports were not available; in the third case, we received no response. We would be greatly surprised if, assuming the litigation proceeds that far, one or more of these doctors did not turn up as expert witnesses for the defense in any one of the various lawsuits brought against Union Carbide as a result of Bhopal, the burden of their testimony being that of trying to minimize the adverse health impacts of the Bhopal disaster.

Carbide's effort at containment is not confined to members of the

American medical profession. In an article headlined provocatively "Carbide Buys Up Bhopal Doctors," one of India's leading English language newspapers, *The Indian Express*, reports (Bangalore edition, June 21, 1985) that "a team of Bhopal doctors has allegedly gone to the United States on the invitation of Union Carbide to depose in American courts that there is a high incidence of tuberculosis in Bhopal." It is a neat tactic in Carbide's containment strategy: seeking to establish that the extensive lung damage caused by the gas leak is primarily attributable to the prevalence of TB in the congested, low-income areas surrounding the plant.

Allegations, always difficult to prove in such circumstances, go much beyond that in the view of some of the leaders of voluntary agencies seeking to provide help to Bhopal victims. Dr. Anil Sadgopal of the Zahreeli Gas Kand Sangharsh Morcha (Poisonous Gas Disaster Struggle Movement) is a scientist with a PhD. from the California Institute of Technology. He was once a member of the faculty of one of India's most prestigious research bodies (Tata Institute of Fundamental Research, Bombay) but has spent the last decade and a half developing innovative approaches to science education in the villages of the state of Madhyra Pradesh. He contends that there is a strong pro-Union Carbide lobby within Indian government circles, at both the national and state levels, which has manufactured what he calls "a string of lies" to conceal information about the number of deaths, the nature of the gas, and rehabilitation and relief efforts.

Much of this criticism centers on key medical officials in government institutions and agencies in Bhopal, particularly on Dr. M.N. Nagu, Director of Health Services for the Madhya Pradesh state government, whose brother, R.N. Nagu, is Chief of Security Services for Carbide's Bhopal plant (and former Inspector General of Police, a powerful position in the Madhya Pradesh government). Circumstantial evidence, such as the vigorous opposition of Dr. Nagu and others in government medical circles to recognition of cyanide poisoning among the victims and the need for appropriate therapies, is advanced in support of these contentions.

This strategy of containment—downplaying the medical impact while seeking to avoid legal responsibility—is nothing new at Union Carbide. It often takes a catastrophic event like Bhopal to stimulate more careful scrutiny of the perpetrator's past. Two voluntary organizations—the Highlander Center, located in Tennessee and the Society for Participatory Research, based in Asia in India—have begun to scrutinize Carbide's past, publishing their preliminary findings in *No Place to Run: Local Realities and Global Issues of the Bhopal Disaster* (June 1985).

What they have found is not pretty—the population of a neigh-
boring village laid low by persisting air pollution from a Carbide plant
in Puerto Rico or such a high incidence of mercury poisoning among
workers in a UCC factory in Indonesia that the Carbide Health Officer
resigned in disgust. Nor is this sorry record confined to the Third
World. In Texas City, Texas, Oak Ridge, Tennessee, and theKanawha
Valley in West Virginia, there are numerous instances of Carbide's
injuring workers or polluting the surrounding environment and then
refusing to admit any responsibility. Perhaps the most callous incident
occurred when a Carbide subsidiary was constructing a tunnel at Gauley
Bridge, West Virginia, in the early 1930s. Over a two-year period,
an estimated 476 workers died and 1,500 were disabled from silicosis.
This sorry record is thrown into high relief by the company's attempts
in recent years to pose as the "Mr. Clean" of the U.S. chemical
industry.

The Relief Imbroglio

In the first pre-trial hearing in the consolidated Bhopal litigation
in U.S. federal courts, the presiding Judge, John F. Keenan, was
reportedly so moved by accounts of bureaucratic delays and other
manifestations of neglect of the poor victims of the Bhopal disaster
that appeared in an article on the legal implications of the disaster in
an article by Steven J. Adler in the *American Lawyer* ("Bhopal Journal:
The Voiceless Victims," April 1985) that he asked Carbide as "a
matter of fundamental human decency" to provide an interim relief
payment of $5-10 million. Although contending that, according to
government of India reports, considerable relief had already been extended to the victims (some $8 million in *ex gratia* payments to affected
persons, plus another $4 million allocated to the Madhya Pradesh state
government to cover some of its extraordinary expenses), Carbide
agreed to provide $5 million for this purpose, provided a satisfactory
plan for distribution and accounting of the funds was devised.

For eight months, this sensitive initiative by Judge Keenan came
to nought as various principals in the litigation, including Union Carbide and the government of India, haggled over terms of reference and
conditions for using the $5 millionin interim relief. Finally in Novem-
ber 1985, agreement was reached that the money would be channeled
through the American Red Cross to the Indian Red Cross. But in
Bhopal itself, on the first anniversary of the disaster, no one—not even
the official of the Madhya Pradesh government in charge of relief for

the victims—had any idea just what the Red Cross would do with the money—and certainly, none of the money had yet benefitted any victims.

That the government is making some effort to provide assistance to the victims, few who are familiar with the situation in Bhopal would deny. An independent report, based upon an on-the-ground investigation, by Paul Shrivastava of the Industrial Crisis Institute in New York suggests that by mid-June 1985, somewhat more may have been spent by Indian government agencies on relief than the $12 million mentioned above but with melancholy results. Dr. Shrivastava, Associate Professor of Management at New York University, who grew up in Bhopal, has been one of the leaders in the U.S.-Indian community in organizing relief efforts for the Bhopal victims.

He has updated his mid-June report with local government figures indicating that the following have received *ex gratia* financial payments as of August 1985:

1,073 surviving family members of deceased persons—$830 each
946 "severely affected" persons—an average of $118 each
13,906 "moderately affected" persons—$16 each
4,472 families with annual incomes below $500—$125 per family

Indeed, in a glossy brochure entitled "We Shall Overcome," which was published by the Madhya Pradesh government's public relations department, it is claimed that *ex gratia* payments have been given, through November 20, 1985, to survivors of 1,405 deceased persons. In sharp contrast to the Carbide contention in May that $8 million had been given out in such payments, this same government publicity handout (prepared for the first anniversary of the disaster) states that "till 20.11.1985 [November 20, 1985] a sum of Rs. 1.4 crores [$1.2 million] has been distributed as *ex gratia* relief."

Free food grains, sugar, and other foodstuffs have been widely distributed in the gas-affected areas of the city and surrounding neighborhoods. From December 1984 through May 1985, some $8 million in food was provided by the government. (By the following November, this sum had risen to $12.1 million.) A 30-bed hospital with x-ray equipment and laboratory facilities and 17 medical dispensaries in the gas-affected areas serving several thousand patients daily (some 2,600 as of June 1985) have been set up by the government to provide medical care. In addition, several non-governmental voluntary organizations such as the Royal Commonwealth Society for the Prevention of Blindness, Action for Gas Affected People (AGAPE), Jan Swasthya Samiti

(People's Health Committee) and Self-Employed Womens' Association (SEWA) have set up small dispensaries in affected areas, jointly
serving about 500 patients a day.

Longer term efforts to help those affected by the disaster economically are much more limited but a beginning has been made. The
government has started using in Bhopal an economic rehabilitation
scheme for the urban poor known as STEP-UP (Special Training and
Employment Program for Urban Poor); under this program, loans of
up to $1,000 have been sanctioned to 79 persons to start their own
small businesses. (Dr. Shrivastava does not have information on how
many of the loans have actually been paid out. The government publicity release on efforts to help the victims mentioned above is also
silent on this point. Often in India, there is a long interval between
approving a government loan or a grant and its actual payment.) Various other initiatives such as setting up training centers to help the
victims learn new and less physically demanding skills have been taken
but appear to be reaching only a small fraction of those seriously
affected by the gas leak.

Dr. Shrivastava also provides a picture of Union Carbide's contribution to the relief effort in Bhopal: $10,000 in emergency supplies,
$50,000 in donations to three American charitable organizations for
work in Bhopal, and a $1 million donation to the Prime Minister's
Relief Fund. Another $1.1 million has been "authorized" by the com-
pany for studies of the accident and visits of medical experts such as
Dr. Weill and Dr. Halberg.

Money actually spent on relief operations in Bhopal by Union
Carbide averages out, by Dr. Shrivastava's calculation, to about 3
cents per affected person per day. Total Indian government expenditure
in relief operations by 31 May 1985 came to $13.75 million, which
he calculates as approximately 38 cents per day per affected person.
These various relief measures by Indian government authorities and
Union Carbide give the impression that the victims are getting at least
some help, albeit inadequate, in their misery. "But here lies the fallacy
and the politics of relief operations," concludes Dr. Shrivastava. "The
amount of money being spent on relief operations is not necessarily
going either to the victims or for needed work." He buttresses this
melancholy conclusion with these observations from a July 1985 report
on his June visit," The Politics of Misery in Bhopal":

> The government has based its relief program on an on-going
> medico-social survey of affected neighborhoods which is still not
> completed. On the basis of partial data, it is virtually impossible
> to identify exactly who is affected by methyl isocyanate and who

is not. Hence, government relief is not focused on victims alone. Over half the population of Bhopal is getting the benefit of free food distribution. In fact, the more vocal, aggressive and politically well connected people are getting relief benefits (money and food) quicker and in larger quantities than some of the more needy but powerless victims.

Middlemen and local money lenders have started exploiting victims by taking commissions for their services in procuring relief benefits for illiterate and voiceless persons, and even confiscating the money received, presumably as repayments for earlier loans to the victims. The psychological trauma caused by the accident is just beginning to be acknowledged and goes far beyond those physically affected by the gas. Victims suffer depression, anxiety, impotence, loss of appetite, nightmares, etc. The fear of latent or delayed effects is so pervasive that well-to-do people without any symptoms of gas poisoning are getting themselves checked and even taking sodium thiosulphate injections [for cyanide poisoning—see discussion of this controversy above] as a precaution. Others have become victims of "compensation neurosis," a mental condition in which people exhibit psychosomatic symptoms and even self-inflicted injuries, in order to avail themselves of any benefits and compensation.

Dr. Shrivastava's final judgment about the situation in Bhopal and the outlook for the victims of that awful tragedy is, if anything, more devastating:

Government is the biggest provider of relief in absolute dollar terms.

But government efforts are slow, tangled in bureaucratic procedures, unfocused, on the whole inadequate and primarily aimed at preventing a political crisis. Union Carbide which has the resources to provide relief is managing the situation from a business perspective. Its stock price is now back nearly to the pre-accident level so it does not feel pressured to aggressively seek ways of helping victims. Volunteer organizations have committed workers but no resources to make a significant impact. The result for thousands of permanently injured and incapacitated victims is slow agonizing death.

The People React

As Paul Shrivastava noted, government efforts to deal with the disaster seemed to be directed primarily toward averting a political crisis. For months after the disaster there have been rumblings from the victims and voluntary agencies trying to help them. In late March, for example, some 150 women staged a demonstration on the premises of a government hospital near the Carbide factory, demanding the availability of sodium thiosulphate treatments for victims of cyanide poisoning. In mid-May, the *Times of India* in Bombay reported that "a large number of victims of last December's gas leak, mostly women, were beaten up by the police when they forceably tried to enter the Union Carbide pesticide plant" (May 19). They were participating in a demonstration to press for adequate relief and medical facilities.

The pot continued to bubble until the last week of June when it boiled over. The local government, learning that a demonstration was to be organized on June 25, staged a preemptive strike on the night of June 24, arresting 35 activists and slum dwellers, including 12 women and five doctors. The demonstration the next day nonetheless went on, resulting, according to press reports, in police violence against the demonstrators. Commented the *Indian Express*, one of India's most widely circulated and respected newspapers, in an editorial in its July 2, 1985, New Delhi edition:

> Regrettably the [Madhya Pradesh] State Government seems to view every demonstration as an impudent challenge to its authority. Clearly there can be no other explanation of the brutal scuttling of the gas victims' demonstration for relief and rehabilitation, organized on June 25 by the Zahreeli Gas Khand Sangharsh Morcha and the rude treatment of the activists behind it. The Government seems to forget that people demonstrate only when other means of drawing attention to their plight fails. Or does it think that the people of Bhopal have nothing to demonstrate about? In that case, it has lost all touch with reality. Meanwhile, the rest of the country looks the other way. Is is that the rehabilitation of the gas disaster victims has now become a purely Bhopal problem?

If the rest of India looks the other way, how much more true is it that the rest of the world appears largely to have forgotten about Bhopal—and how remote now seems the goal of achieving justice for the Bhopal victims, the subject to which we now turn.

Chapter 3

JUSTICE FOR THE BHOPAL VICTIMS

Bhopal: A Travesty of Justice

The scale and intensity of the Bhopal disaster boggles the mind. It is not only the thousands of people who have already died but the tens of thousands who, while they may have survived thus far, are experiencing great physical suffering and emotional anguish. Virtually all are very poor and vulnerable. It is also the arrogance and contempt with which these powerless victims have been and are being treated.

For months, their lives were placed at risk while safety standards and maintenance procedures were allowed by the Union Carbide management to deteriorate because the plant was no longer profitable. When the worst happened, this contempt for the well-being of Carbide's neighbors was compounded by blatant acts of injustice to the victims. First insisting there was no leak, then failing to sound the public alarm on the night of the accident, next providing misleading information on treatment for the toxic effects of MIC and other substances, trying to pin the blame on local workers, conducting a media blitz to divert attention from those really responsible—the litany of injustices is long, making the pain of the victims all the greater.

The litigation now before the U.S. and Indian courts will, if it is allowed to proceed, establish clearly and unequivocally whether the

managements of both the parent U.S. corporation and its Indian subsidiary are guilty of gross negligence. But while they may be the
principal agents of injustice to the Bhopal victims, they are not the
only ones. The state government of Madhya Pradesh and the national
government, while they did not cause and are not directly responsible
for the accident, could have prevented it if stronger and more strictly
enforced industrial safety and environmental laws and regulations existed. To underscore how interconnected are the roles of government
and company, strict enforcement would have required far greater co-
operation from Carbide than appears to have been forthcoming, in the
absence of much more sophisticated monitoring mechanisms than now
exist in Bhopal. But that said, the government clearly bears a measure
of responsibility for the disaster because of its failure to enforce the
environmental and worker safety standards that already exist and because of its failure to create or implement effective emergency procedures.

We have already examined the sorry record of government relief
and health care efforts for the victims. To make matters worse, government agencies have withheld information and restricted the availability of drugs that would have helped in the treatment of the surviving
victims, paralleling the Union Carbide refusal to release information
about the toxic character of MIC and the nature of other chemicals
involved in this tragedy. A large number of the victims, because of
both their injuries and the dislocation of Bhopal's economic life caused
by the disaster, are unable to resume normal working lives, making
all the more critical the need for rehabilitation and employment generation schemes.

Other perpetrators of injustice to the Bhopal victims surely include
the American personal injury lawyers who swooped like vultures down
on the city of Bhopal soon after disaster struck. Motivated by greed,
rather than compassion, as a few of them were at least candid enough
to admit, they secured representation agreeements from large numbers
of victims, using Indian accomplices as go-betweens. The antics of
these scavenging lawyers has kept attention overly focused on the
question of financial compensation, with the resulting neglect of other
actions needed to bring about true justice to the victims.

This travesty of injustices to the Bhopal victims led Judge John
F. Keenan, before whose Federal District Court in New York all
lawsuits in the federal courts on behalf of Bhopal victims have been
consolidated, to ask Union Carbide Corporation as a matter of "fundamental human decency" to provide an immediate fund of $5-10
million for immediate aid to the victims. The difficulties involved in

finding an acceptable channel for using this money to provide meaningful help to the victims have already been discussed in the preceding
chapter.

Somewhat more hopeful are the modest initiatives that have been
mounted by Indian voluntary organizations to help the victims. These
initiatives could be greatly expanded with support from international
relief organizations and voluntary agencies in other countries. But even
the efforts of voluntary agencies have not been above criticism. Squab-
bling among voluntary agency leaders and confused and sometimes
seemingly contradictory priorities have been compounded by government harassment when the political challenge posed by some of the
agencies was perceived by key goverment officials as a threat to public
order and their own positions of power and authority.

We fervently hope that, by the time this book is published, that
Judge Keenan's concern for "fundamental human decency" will have
borne fruit and a comprehensive program of assistance that actually
reaches and gives genuine aid and comfort to the Bhopal victims will
be underway. The victims urgently need real help, not talk or promises,
and not only for immediate needs such as nutrition and health care but
also for longer term problems such as housing rehabilitation, vocational
training for the handicapped, and employment generation.

The Concept of Justice

Providing immediate help, important as it is, is only one element
in securing justice for the Bhopal victims. The magnitude of the Bhopal
disaster and the apparent negligence that caused it surely rank this
tragedy among the major twentieth-century crimes against humanity.
Because of its historic and unprecedented character, Bhopal thus gives
us an opportunity to reexamine the most basic meanings of justice and
to break new ground, legally and morally, in redefining and extending
those meanings to encompass the manifold harms inflicted on the poor
and powerless Bhopal victims.

The concept of justice has at least two fundamental dimensions.
One concerns application of the law according to the rules of equity
or fairness. The other is broader, involving the principles of rectitude
and integrity in the dealings of human beings (and institutions they
have created such as governments and corporations) with one another.

In any discussion of justice for the Bhopal victims, it is critically
important that this broader definition should be applied in judging the
adequacy of whatever has been and will be done for the victims. For,

with very few exceptions, they are not only very poor but singularly vulnerable to and innocent of the awful tragedy that has befallen them.

Thus far, it must be said that precious little has been done to fulfill this larger concept of justice as a moral obligation—what Judge Keenan called "a matter of fundamental human decency." Most attention has focused on narrower, legalistic definitions of justice. But even here there is much scope for socially creative initiatives which are sensitive to the plight of poor and innocent people whose lives have been rent asunder by an event over which they had no control. The scope for developing new law through further evolution of the legal concept of justice exists, furthermore, in at least three different contexts—under Indian law, U.S. law, and international law.

That there should be a pluarality of concepts of justice in the Bhopal tragedy is only natural, given the nationality of the key actors involved and the transnational context in which they were operating. The victims are entitled to the fullest measure of justice under any and all concepts. Singularly inappropriate, given the enormity of their injuries and suffering and the apparently negligent behavior of Carbide, is the proposition advanced in a May 1985 *Wall Street Journal* article on compensation of the victims discussed below, which is based on the most restricted definition of justice.

Certainly, any defensible definition of justice must banish, once and for all, the chauvanism implicit in double standards for industrial safety where human lives are at stake. The protestations of the Union Carbide management to the contrary notwithstanding, the *actual practice* has been to observe two standards in operation of Carbide plants—one for the U.S. and the other for India. (Specifics of double standards in Bhopal and the sister Carbide plant in Institute, West Virginia, are given in the first chapter.)

But surely human life is as precious in Bhopal as it is in Institute. The Nuremberg trials after the Second World War clearly establishd the principle that those who kill, maim, or otherwise victimize innocent people have committed crimes against humanity and can be held accountable for those crimes not only under the laws of individual states but also under international law as created by the human community as a whole. Justice for the Bhopal victims demands nothing less in this, the worst industrial disaster in history.

Beyond legal definitions of justice lie the broader principles of human conduct mentioned above such as rectitude, integrity, and fairness. Warren Anderson, Chairman of Union Carbide, while disclaiming any legal liability on the part of the U.S. company for what happened in Bhopal, accepted for Union Carbide "moral responsibility for the whole issue [i.e., the tragedy in Bhopal]'' (December 10, 1984, news conference as recorded by BBC). We need to know what this self-assumed standard really means for Anderson, the other Carbide officials concerned, and the company itself. What are they going to do to see that justice in the most fundamental sense of human decency is provided to the poor victims of Bhopal?

There is little evidence thus far that this self-assumed responsibility is anything more than a public relations ploy, no matter how genuinely Warren Anderson may personally feel for the plight of the victims. The dominant pattern of his actual behavior as Chief Executive Officer of Carbide has been, so far as we have been able to observe it, precisely the opposite—namely, seeking to frustrate efforts to bring true justice to the victims by giving primacy to protecting the assets of the company. Indeed, his true feelings appear to be more accurately reflected in his statement to the press as the first anniversary of the tragedy approached that he ''overreacted'' in his expressions of concern over the impact of the disaster on the company in the first few weeks after the disaster occurred.

What Needs to Be Done

What follows is a minimum action program necessary to bring justice to the Bhopal victims. Litigation in the courts is only one means of achieving justice for the Bhopal victims, albeit an important one. Others include use of the political process, actions by non-governmental agencies and institutions, including groups within the community, and public education. Whatever the means used, the objective should be to secure the fullest measure possible of justice for the victims and to hold those responsible for the tragedy accountable.

1) Relief

The most obvious and immediate aspect of justice to the Bhopal victims is precisely what has engaged Judge Keenan's attention—namely, relief—i.e., efforts to sustain the victims and help them cope with the harsh new day-to-day realities confronting them. Relief includes the provision of adequate nutrition, health care services, housing and community rehabilitation, and for those able to work, generation of suitable employment.

Judging from the experience of the victims so far, realizing a just measure of relief as defined here will not be easily accomplished. By using a combination of legal, administrative, and political processes, voluntary agencies and public interest law groups concerned about achieving justice for the victims can play a significant role. Thus, they can move to secure more access to information from both government and Union Carbide sources that will facilitate proper medical treatment of the victims and remove constraints on their treatment (for instance, the results of autopsies, data on the different chemicals involved in the atmospheric leak, availability of suitable medicines).

In a similar manner, public interest lawyers and citizen action groups should be monitoring what the government of India, both directly and through the state government, is in fact providing for the victims' nutrition—both the adequacy of foodstuffs allotted and their *actual* delivery to the victims. Similar roles need to be played in the realm of employment, invoking such protection as exists under Indian labor and social welfare legislation and working toward the resolution of all of the many problems involved in creating alternative employment for the victims and their retraining and rehabilitation to qualify them for such employment.

2) Reparations

Beyond relief is a much more comprehensive consideration of reparations to the victims for the harms they have experienced. Reparation is a multifaceted component of justice which involves at least five major elements:

1. Restitution—i.e., giving back, to the extent possible, what was lost by the victims. (There is, of course, no restitution for death or permanent personal injury.)
2. Compensation for direct and ancillary losses, not only to date but as far into the future as the impact of the disaster will continue to affect the victims. (Because of the nature of the Indian joint family, in which one wage earner may be responsible for supporting two or three generations, such compensation will need to be calculated, if it is to be fair, beyond the expected lifetimes of those who died and the surviving but disabled victims. Evidence of chromosomal damage to some victims gives even greater force to this proposition. Unborn children of gas-leak victims are surely entitled to compensation if they have serious genetic deformities attributable to the exposure of their parents to MIC.)
3. Damages, which go beyond actual compensation and seek to assess the intangible losses suffered by the victims, both physical and emotional.

4. Accountability. Justice for the victims, who have suffered so much, must surely include strict accountability for those responsible for their suffering.
5. Punishment. To hold those responsible accountable, concrete actions must be taken if justice is to be done. In jurisprudence there are four objectives of punishment—1) prevention, 2) deterrence, 3) retribution, and 4) reformation. Punishment in the Bhopal disaster should certainly include prevention (e.g., shutting down the Carbide plant or outlawing use of MIC in India), deterrence (i.e., punitive damages), and reformation (i.e., efforts to change the industrial environment so that extremely dangerous chemicals would no longer be manufactured or used). Retribution has increasingly been replaced with the concept of "doing right by the victims," which is the overriding objective of the minimum action program being described here.

3) Investigations

Investigations are key to assuring that there are adequate reparations as defined above. These investigations, in which public interest lawyers and citizen action groups have a vital role to play, should also lead to better preventative measures to diminish sharply the likelihood of such a catastrophe occurring again.

These investigations should include the causes of the accident and what occurred during and following the runaway reaction and emission of MIC and other chemicals from the Carbide plant (including the design, safety, and maintenance of the plant and toxicology of MIC and other possible reaction products), deaths, personal injuries, and damages from the accident, and continuing in long-term tracking of health and environmental impacts.

Various official and unofficial investigations and inquiries have been launched, such as the government of India's Central Bureau of Investigation, the Madhya Pradesh Government Enquiry Commission, Union Carbide's own "investigation" into the accident, and hearings of different U.S. Congressional committees and inquiries of governmenment agencies such as the Environmental Protection Agency and the Occupational Safety and Health Administration, not to mention different citizens' groups in Bhopal, the U.S., and elsewhere. The completeness and accuracy of these investigations need to be critically assessed by independent sources, and pressure asserted through public disclosure when shortcomings or omissions are identified. Litigation itself becomes, through the discovery process in a court of law, an important tool of investigation.

A sharp distinction should be drawn between genuine investigations and those which masquerade as "investigations" but are in fact exercises designed to obscure what really happened in pursuit of self-serving objectives of those undertaking or commissioning the so-called investigations. A classic illustration of the latter type of "non-investigation" is the Union Carbide report on the accident at its Bhopal plant, which was released in March 1985 and which advances the spurious theory that the accident was caused by "sabotage" without producing any evidence whatever to support such a hair-brained proposition.

It appears that there are a number of gaps in the investigations underway and considerable scope for more thorough and extensive studies and inquiries if there is to be meaningful justice for the Bhopal victims. For example, to the best of our knowledge at the time of writing, there has yet to be constructed an atmospheric diffusion model (a technique used in air pollution studies) to determine what was the likely exposure to different substances in different localities around the Carbide plant, although the Air Pollution Control Board has gathered some of the needed data in the report mentioned in the preceding chapter. Nor have there yet been any *serious and comprehensive* epidemiological studies to determine the incidence and the extent of injuries to the surviving victims (although the Indian Council of Medical Research has reported that such a study is underway). Such steps as these are crucial if there is to be meaningful justice for the Bhopal victims. In filling gaps such as these, public interest lawyers can help citizen groups gain access to vital information such as the current condition of the victims and the actual status of relief, health care, and other efforts to assist the victims. They can also take steps to see that properly organized and financed studies are made.

4) Public Education

Yet another element of justice for the Bhopal victims involves public education and consciousness-raising among the community at risk—i.e., victims, workers, and users. Only when such affected groups understand fully the situation will they be in a position to determine whether justice has been done, and if it has not, to insist that it be done. Such public awareness is, furthermore, a crucial prerequisite to yet another dimension of justice for the Bhopal victims—namely, pressure for changes in existing institutions, both governmental and private, and in productive activities that will make another Bhopal truly impossible.

Public interest lawyers and citizen action groups have a major role to play in helping communities and groups of persons whose lives are placed at risk to assert their rights to know and to act in protecting themselves. To give an especially poignant illustration where these rights have not been effectively exercised in Bhopal, pregnant women exposed to the gas leak clearly had a right to know in time about the possible impact of such exposure on their pregnancy and, if they so chose, to have an abortion. Workers have similar rights to adequate safety and maintenance when handling hazardous substances, rights that were flagrantly abused in the Carbide plant. And the right to know of consumers about hazardous products should be manifested in adequate labeling and specific warnings about harmful effects and what should be done in the event of exposure.

We have a long way to go in both India and the United States, as well as many other countries, before the rights of workers, communities, and consumers at risk from hazardous products are fully realized, and even farther to go before their rights to participate in decisions affecting their well-being, if not their very survival, are fully granted. Meaningful justice to the Bhopal victims requires that these rights to know and to act should be fully respected, clearly a major challenge for public interest lawyers and citizen groups not only in India and the U.S. but all around the world. At a still more fundamental level, justice to the Bhopal victims requires that their choices in life, especially in where they live and what kind of work they do, be substantially enlarged. The poor and vulnerable are frequently compelled to live and work in hazardous environments because they lack any real choice.

Compensation and Punitive Damages

The question of the criteria and methods to be used in calculating compensation for the victims has occupied considerable public attention, as much with an eye to its possible impact on Union Carbide's financial fortunes as to what it will do for the victims. While there is much more to securing justice for the Bhopal victims than payments of money, as we have tried to demonstrate, the adequacy of compensation is obviously an important element in realizing true justice for the victims. Estimates of possible compensation vary widely and depend in part on whether Indian or American standards are used.

Recent cases in American courts involving comparable circumstances such as the Karen Silkwood case have resulted in jury awards on the order of $500,000 as compensation for the suffering involved. (In Silkwood, the Kerr-McGee Corporation allowed plutonium, a highly poisonous radioactive substance, to escape from its plant; Silkwood's lungs were contaminated with a dose sufficient to give her cancer, and she suffered with this knowledge for one week before she died in a car crash.) If a U.S. jury awarded $500,000 for mental distress for one week as in the Silkwood case, what would the court award for the tens of thousands of Bhopal victims who have endured not only physical injury but also great emotional anguish for many months?

The range of possibilities is very wide. At one extreme, Douglas J. Besajrov and Peter Reuter argue in the *Wall Street Journal* ("Averting a Bhopal Legal Disaster," May 16, 1985) that a U.S. court would take into account the differences betwen U.S. and Indian costs and standards of living. Since Indian per capita income is less than two per cent of the comparable U.S. figure (about $250 vs. $15,000), a U.S. court might award only $8,500 for an Indian's death in contrast to $500,000 for an American's death. Applying the same adjustment to injuries and using as a standard the $64,000 average payment to asbestos victims in recent litigation, the authors calculate that the average for each injury would be $1,100. If these figures were the basis for compensation, the total would come to between $200 million and $300 million. The former figure is said to have been the first offer made by Union Carbide in its negotiations with the government of India which promply rejected it as too low.

There are good reasons for the government of India having done so. This per capita income method is inappropriate. It does not take into account, for example, the needs of the surviving victims for health care, the costs of which are very likely to be comparable to what such costs would be in the U.S. Medical costs are largely dictated by the character of the care involved, not by the geographical location where it is needed. Medical costs may well be lower in India for treating certain types of known conditions, but the health problems of the Bhopal victims are clearly not well understood and will require a variety of treatments novel in the Indian context and therefore much more costly to provide. Beyond that, however, is the consideration that truly thorough and comprehensive epidemiological studies over long periods of time are very expensive. Witness the assertion by Union Carbide, in a letter from its lawyers to Judge Keenan on May 8, 1985, that it has spent $129,000 just for fees and expenses of three internationally recognized medical specialists who went to Bhopal at Carbide's request immediately after the accident and for related expenses of several other experts on MIC exposure.

Nor does the per capita income method take into account the family structure dominant in Indian society, in which one wage earner is often responsible for the maintenance of two or three generations of a joint family. Obviously, the earning potential of future generations of that family are going to be adversely affected by the death or disablement of the key wage earning member, introducing a significant multiplier effect.

The Besajrov/Reuter proposal is even more fundamentally flawed. There can, of course, be different figures in different societal contexts for economic losses due to injury—i.e., restitution on purely economic terms. To use per capita income figures for a country as large and diverse as India as a basis for determining economic losses to the actual victims in the city of Bhopal is ridiculous. It is like using per capita income figures for the U.S. as a whole to calculate lifetime income loss for residents of one of America's major cities. More precise data on income levels in Bhopal, which reflect the wide gap between urban and rural consumption patterns and living standards (even for the urban poor) can and should be collected.

But even more importantly, by failing to include non-economic factors which would ordinarily be considered by U.S. courts for American victims, they have invidiously introduced a double standard. And when it comes to calculating monetary amounts for such phenomena as loss of life, mental distress, and deprivation of companionship for the survivors, there can be no double standard if we truly subscribe to the proposition that human life is as valuable in the Indian subcontinent as it is in North America. Indeed, given the extended nature of the Indian joint family, it could well be argued that loss of life leads to even greater deprivation of companionship than with the American nuclear family and that, therefore, still more substantial awards are in order for survivors of the Bhopal victims.

A more comprehensive calculation has been made by Professor Alfred DeGrazia, formerly on the faculty of New York and Stanford Universities, in one of the first books about Bhopal to be published (*A Cloud Over Bhopal*, Bombay: Kalos Foundation, 1985). Based also on Indian economic conditions (the basic multiplier is an annual wage of $1,500, roughly equal, according to Professor DeGrazia, to a worker's pay and benefits at the Union Carbide plant in Bhopal), he arrives at the following bill of particulars:

Category of Damages	Amount of Damage
	(in U.S.$ millions)
Survivors of Dead (estimate of 3,000 persons, loss of 85,000 human years of productive work at $1,500 per work year)	127.50
50% + Disabled (estimated 10,000 persons and 265,000 work years at $750 per year)	198.75
25% + Disabled (estimated 20,000 persons with total loss of 553,360 work years at $325 per year)	179.84
10% + Disabled (estimated 180,000 persons x $150 per year x 10 years)	720.00
Business Losses (at least two-weeks' loss of work for much of the city of Bhopal, calculated at 1/30th of the city's annual gross product of goods and services of approximately $2 billion)	64.00
Animal and Property Loss	1.00
Awards to Helping Groups	1.00
Costs of Executing Judgments/Settlements	20.00
Fees and Costs of Attorneys	6.56
	————
Total	$1,318.65

Professor DeGrazia's total thus comes to $1.3 billion for compensation for economic losses alone, even though the bases for his calculations are very modest. In sharp contrast, Carbide's New York lawyers have cited, in their May 8 letter to Judge Keenan, two earlier disasters in India—a collapsed dam in 1979 and a serious train wreck in 1981—by way of demonstrating how little is typically awarded to victims or survivors of victims of catastrophic accidents. (Compensation for each death in the dam incident was approximately $250, and in the train wreck two years later, $1,825.) But this is an inappropriate analogy for at least two reasons. First, the party ultimately liable in these two disasters was the government itself, and the government is notoriously stingy about providing adequate compensation. In the Bhopal tragedy, the party ultimately responsible is a well-heeled, U.S.-based multinational company.

Second, and much more important, the circumstances in all three disasters are markedly different. Furthermore, there is a clear trend in level of compensation from the dam tragedy in 1979 to the railway accident in 1981. Compensation in the latter instance is seven times greater than in the former. Thus, these two disasters provide very dubious precedence for calculating what would be appropriate as compensation in the Bhopal tragedy.

But even if Professor deGrazia's more comprehensive calculations were to be taken as a basis for determining compensation for economic losses, his method of calculation is flawed in one vital respect, leading him to substantially understate the actual economic loss suffered by the victims and their survivors. He neglects to allow for inflation which, over time periods measured in decades rather than years, is very substantial. From 1960 through 1984, by way of illustration, the Consumer Price Index for industrial workers on an all India basis increased from 100 to 586—in other words, an increase of almost six times. While the government of India does not report a separate Consumer Price Index for Bhopal, it does for another city in Madhya Pradesh, and the increase there is even slightly higher—595.

Nor does Professor deGrazia include any provision for other aspects of relief and rehabilitation discussed above such as health and nutrititional care or building and maintaining community infrastructure and facilities to assure the physical well-being of the disabled. Our calculations, based on conservative assumptions of what we now know about the extent and character of the impact of the gas leak from the Union Carbide plant and with an extremely modest allowance for inflation over the next two to three decades, come to a *minimum* of $4.1 billion for *economic losses and relief and restitution alone* (i.e., not including compensation for intangible damages such as pain and suffering and emotional anguish or punitive damages). The accompanying table gives particulars, category by category.

Several additional comments are in order on these calculations. One is their conservative nature. The Madhya Pradesh Commissioner of Relief told us on the first anniversary of the disaster that the government has already registered 350,000 claims against Carbide, and the claim registration process (conducted under large tents erected in open areas near the slum colonies around the Carbide plant) is still going on. He was not yet able to characterize the magnitude of these complaints, but they suggest that the numbers we have used in making the foregoing computation of likely compensation are quite cautious. How many of these claims can be sustained in a court of law or will be encompassed in any overall out-of-court settlement is, naturally, another question.

Another indication of the conservative nature of these calculations concerns business losses. One of the other major industrial concerns in Bhopal, a government-owned corporation, Bharat Heavy Electricals Ltd. (BHEL), is said to have registered a claim for one month's business loss at Rs.250,000,000 ($20.8 million). This claim alone is two and a half times the total figure we have used of $8 million and does not include claims registered by some 19,000 small businesses, not to mention a number of medium-sized companies.

Calculation of Compensation for Economic Losses, Relief, and Restitution for the Bhopal Victims

Category of Compensation	Amount (in U.S. $ millions)	

A. *Statistical mapping* of the tragedy (determining as precisely as possible the number of fatalities, the extent of impairment of survivors, their age distribution, employment status, number of wage earners per household lost through death or disablement, average number of dependents per family, etc.) $10

B. *Survivors of the dead* (estimate of 5,000 fatalities; average remaining life expectancy of 10, 20, and 30 years; estimate of average "lower middle class" *household* income in Bhopal of Rs2,660 per month [U.S.$222] or Rs31,920 per year [U.S.$2,660]; number of fatalities diluted by 25 per cent to 3,750 to account for multiple fatalities in the same household, death of person other than actual or potential prime cash income provider, etc.)[1]

Loss of income per fatality per year = $2,660

1,250 persons x $2,660 x 10 years =	$33	
1,250 persons x $2,660 x 20 years =	66	
1,250 persons x $2,660 x 30 years =	99	198

C. *Disabled* (estimate of 60,000 persons, average of 25 percent disability, assumptions regarding remaining working life, household income, dilution to account for multiple personal injuries in the same family, etc., as in B. above)

Loss of income per fatality per year = $2,660
60,000 disabled x 25 per cent disability = 15,000 full-time equivalent disabled x .75 dilution for multiple injuries in same household, etc. = 11,250 equivalent fully disabled persons

3,750 persons x $2,660 x 10 years =	$ 99.8	
3,750 persons x $2,660 x 20 years =	199.6	
3,750 persons x $2,660 x 30 years =	299.4	599

D. *Health care* for and monitoring of 200,000 victims and their survivors for the next

30 years (calculated on the basis of $100
per person per year, a very low figure
for modern health care costs)[2]
    200,000 persons x $100 = $20 million a year x 30
        years =   600

E. *Food and nutrititional support* (based on
government of India estimate of $7 mil-
lion for 200,000 for six months or an
annual per capita cost of $70)[3]
    First 5 years after the accident:
    200,000 persons at $70 a year x 5 years =   70
    Next 5 years: 100,000 persons at $70 a year x 5 years   35   105
    =

F. *Building and maintaining community infrastructure* and facilities to assure
physical well-being of significantly disabled victims (sanitation, water supply,
housing, etc.)[4]
    $12 million x 10 years =   120

G. *Vocational rehabilitation and alternative
employment* of disabled victims (based
on $150 per year per person for new job
creation)[5]
    50,000 persons for 5 years = 250,000 person years
    x $300 ($150 retraining; $150 new job creation) =   75

H. *Epidemiological surveys* (sample of 85,670
individuals now being surveyed by Indian Council of Medical Research; annual cost of $100 for clinical
examinations, medical record keeping,
etc. or 25 per cent of equivalent U.S.
per capita figure for similar epidemiological surveys)[6]
    85,670 persons x $100 per year (for clinical exami-
    nation, medical record keeping, etc.) x 20 years =   173

I. *Unidentified and future victims* (based on
the assumption that one out of every 10
persons in the city of Bhopal will manifest long-term health effects and will
involve health care costs and other support services such as items E and G of
$200 per year per person for a period
of 10 years)
    67,000 persons x 10 years x $200 per year =   134

J. *Business losses* (at least two weeks' loss of
    work for much of the city of Bhopal,
    calculated at 1/26th of the 1984 per cap-
    ita GNP)
        $306/260 = $12
        $12 per person income loss x 671,000 =   8

K. *Animal losses* ($250 each x 2,000 larger
    animals lost in the disaster)   1

        Subtotal $2,023

Allowance for inflation (doubling over an average time period of 20 years, a mere fraction
of historical inflation rates which increased
almost six times from1960 to 1984)[7]   x 2
                             $4,046

Costs of executing judgments/settlements and
attorney's fees   20
Minimum compensation for economic losses,
relief, and restitution $4,066

Note: Data on per capita income, household size, life expectancy, and population of
Bhopal are taken from the World Bank, *World Development Report, 1985* and the
Statistical Outline of India, 1983/84, (Bombay, Tata Services Ltd., 1984). Other
sources are indicated in the notes below.
[1] Based on discussion with Professor Paul Shrivastava, New York University, a native
of Bhopal, who estimates minimum residential accommodation cost for a "lower
middle class" family (a standard to which even the very poor might reasonably
aspire and some achieve) of Rs.400 per month. Accommodation costs are typically
15 per cent of an urban family budget. More refined numbers on living costs are
being developed by competent authorities in Bhopal.
[2] Indian health care costs are only marginally relevant in making this calculation
because the victims face new kinds of health problems never before dealt with in
India. This means that expertise, equipment, and in some cases, drugs will need to
be brought to Bhopal from other parts of the world, and this is very costly. For
example, the Union Carbide Corporation, by its own admission, spent $129,008 to
bring three medical specialists to India right after the disaster.
[3] Letter from Kelley, Drye and Warren (Union Carbide Corporation attorneys) to
Judge John F. Keenan, May 8, 1985.
[4] While comparisons are difficult because each situation is distinctive, this cost calculation reflects UNICEF's experience in implementing comparable programs for
the urban poor in India.
[5] Here again comparisons are difficult, but these estimates reflect the experience of
UNICEF and other international agencies in India.

6 Based on discussions with staff members of the Department of Community Health and Social Medicine at the City University of New York Medical School and the Mt. Sinai Medical Center Department of Environmental Medicine. The above figures are only rough approximations. More precise calculation requires greater specificity in identifying the number of variables to be surveyed and the characteristics of the target populations.

7 A more precise calculation of total compensation would involve determining the rate of inflation for each category of compensation. In some instances, where the costs involved are immediate or very short term, little or no allowance for inflation will need to be made. In other instances, such as the calculations for income loss for fatalities and injured persons, inflation over periods as long as 30 years will require a major adjustment in.current dollars or rupees. The same applies to health care costs and nutrititional support. Since these categories constitute a substantial proportion of total compensation, the inflation factor used above—i.e., doubling total compensation calculated in current dollars—appears very conservative.

While the income figures we have used may at first glance seem high, certainly in relation to per capita income in India, several factors need to be taken into account. One is the disparity in income levels between urban and rural areas which we have already mentioned. Another is the need to take into account (which we have tried to do) non-cash income of the victims. Like the poor elsewhere in the world, these slum dwellers in Bhopal worst affected by the gas leak meet their living needs in a variety of ways, including barter, non-monetized work, and facilities for which they may not have paid cash but which nonetheless have a real monetary value (for example, self-constructed squatter housing). Any fair method of calculating income loss from death or permanent disability will need to take all of these factors into account, then translating them into monetary amounts since that is presumably the principal form which the compensation will take.

The complexity of determining loss of lifetime income is underscored in one of the standard authorities in U.S. personal injury litigation, the massive three-volume work by Stuart M. Speiser, *Recovery for Wrongful Death* (Rochester, New York: Lawyers Cooperative Publishing Company, 1979, 2nd edition), especially the third volume entitled *Economic Handbook*. Take, for example, the changes in income levels during a person's lifetime embraced in what the U.S. Census Bureau refers to as ''aging,'' a concept which encompasses changes in experience, knowledge, skill, exertion, and mobility. What would be the impact, in terms of income earned, of a significant skill acquisition by one of the Bhopal victims which would increase substantially individual productivity. We believe, therefore, that the income figures we have used in making our calculations for compensation are in fact reasonable when all of these different variables are taken into account, although there is certainly a need for a better empirical base for making lost income determinations as the local authorities in Bhopal are now doing.

It should be emphasized again that the $4.1 billion figure does not include any compensation for intangible or non-economic losses such as pain and suffering or emotional anguish. If the double standard in matters of the quality of human life (not its presumed economic worth) is to be eschewed in the cause of justice for the Bhopal victims, prevailing standards in comparable personal injury cases in American courts such as the Silkwood case should apply. This would clearly multiply the total figure several times over.

Moreover, if punitive damages are also awarded, the total figure would be *very much higher still*. In the Karen Silkwood case, the jury awarded her estate $500,000 in compensation and $10 million in punitive damages. That punitive damages of some sort would almost certainly be awarded to the Bhopal victims if their case was litigated to the ultimate end of a decision seems almost certain. As Rob Hager, an American public interest lawyer, points out in the March 25-April 7, 1985 issue of *BusinessIndia*, "The reckless conduct for which the punitive damages were awarded in Silkwood was not as grave as that already revealed by Carbide at Bhopal before and after the release of MIC."

Punitive damages are intended to deter the perpetrator of the disaster from future behavior that might lead to another catastrophe in instances where gross negligence on the perpetrator's part can be established. The magnitude of punitive damages in personal injury cases depends upon how gross and willful the negligent behavior of the defendant is determined by the court to be. The fairest way to determine punitive damages, as well as compensatory damages for pain and suffering, is through the collective judgment of a jury.

Whatever the figure is, however, it is clearly of an entirely different order of magnitude than the numbers reported in the press as being discussed between Carbide and the government of India. The government of India is said to be holding out for at least $1 billion—a totally inadequate figure—but even if it were two or three times as great, it would still be insufficient. If there were a settlement at that level, it would represent a travesty of justice for the Bhopal victims—and the difference between that figure and the reported maximum offer by Carbide ($230 million) is very, very wide.

What is finally determined will depend on which courts end up being principally involved in the litigation and whether or not the litigation is carried through to the stage of judicial decision. Because there is always the possibility that Judge Keenan may dismiss the suit on the grounds of *forum non conveniens*, thus moving it into the Indian courts, there is likely to be enormous pressure by the American personal injury lawyers to reach a settlement before that happens. (This is because these lawyers, who are working on a contingency fee basis, feel that they would get nothing at all or very little if the litigation were to go into Indian courts where contingency fees are not permitted.) Ordinarily, according to Melvin Belli, one of the leading U.S. personal injury lawyers in the case, the management and directors of a major corporation will not settle for any amount in excess of the company's insurance and bank loans. In Union Carbide's case, these have been estimated to come to some $600 million, substantially less than the $1 billion minimum asking figure of the government of India and not even in the same realm of magnitude as our minimum of $4.1 billion for economic losses alone, or $15-20 billion if non-economic damages for pain and suffering and punitive damages are included.

While there are some advantages to the principal litigation over compensation and damages remaining in the U.S. courts, we are by no means convinced that all would be lost if a ruling of *forum non conveniens* were made by Judge Keenan. For one thing, a condition of such a ruling would be that the parent Union Carbide Corporation would have to agree to submit to the authority of the Indian courts, where a concept equivalent to punitive damages—called "exemplary damages"—does exist. Under Indian judicial procedure, the case could go directly to the Indian Supreme Court. And there, given the character of the court and the considerable possibilities that "socially concerned" justices have in developing new law to apply to an extraordinary and unprecedented case, the decision might come more quickly and be every bit as comprehensive in terms of awarding compensation and damages to the victims as would a decision from a U.S. court.

One additional advantage to having the case played out in the Indian court system is that contingency fees for legal services are not allowed. Consequently, there would be no way that the American personal injury lawyers in the case would be able to walk away with huge fees for their part in representing the poor and hapless victims of Bhopal.

Consequences for Union Carbide, Hazardous Industries—and the Bhopal Victims

Two critical questions need to be addressed: What can Union

Carbide afford to pay and what would be just and fair to the Bhopal victims? Since Union Carbide's total assets are approximately $10 billion, it might be assumed that damages in excess of that amount are simply beyond the capacity of the company to pay and would only result in its liquidation. But this is not the case, and our calculations on compensation above are made with due regard for Union Carbide's capacity to pay.

Some categories of compensation involve activities extending over 20 to 30 years (e.g., epidemiological surveys, provision of health care services). Others could be structured, as part of negotiating a compensation package, so that they were payable over longer periods of time (e.g., compensation for income loss for families of the dead and for the disabled).

Because of the number of variables involved, it is not possible now to make a precise calculation, but we believe that an initial sum of less than $3 billion set aside at the beginning and administered on the insurance principle of an annuity (i.e., with reinvestment of interest) would be sufficient to meet a total damages award of $15-20 billion extended over 20-30 years—assuming that a jury would award roughly the equivalent of economic losses for pain and suffering and the equivalent of the total of those two categories of compensatory damages to cover punitive damages. (At 10 per cent interest, the principal would be doubled in seven years and doubled again in five more years. Additional funding could be provided in subsequent years should experience indicate that trust funds established initially are inadequate to meet future obligations in the compensation package.)

We think that the minimum action program set forth in this chapter is just that—the minimum effort required to see that justice is done to the victims. And that, we calculate, will require at least $4.1 billion, without even compensating the victims for their pain, suffering, and emotional anguish. While that is a substantial sum of money, the injury and devastation experienced by the victims has occurred on an historically unprecedented scale.

But more than money, even a substantial amount like $4.1 billion, is involved in assuring that justice is provided to the victims. Compensation, after all, is a means to an end, not an end in and of itself. Attention must also be given to mechanisms for assuring that the ends of justice as outlined here are served. Delivery of justice to the victims thus becomes a second critical question.

That delivery will not be easily accomplished, judging from the experience with relief operations in Bhopal since the December 1984 disaster. Let us start with what should not be done if the Bhopal victims are to be justly treated. There should not be a single, bureaucratically administered program for the victims. That program should not be distributing large-scale cash payments to the victims who will almost immediately be subject to extortion and exploitation even if they should get what is due them. While calculations of monetized damages are inescapable, it is not the payment of money as such that matters but rather the efforts made to restore the lives of the victims, to the extent possible, to what it was before and then to try to compensate them for loss and suffering which cannot really be covered by money.

Implementing a program of justice for the Bhopal victims should not be constrained by the limitations of past experience. There has never been a disaster of this magnitude so that it is simply impossible to use responses to past disasters as a guide for what is appropriate in this instance—for example, the nutritional needs of the surviving victims may be far different and much greater than they were before the disaster struck.

The virtually total exclusion of the victims from decisions affecting them thus far must be rectified in subsequent efforts to provide justice. In a similar fashion, the notable lack of partnership—with government agencies, non-governmental organizations, and international agencies seemingly all going their separate ways—must be overcome, as must the lack of personal and organizational accountability on the part of those involved in ministering to the victims.

There are a number of characteristics, flowing in part from what has already been said should not be done, in any efforts to bring justice to the Bhopal victims. Administratively, in addition to the ongoing programs of existing government and voluntary agencies, what is required is the creation of a trust fund (involving, of course, the government of India, as well as other appropriate agencies, international or voluntary) which will seek to stretch the financial resources finally provided through a judgment or settlement of the claims of the victims as far as they can go. Certainly some of the funds should be invested as an endowment, so that there will be income long into the future to help meet as yet unknown needs of the victims.

There is also a third issue at stake, and it involves more than just Union Carbide and the Bhopal victims. This disaster in fact confronts us with a critical choice. On the one hand, if justice is done, the award of damages against Union Carbide, amounting to a substantial segment of its assets, will deliver an unambiguous message to hazardous industries all over the world that they no longer can give the quest for profit priority over human life.

On the other hand, if Carbide is allowed to settle for a fraction of the amount that a jury would award and an amount that does not materially affect its financial position, the opposite message will be conveyed. Hazardous industries may continue business as usual, comfortable in the knowledge that they can expect to survive and escape meaningful liability when catastrophic accidents occur.

The impact of the litigation involving Union Carbide and Bhopal victims will thus determine the standard of conduct for hazardous industries around the world for many decades to come. What happens to this litigation will determine how frequently death and disabling injury on such a scale will be repeated and with what consequences for those responsible.

For all of its uncertainties and the inordinate length of time it will almost certainly take, litigation seems to be the only route through which there is any possibility of meaningful justice for the Bhopal victims. Whether they are dealt with justly will depend not only on the skill of the lawyers, the disposition of the judge, and the fine points of the law, but also on public opinion and the political climate in both India and the U.S. and how these phenomena will shape what is considered to be "fair and reasonable" to the victims.

Criminal Liability and Corporate Responsibility

One other issue in this exploration of justice for the Bhopal victims that is beginning to emerge in the wake of the Bhopal tragedy merits discussion. This is whether corporate executives should face criminal charges when they make decisions that lead to large-scale personal injuries and fatalities or when death or serious injury occurs through their deliberate actions. *BusinessIndia*, in its cover story on the first anniversary of the Bhopal disaster (December 2-15, 1985) puts it this way:

> Given that modern corporations control technologies that can have such devastating consequences, how, then, are we to ensure that these corporations will always act with the highest standards of responsibility and care? When corporate managers take decisions that might endanger other people's lives, how can we be sure that the risks they expose others to are going to be "acceptable" risks? When they weigh the risks and benefits of their decisions, what is the guarantee that what seems "rational" to the corporation will also be "right" for the rest of us?

There is indeed a view surfacing in some corners—including the editors of *BusinessIndia*—that criminal sanctions on corporate executives constitute a more effective means of accomplishing the goals of punitive damages in civil litigation such as deterrence than the prevailing pattern of tort litigation, particularly as it has been evolving in U.S. courts in recent decades. *BusinessIndia* argues that the large element of unpredictability in tort litigation, where large-scale punitive damages are becoming more and more frequent when gross and willful negligence of company managements can be established, is becoming a severe drag on ''normal'' business activity. It is also arousing widespread opposition to the principle and practice of tort litigation in which injured parties sue for large sums in cases that often take years to resolve and result in a substantial proportion, if not the lion's share, of the damages going to the lawyers involved.

> *BusinessIndia* sums up the case for holding corporate executives criminally liable where unusual hazards are involved in these words: First and foremost, it has the strongest deterrent value and can become a powerful means of restraining behaviour that exposes others to large scale risk. The prospect of a period of imprisonment, no matter how short, and the social stigma it implies, would induce corporate managements to be very careful indeed about taking decisions that may endanger other peoples' lives. Secondly, there is a discretionary element in the imposition of sanctions during the sentencing procedure. This discretionary element allows the court to impose the necessary sanction in a particular case without imposing absurdly high standards across the board. In other words, it makes the punishment fit the crime by taking account of the gradations involved. Thirdly, as compared to civil litigation, criminalisation offers the advantage of speedier resolution of the case.

This approach to assuring that those responsible for the kind of death, injury, and devastation that occurred in Bhopal are held accountable for their actions took a major step forward in a recent case in Chicago. In that case, involving a company known as Film Recovery Systems and three of its executives, Circuit Court Judge Ronald J.P. Banks found the three company officials ''guilty of murder both as individuals and also as officers and high managerial personnel of Film Recovery Systems.''

A New Post-Bhopal Jurisprudence

What, then, might we hope would emerge from this tangle of

litigation, investigations, and other actions that seek to secure true justice for the Bhopal victims? Is it possible that a new jurisprudence will emerge, more fully and effectively protecting the rights of victims of such crimes against humanity?

If such a new jurisprudence does emerge, it will of necessity contain at least two critical elements. One is effective articulation of the rights of workers, consumers, and communities at risk to know and to have *accessible* remedies that will enable them to protect themselves when their well-being, indeed their very survival, is threatened. This dimension to a post-Bhopal jurisprudence might well be characterized as a kind of "people's law," incorporating some of the key elements of the approach to social action litigation enunciated by Justice P.N. Bhagwati, the new Chief Justice of the Indian Supreme Court, and described by the Indian legal scholar, Dr. Upendra Baxi, in "Taking Suffering Seriously: Social Action Litigation in the Supreme Court of India" (*Delhi Law Review*, Nos. 8 and 9, 1979).

Yet another vital dimension of this new jurisprudence will be meaningful and enforceable international standards for hazardous industries where the risk of catastrophic disaster is present. No one is under any illusions that this will be easily achieved. But only through such international standards, effectively enforced, will it be possible to banish for all time the invidious practice of double standards where the safety of workers, consumers, and communities are involved—standards which in effect state that human life is more precious in some parts of the world than it is in others. In the meantime, even without strict enforcement, international standards will provide a useful norm against which to measure the performance of individual companies in extremely hazardous industries.

Justice for the Bhopal victims includes not only prompt relief, full rehabilitation, adequate compensation, and all the other issues we have discussed in this chapter. It is also crucial that their anguish and suffering shall not have been in vain. And for that condition to be fulfilled requires the emergence of a new post-Bhopal jurisprudence along the lines set forth here.

Chapter 4

THE TANGLED WEB OF LITIGATION

A Lawyers' Bonanza?

Issues of compensation, damages, and accountability discussed in the preceding chapter are all subject to a mass of litigation spawned by the worst industrial disaster in history. On the face of it, Bhopal is a bonanza for lawyers.

Legal actions against Carbide have been initiated in both India and the U.S. on a grand scale. Almost 3,500 cases have been filed by victims in the civil and criminal court in Bhopal, although further action in these cases has been delayed when the Indian government, in February 1985, promulgated the *Bhopal Gas Leak (Processing of Claims) Ordinance* under which the government claims the exclusive right under Indian law to represent all claimants against Union Carbide.

In the U.S., legal actions have been initiated in several state courts on behalf of the victims, not to mention some 100 suits initiated in different federal courts. The federal court actions have been consolidated, by a judicial panel on multidistrict litigation, and assigned to the United States District Court for the Southern District of New York before Judge John F. Keenan.

In addition to all of this litigation seeking damages for the victims, there are suits by Union Carbide shareholders against the Carbide

73

management in U.S. courts, alleging that negligence by the management has significantly diminished the value of shareholders' equity in the company. These cases are also before Judge Keenan. There is also an action by some of the American personal injury lawyers involved in the consolidated action before Judge Keenan's court in New York, challenging in the Indian courts the constitutionality of the ordinance-mentioned above (subsequently adopted as an act of Parliament) that grants the government the exclusive right to represent the Bhopal victims.

While some of the other actions may turn out to be significant—at a minimum, they give the lawyers involved something to do—main attention for the moment is centered on Judge Keenan's court in New York. It is here, at least until some key procedural issues are resolved over the next several months that the struggle to secure justice for the victims will be played out.

Dramatis Personae in MDL #626

The consolidated action in Judge Keenan's court has been assigned an identifying number—MDL (Multi-District Litigation) #626—which appears on all of the briefs and other submissions to the court by attorneys for the plaintiffs and the defendant. That impersonal designation masks the drama inherent in a situation in which accountability will be established and compensation determined for the 200,000 or more persons killed or injured by the disastrous gas leak from the Union Carbide plant in Bhopal early on the morning of December 3, 1984. At issue is the future well-being of all those innocent victims and survivors, most of them poor and highly vulnerable to adversity under the best of circumstances.

The claims of these victims against the Union Carbide Corporation have been calculated to total some $150 billion, raising the stakes to a level that puts this consolidated action in the same league as the U.S. government's budget deficit. Such claims will never, of course, be awarded to the victims—they are 15 times Union Carbide's total assets—but they underscore what is on the table in Judge Keenan's courtroom. For Union Carbide, the issue in its ultimate terms is survival of the company.

By any measure, legal action stemming from the worst industrial disaster in history is bound to be momentous. Judge Keenan, a former public prosecutor appointed recently to the federal bench by President Reagan, is clearly aware that his handling of the case will, because of the historic character of the event that provoked it, also make history.

Before him are arrayed a sometimes rancorous and often contentious babble of lawyers. For the defendant, Union Carbide Corporation, is one of the more prestigious of the big New York City law firms representing Fortune 500 companies, Kelley, Drye and Warren. Solid and respected in legal circles, Kelley, Drye and Warren has long represented Union Carbide in a great variety of matters, but this is by far the most consequential of any legal problem heretofore facing its client. As in any large law firm, a lot of people are involved behind the scenes, especially when the stakes are as big as they are in MDL #626, but there always is at least one person up front who signs the letters to the judge and appears in court. In this instance it is a senior partner, Bud G. Holman, a product of City College with solid legal credentials from the Yale Law School.

For the plaintiffs—the voiceless victims half a world away—Judge Keenan is confronted by a motley crew. Indeed, so numerous are the personal injury lawyers who claim to have secured representation agreements from victims in Bhopal—some 100 law firms are involved—that in order to make the whole proceeding manageable, Judge Keenan, at the first pre-trial hearing in April 1985, directed the lawyers for the plaintiffs to establish a representational mechanism with which he might deal, warning them that if they failed to do so he would take action himself. Predictably, they were unable to reach agreement, so Judge Keenan did what he said he would— namely, designated a three-person executive committee plus a New York-based lawyer (Jack Hoffinger) as liaison between the court and the executive committee.

Two of the members of the executive committee are well known American lawyers—F. Lee Bailey and Stanley M. Chesley. (Bailey, whose area of expertise is criminal law, is usually represented in this case by his partner, Aaron Broder.) The third member of the executive committee is Michael Cerisi, a partner in Robins, Zelle, Larson and Kaplan, the Minneapolis law firm selected by the government of India to represent it (and through it, the victims) in MDL #626.

When Robins Zelle was chosen by the government of India, there were some raised eyebrows among some American lawyers following the case. Robins Zelle has a reputation for being aggressive—some would say overly aggressive—in representing its clients' interests. Its zeal in doing so has from time to time resulted in its getting its wrist slapped in different U.S. courts.

Contingency fee lawyers, who most of the 100 attorneys representing Bhopal victims are, constitute a controversial phenomenom on the American legal scene. Their fees are ordinarily a percentage of the damages awarded by the court to their clients. If their clients lose, they get nothing, but if the clients win—either through a trial or an out-of-court settlement—they are rewarded, in some cases very handsomely. Critics say that the contingency fee system results in excessive litigation and settlements that are too costly where personal injuries are involved. Defenders of the arrangement insist that contingency fees mean that many victims of irresponsible actions by others, especially large corporations, get legal representation which they would otherwise never be able to afford, and in many cases, at least some satisfaction of their claims against those who have done them wrong.

Be that as it may, almost all of the 100 lawyers representing the Bhopal victims—with the notable exception of Robins Zelle, which has been hired by the government of India as its attorney in the case—are working on a contingency fee basis. They have been called international ambulance chasers and accused of being vultures, descending on the city of Bhopal in the wake of that enormous tragedy to prey upon its victims. The best of them, regardless of what names they are called, are very skilled at litigating actions involving personal injury in U.S. courts—and have long records of multi-million dollar settlements to prove it. Stanley Chesley and Aaron Broder, F. Lee Bailey's partner, are among the best American tort lawyers—bright, articulate, sometimes abrasive, always ready to take advantage of whatever opportunities the law provides to press for ultimate satisfaction of their clients' claims.

There are, in addition, two or three *pro bono* lawyers serving without fee. There is also one lawyer who has been both *pro bono* and public interest—i.e., serving without fee in seeking satisfaction of the claims of those victims who are his clients and also concerned with broader public issues raised by the case—Kevan Cleary formerly with the New York law firm, Rubin, Baum, Levin, Constant and Friedman. Cleary, who was participating in the Bhopal case in his individual capacity, has recently been appointed an Assistant U.S. District Attorney for the Eastern District of New York, and has been replaced by Robert C. Cheasty from Berkeley, California.

Pre-Trial Maneuvering in MDL #626

The first pre-trial hearing before Judge Keenan occurred in April. On that occasion, Judge Keenan took the steps, described above, to make more manageable the conduct of MDL #626 by creating the executive committee mechanism for the numerous plaintiff's lawyers. At that time, the judge also made his plea for $5-10 million from

Union Carbide to provide for immediate help to the victims (further discussed in Chapter 2) "as a matter of fundamental human decency." As an experienced man of the law, both as lawyer and as judge, he recognized from the beginning that a complex legal proceeding with the enormous stakes of this one will take time—very large amounts of time. (Five to ten years is a reasonable forecast, allowing for the inevitable appeals that will be made by either one side or the other.) Something, he clearly argued to himself, must be done in the meantime to look after these poor people.

The second pre-trial hearing was held in August 1985 after several postponements. On this occasion, the attorneys for Union Carbide made, as anticipated, a motion for dismissal of the suits before Judge Keenan on the grounds of *forum non conveniens*. In the memorandum of law submitted to the court in support of this motion, Kelley, Drye and Warren argued that:

> These actions do not belong in the courts of the United States. They belong in India, and under the sound policy and rule of *Piper Aircraft Co. v. Reyno*, 454 U.S. 235 (1981), and *Gulf Oil Corp. v. Gilbert*, 330 U.S. 501 (1947), this Court should dismiss them in favor of the Indian forum. India is the only appropriate and clearly the most convenient forum in which these actions should proceed.

We shall return to the key question of determining the most appropriate forum for these lawsuits, but it should be noted that *forum non conveniens* does not exhaust the grounds on which Union Carbide can—and doubtless will—if the *forum non conveniens* question is decided against them—move to dismiss these actions as the Kelley, Drye and Warren brief puts it:

> Union Carbide has not briefed the other grounds upon which it has moved to dismiss these actions because the *forum non conveniens* motion is dispositive and the reasons for granting it are overwhelming. Thus, this court need not reach the issues of the propriety of the U.S. lawyers' engagements, their multiple and duplicative proported representation of Indian claimants or the lack of standing or authority of the plaintiffs to bring these suits in the United States. This court is not an appropriate or convenient forum and should defer to the Indian forum where these and other issues may be academic or appropriately dealt with. However, if the court wishes, Union Carbide will also brief these other grounds for dismissal.

Pre-trial maneuvering has continued since the August hearing.

During September and October, discovery limited to the *forum non conveniens* issue took place, based on Judge Keenan's Solomonic ruling between the plaintiffs' lawyers' request for complete discovery and Carbide's demand for none. Answering briefs were filed by the plaintiffs' lawyers in early December, and oral arguments before Judge Keenan on the *forum non conveniens* motion took place on January 3, 1986.

One new dimension to the litigation has surfaced in the pre-trial maneuvering—namely, a more visible "public interest" presence. The Citizens Commission on Bhopal—a broad coalition of environmental, consumer, church, worker, and medical organizations—filed a friend-of-court or *amicus* brief on the *forum non conveniens* motion on behalf of the Commission as well as the National Council of Churches and the United Church of Christ. At the January 3 hearing, Rob Hager, a public interest lawyer from the Christic Institute in Washington with considerable experience in personal injury litigation (for example, the Karen Silkwood case mentioned above), appeared on behalf of the Commission. He was also asked by Judge Keenan to make the summation for the plaintiffs.

Judge Keenan has promised an early decision on the *forum* motion. Even before he makes that ruling, he is reportedly seeking to use whatever leverage he can to push the parties to the litigation in the direction of a settlement.

In the meantime, the plaintiffs' lawyers have adopted a strategy that seems to contemplate a long struggle rather than a quick settlement. Steven J. Adler, Executive Editor of *The American Lawyer*, reports, in a discerning piece in that magazine ("Carbide Plays Hardball," November 1985) that they have amassed a "war chest" by levying an assessment of $3,000 on each of the 100-odd firms that have collected representation agreements from Bhopal clients. With those funds, they have opened a Bhopal litigation office in New York.

The Key Legal Issues

There are three clusters of key legal issues in the Bhopal tragedy which will need, sooner or later, to be resolved. The first cluster involves issues of jurisdiction, the second concerns the nature of Union Carbide's liability, and the third (discussed in the previous chapter) deals with damages and the compensation of the victims.

Regarding jurisdiction there are two major issues: the relationship of the parent Union Carbide Corporation to its Indian subsidiary and the appropriateness of the place where litigation is being conducted. Thus, determination will need to be made over the issue of which courts in which country should have jurisdiction over what kinds of litigation. Equally pressing is the matter of piercing the corporate veil—that is, determining that a subsidiary corporation is effectively controlled by the parent, even if the subsidiary has a separate legal character. Failure to pierce the corporate veil would leave only the very much more limited assets of Union Carbide India, Ltd. to satisfy any judgment rendered by a court or the terms of any out-of-court settlement.

As might be expected, the parent corporation and its Indian subsidiary are going to some lengths to maintain their separate identities. According to Steven Adler in an earlier article on Bhopal in *The American Lawyer* (''Bhopal Journal: The Voiceless Victims,'' April 1985), the standard response by Carbide's Indian lawyers responding to lawsuits in the Indian courts is:

> It is incorrect that defendant [Union Carbide India, Ltd.] is controlled by foreigners and outsiders and can transfer its property to foreign countries. The correct position is that approximately 51 per cent of the shares are held by non-residents and the balance of 49 per cent are held by Indian citizen/Government of India financial institutions.

Vijay Kumar Gupta, UCIL's chief counsel in Bhopal, who is vigorously engaged in fighting suits brought by Bhopal victims for interim relief in the Bhopal High Court, is even more explicit. Adler quotes him as saying:

> Union Carbide India, Ltd. is an Indian company regulated under the Indian Companies Act. Therefore the Union Carbide Corporation cannot be held liable for any of the acts of the Indian company. It is wrong to say that the American company is the parent company. It holds some shares, but it is not the proprietor. The Indian company has nothing to do with the U.S. company.

The reality, however, is different. The parent company includes the Indian subsidiary in its consolidated balance sheet and lists in its annual report Carbide India as one of the divisions, subsidiaries, and affiliates through which ''Union Carbide Corporation's business worldwide is conducted principally.'' In the design of the MIC plant, as we noted previously in the Edward Munoz affidavit filed in the U.S. Federal District Court in New York, a dispute arose between the Indian subsidiary and the U.S. company over whether MIC should be stored only in small quantities or in large tanks at the Bhopal plant; the parent company's view prevailed. (Munoz is a former Managing Director of UCIL and a former Vice President of UCC.) For reasons not yet explained (in all likelihood, the hope of developing an export market from India), the U.S. company insisted on the installation of large tanks, and so they were installed. If the Indian subsidiary's position had been followed, the Bhopal tragedy would never have happened.

There are many other indicators of a close supervisory relationship between the U.S. parent and the Indian subsidiary—for example, the inspection team sent by the U.S. company to Bhopal in 1982 to review safety and maintenance at the Carbide plant there (with UCIL management dutifully reporting over the next two years its progress in correcting the deficiencies found by the team), monthly reports on operations submitted to the parent company, and approval by the parent company of the Indian subsidiary's annual budget. Perhaps most telling is a decision by the parent corporation (documented with an internal Carbide telex dated November 21, 1984, just before the accident) to explore whether or not to dismantle the Bhopal plant and ship it to another country or countries. With these and similar pieces of evidence, the plaintiffs' lawyers have sought to establish the close supervisory relationship between the U.S. parent and its Indian subsidiary as a critical element in the larger argument that the trial belongs in the U.S. because that is where all the key decisions related to the tragedy were made.

There is, furthermore, considerable legal precedent for insisting that the Union Carbide Corporation is responsible for the actions of its subsidiary. Perhaps the most well known case involves an oil spill caused by the grounding of the tanker *Amoco Cadiz* off the coast of France in 1978. In a decision recently made for the northern district of Illinois, Standard Oil of Indiana was found to be liable for the acts of its subsidiary, involving an accident which occurred in another country. Key factors in determining that Standard was liable in *Amoco Cadiz* included the flow of benefits, assignment and accountability of key personnel, and pattern of operation of Standard as a whole, in which it was clearly established that responsibility for key decisions rested with Standard and not any of its subsidiaries. On the face of it, if the findings in *Amoco Cadiz* were applied to Union Carbide, there is little doubt that the parent corporation would be held liable for the acts of its Indian subsidiary.

Another cluster of legal issues revolves around questions of liability. The complaints filed on behalf of the victims with Judge

Keenan's court (both the government of India complaint and the consolidated complaint of the personal injury lawyers) charge Union Carbide with multi-enterprise liability, absolute liability, and strict liability
(the principle of law enunciated in the famous 1868 House of Lords
case in Britain of *Rylands v. Fletcher*), not to mention negligence,
breech of warranty, and misrepresentation. The plaintiffs' lawyers are
seeking not only compensatory but also punitive damages. Whether
they will be able to sustain all of these charges in the litigation remains
to be seen. Obviously, if the case does go to trial before Judge Keenan,
Union Carbide can be expected to resist vigorously all of these charges.
How they are ultimately resolved will have an important bearing on
the character and magnitude of damages awarded to the plaintiffs.

Is Union Carbide Beyond the Law?

The first legal issue to be confronted in the litigation is, as we
have noted, the *forum non conveniens* question. As might be expected,
the two cases emphasized by Carbide's attorneys in their submission
to Judge Keenan's court— *Piper Aircraft* and *Gulf Oil*—support their
position that the case should be tried in Indian courts. In general, there
is a rule in law which states that a court which has jurisdiction over
a case is also under duty to exercise that jurisdiction. *Forum non
conveniens* is a qualification of that rule, permitting courts at their
discretion to decline jurisdiction under certain circumstances. The considerations involved in applying the doctrine of *forum non conveniens*
include such matters as access to evidence in the place where the injury
occurred, availability of evidence and witnesses, or the adequacy of
another court as an alternative forum.

At first glance, it would appear that there were persuasive grounds
for having the case tried in India. The disaster itself which provoked
the litigation occurred in India, and certainly some witnesses and evidence exist in India. But there are countervailing arguments which
attorneys for the plaintiffs hope will persuade Judge Keenan that the
trial belongs in his court.

Thus, in the Robins Zelle complaint on behalf of the government
of India, it is argued that:

> Multinational corporations, by virtue of their global purpose,
> structure, organisation, technology, finances and resources, have
> it within their power to make decisions and take action that can
> result in industrial disasters of catastrophic proportions and mag-

nitude...Key management personnel of multinationals exercise a
closely held power which is neither restricted by national bound-
aries nor effectively controlled by international law. The complex
corporate structure of the multinational, with networks of subsidiaries and divisions, makes it exceedingly difficult or even impossible to pinpoint responsibility for the damage caused by the
enterprise...Persons harmed by a multinational corporation are
not in a position to isolate which unit of the enterprise caused the
harm, yet it is evident that the multinational enterprise that caused
the harm is liable for such harm... A multinational corporation
has a primary, absolute and non-delegable duty to the persons and
country in which it has in any manner caused to be undertaken
any ultra-hazardous or inherently dangerous activity.

The government of India's petition argues that insofar as Union
Carbide designed, constructed, owned, and operated the plant from
which the chemical escaped, the company should be held absolutely
liable for all the resulting damage. Second, the company, in undertaking an activity that it knew was ultra-hazardous to the public at
large, is strictly liable for the harm that was the material consequence
of such activity, regardless of whether the harm resulted from a fault
on its part or negligence. Third, the company was negligent in de-
signing, constructing, operating, and maintaining its plant and thus
failed to exercise its duty of care to protect the public from the dangers
inherent in its plant and processes.

Fourth, the company is liable for a breach of warranty, in that
it had expressly warranted that the design, construction, operation, and
maintenance of its Bhopal plant would be undertaken with the best
available information and skills in order to ensure safety, and that it
failed to do so. Finally, that the company, in doing so, and in intending
that the plaintiff would rely and act upon such assurances, is guilty
of misrepresentation.

Thus, the government argues that all the decisions that are material
to the case and whose execution set off the chain of events which
culminated in the Bhopal disaster, were taken by Union Carbide Corporation, headquartered in the U.S. The evidence that the plaintiffs
would require to substantiate their charges, whether relating to the
design and manufacture of the equipment in question, or the structure
of decision making within the corporation, is available only in the U.S.
The same would hold in the case of witnesses. Thus, the transfer of
the case to India would prejudice the plaintiffs' case as well as increase
the cost and administrative difficulties that the trial is bound to entail
because much of the evidence and key witnesses are in the U.S.

The court could agree to a trial in the U.S. even if it refrains from ruling on the government's contention regarding multinational enterprise liability. The breach of warranty referred to earlier allows the plaintiff to bring a suit against Union Carbide on grounds of product liability, and every state in the U.S. where the company conducts business can be assumed to have jurisdiction over the case.

But there is a more basic presumption involved in invoking the doctrine of *forum non conveniens*. In declining to exercise jurisdiction over a case, the court must be satisifed that an alternative forum exists, which would be more suitable for the adjudication of the case. More important, the defendant must be willing to submit to the jurisdiction of the alternative forum. What is most intriguing about Union Carbide's efforts to get the case thrown out of U.S. courts on grounds of *forum non conveniens* is that such efforts were preceded by Union Carbide's express refusal to submit to the jurisdiction of Indian courts!

In the case of *Yunus Farhat v. Union Carbide Corporation and 56 Others* (where UCC is named defendant No. 1 and UCIL defendant No. 2), Carbide's reply goes one step further in arguing that "the suit against defendant No. 1 is not maintainable at Bhopal." In other words Union Carbide Corporation is not subject to the jurisdiction of the Bhopal court.

This position, as we have already noted, is entirely consistent with what Union Carbide has always argued. According to Carbide, UCIL is an Indian company, managed by Indians, over whom UCC exercises no control whatsoever. That Union Carbide would do everything in its power to avoid liability in the Bhopal litigation is only to be expected. After all, its very survival would be threatened, were its liability to be proven.

But what Union Carbide also appears to be attempting is to avoid facing trial altogether. To argue for the dismissal of the case in U.S. courts on the ground of *forum non conveniens* implies the acceptance of a *prima facie* case against the company. The Union Carbide brief for Judge Keenan's court makes it clear that the preferred forum, as far as Union Carbide is concerned, is India. But with the other hand, Carbide argues that the Indian courts are not suitable either. Union Carbide, it would appear, finds no court suitable, arguing in effect that it is beyond the law.

The Victims' Claims: Settle or Litigate?

Much has been said about the alleged desirability of settling the claims of the victims as soon as possible. Perhaps the most vigorous proponent of this viewpoint is the Union Carbide management itself which stated in its 1984 annual report that ''a quick and fair settlement of the claims of all victims would serve their needs far better than prolonged and expensive litigation.'' Implicit in this line of argument is that the victims will continue to suffer from neglect while litigation proceeds in courts in the U.S. and India, a process which almost certainly will take years to complete.

There is little doubt that the victims have thus far not been treated well by any of the key actors in the tragedy. But the solution to that situation is not a quick settlement of the claims but rather immediate provision of relief and rehabilitation funds, precisely as Judge Keenan has urged.

It will be argued that $5 million will not last very long if truly effective relief and rehabilitation, including proper health care services, are provided to all of the Bhopal victims and that Judge Keenan's initial request to Carbide is only a stopgap. But there is no reason why periodic payments cannot be made by Carbide as the litigation proceeds through the years. According to Warren Anderson, the Union Carbide Chairman (in a December 10 press conference recorded by BBC mentioned previously), Carbide has admitted ''moral responsibility,'' if not legal liability, for the disaster and has agreed to compensate the victims at least to the extent of $230 million (this being the highest Carbide offer for a comprehensive settlement thus far reported). Periodic payments for ongoing relief and rehabilitation for the Bhopal victims as the litigation proceeds can be charged against the amount to be paid by Carbide, whatever it finally turns out to be.

There are some additional advantages to such an approach to interim relief and rehabilitation of the Bhopal victims. Experience will be gained, as the litigation proceeds in the years ahead, regarding the absorptive capacity for varying dollar amounts of assistance, and the adequacy of administrative machinery and institutional arrangements in Bhopal for handling such assistance. In a similar manner, the court will acquire a better fix on actual needs of the victims and costs of meeting those needs.

One thing is abundantly clear: The cause of justice for the victims of Bhopal will not be well served by a premature and inadequate out-of-court settlement. On the compensation issue alone, the amounts reportedly being offered by Carbide are ludicrously low, as our discussion of compensation in the preceding chapter underscores. Even the reported asking figure of the government of India is totally inadequate.

But more fundamental arguments against settlement need to be considered. One of the most pervasive is the large measure of shared interest of the two principal negotiating parties—i.e., Union Carbide and the government of India—in a settlement. While Carbide's hands are much dirtier, neither is entirely clean with respect to this disaster.

But there are still more persuasive arguments against a premature settlement. Only through the discovery process in litigation and through the rigorous rules of evidence that apply in a court of law will it ever be possible to determine, once and for all, what really happened in the Carbide plant in Bhopal and who is responsible. The dissembling performance thus far by Union Carbide underscores the importance of this point.

Determining through litigation who is responsible is essential to fixing accountability. While such accountability is a crucial element in achieving justice for the Bhopal victims, it also relates to issues which transcend Bhopal and Union Carbide and which were stressed in the *amicus* brief by the Citizens Commission on Bhopal mentioned above. How else will a powerful message be sent to the chemical and other industries involved with high-risk technologies and to governments responsible for assuring public safety that the kinds of conditions that have existed in the Bhopal plant will never be tolerated again?

Anyone who doubts the need for pressing forward with litigation should ponder the fine print in Carbide's 1984 annual report. The ritual statement of regret and concern at the beginning of the annual report is undercut by one of the footnotes (on "commitments and contingencies") to the financial statements on page 36. After noting the various lawsuits brought against the company on behalf of the Bhopal victims and by shareholders in the U.S. and India, the management concludes that *"no charge or accrual* is required for *any liabilities* or for *any impairment of assets* that may result from the lawsuits described above relating to the Bhopal plant"* (emphasis added).

Clearly, given this position by the Union Carbide management, accountability will never be achieved—and, therefore, justice never done to the victims of Bhopal—if the claims against Carbide are settled out of court. Of course, opposing a settlement as a matter of principle is a difficult position to sustain. Obviously there would be advantages to the plaintiffs in a prompt settlement. If nothing else, lawyers fees and claims would be much less.

The key issue is not a settlement as such but rather a *premature and inadequate* settlement that would frustrate the cause of justice to the victims and leave confused and unclarified what happened and who was responsible.

Unfortunately, in a case like this, where the plaintiffs do not control their own lawyers (except, of course, for the government of India), the possibilities for manipulation of those lawyers are substantial. Furthermore, although the compulsions for an early settlement are quite different, they are by no means absent in the case of the government of India which has its own reasons for not wishing to see all the relevant facts of the case exposed to public view in a trial.

If in fact justice were to be done to the victims along the lines set forth in the preceding chapter and rigorous investigation would continue to determine what happened and who was responsible, an early settlement of the case would be welcome. But the likelihood of these conditions being met in the event of such a settlement seems, to put it mildly, highly remote.

Litigation and Justice

In the final analysis, this tangled web of litigation and legal issues must be judged for its instrumental result: Will it bring true justice to the innocent victims of the worst industrial disaster in history? The search for parallels and precedents to help answer this question yields only confusing signals and uncertanties.

The saga of the asbestos industry and the terrible injuries it inflicted on millions of workers and other victims of its products comes readily to mind. The circumstances involved in asbestos litigation and in the Bhopal tragedy are, of course, vastly different. Asbestos is slow-acting, often taking two or three decades to show up in a victim's lungs, and asbestos litigation has stretched over 50 years, involving dozens of different companies in thousands of different cases with different victims suffering in different ways. Bhopal, by contrast, was concentrated on a single event with one company as the clear and uncontested perpetrator. But there are also striking similarities, particularly in terms of the possible impact on the defendant companies for the injuries they have inflicted.

As the cumulative impact of a growing number of asbestos lawsuits involving larger and larger amounts (not only reflecting inflation but also growing awareness by judges and juries of the wanton and willful behavior of the defendant companies) has taken effect, several companies—Manville is the best known—have taken refuge behind the bankruptcy code. This in turn has intensified the search for some alternative to litigation as a means of making more manageable to the companies involved the enormous contingent liabilities that are now descending upon them for their past behavior.

In his penetrating series on asbestos litigation in *The New Yorker* ("The Asbestos Industry on Trial," June 10, 17, 24 and July 1, 1985), Paul Brodeur concludes that rather than reform the private enterprise system in order to stem the onslaught of environmental pollution and accompanying illness, we will opt for some kind of "manageable" administrative solution that will enable the perpetrators of this pollution and illness to "cope" with the havoc they have created without adversely affecting their profitability or preventing them from earning a satisfactory rate of return on their investments. He calls this kind of solution "ethical bankruptcy," quoting Anthony Mazzocchi, former official of the Oil Chemical and Atomic Workers International Union and now Director of the Workers' Policy Project, to make his point:

> History shows that the lawsuit is the only adequate preventive measure against occupational and environmental cancer. Take away the lawsuit, replace it with a compensation schedule or some other administrative scheme and you pave the way for cancer to become just another commodity to be costed out. The solution now being negotiated for the asbestos problem can then be applied across the board to future problems, such as the widespread contamination of the nation's drinking water supplies with cancer-producing chemicals. In this manner, you can institutionalize occupational and environmental cancer as a way of life.

Chapter 5

CAN IT HAPPEN HERE?

More Bhopals in the U.S.?

After the Bhopal disaster, the standard line of the U.S. chemical industry to the American people was one of reassurance. Relax, their spokespersons said. In our plants, we have high safety standards, better trained operators, more stringent government standards—so that it is simply impossible that an accident of this magnitude could happen here. Bhopal was just that—an accident—and not the result of any inherent shortcomings in the way chemical plants are designed or operated or the processes or products they use.

American workers in chemical and other plants where high-risk technologies are used have a different view. So do people from surrounding communities. And their concerns are increasingly supported by evidence being systematically accumulated in recent decades by experts on occupational health and industrial accidents.

Their answer to the question, "Can it happen here?," is yes. Not only will it happen. It does happen—regularly, even though not on the same awful scale as in Bhopal. To probe this question further, the Workers' Policy Project, in cooperation with a number of labor, church, public health, and other professional and citizen groups, organized in March 1985 in Newark, New Jersey, a conference on the theme, "After Bhopal: An Accident Waiting to Happen?". At this conference some of the leading authorities in the U.S. in occupational, health, environmental, medicine, industrial, safety and related fields were assembled. Here is what they have to say on the possibility of Bhopal-type accidents in the United States.

In his major new work published shortly before Bhopal, *Normal Accidents* (New York: Basic Books, 1984), Charles Perrow of Yale University studied accidents in a number of "high-risk systems" such as chemical plants, nuclear power plants, nuclear weapons systems, and air and marine transport. These systems, he reported to the Newark Conference, have two important characteristics. First, they are inter-active in complex ways so that multiple failures, often trivial in and of themselves, can build on one another in an unexpected manner. They are thus able to overcome the most finely designed safety mech-anisms and most carefully trained operators.

Second, these high-risk systems are usually designed in a very "tight" configuration so that either there is no time for recovery from a series of interacting multiple failures or substitutes and buffers that will permit recovery from the accident are lacking. If the systems have the potential for causing a catastrophic accident, as those studied by Perrow do, such an accident, while rare, is inevitable, given a sufficient number of systems and sufficient time.

"An accident such as Bhopal is bound to occur, sometime and someplace," Perrow concluded. "It is only marginally more likely to occur in a lesser developed country than in a developed one."

A chemical plant like the one in Bhopal or a similar Union Carbide plant manufacturing MIC in Institute, West Virginia, shares roughly similar probabilities of minor, major, and catastrophic accidents with other complex, tightly coupled systems which can give off large and sudden releases of energy, use highly toxic substances, or operate in hostile environments. Minor accidents are almost continuous, Perrow pointed out, but safety devices prevent their spread. Three or four times a year a chemical plant will have a series of minor accidents which interact in an unexpected manner and bring down a major sub-system. This constitutes a major accident.

At the present level of plants with these characteristics and vol-umes of production, Perrow insisted that we can expect catastrophic accidents, which he defines as those that kill or seriously injure 100 or more bystanders, at the rate of about four a decade. There are literally thousands of chemical plants all over the world which are responsible for this figure; many of them are in the U.S., which has by far the largest overall production capacity of any country. There are only a few hundred nuclear power plants and even fewer nuclear weapons systems, so the frequency of catastrophic accidents in those cases is much lower.

Industrial accidents are much more frequent than most people realize. According to Perrow, the average petroleum refinery has a fire every 11 months, and most of these are major accidents according to Perrow's definition since they involve shutting down major subsystems. The average ammonia plant, which involves a very well established technology, also has a fire on the average of every 11 months. Even what might be called passive systems like oil and gas tank farms have some 1,400 fires a year in the U.S. "Only fortuitous and largely unplanned conditions and events," observed Perrow in Newark, "stand between these commonplace accidents and those rare catastrophes such as Flixborough, Seveso, the recent Pemex explosion, and Bhopal."

Further and compelling evidence of Perrow's insistence on the frequency of serious industrial accidents comes from numerous other sources. Henri Smets, a senior environmental official at the Organisation for Economic Co-operation and Development (OECD) in Paris, has provided extensive documentation of many different kinds of industrial accidents in a major paper prepared for aconference on transportation, storage, and disposal of hazardous materials held in Austria in July 1985. To underscore the point, we have included a list compiled by Smets of gas leaks (but one type of industrial accident, of course) which occurred in a recent period of only six months (see accompanying box)— 12 serious accidents (not counting the most serious of all in Bhopal) in that short time period, seven in industrialized countries and five in the Third World.

But there is even more compelling evidence closer to home. On October 3, 1985, Stuart Diamond reported in the *New York Times* that a report commissioned by the Environmental Protection Agency, but not yet released, documents at least 6,928 accidents involving toxic chemicals which have occurred in the U.S. in the last five years. These accidents have killed more than 135 people and injured nearly 1,500. And this report is, by its own admission, based on an incomplete listing of such accidents. From this we can only infer that if a truly comprehensive report were prepared, the number of accidents, the number killed, and the number injured would only be higher.

But the argument that chemical plants based on complex modern technology and handling highly toxic materials are inherently prone to have accidents is still more compelling. For in the period since the awful tragedy in Bhopal, there have been two further accidents in, of all places, the Carbide plant in Bhopal and its sister plant in Institute,

Major Gas Leaks in Six-Month Period (September 1984 - February 1985)

1) September 1984	A bromine leak at Fawley (Southampton) affected between 60 and 70 people and will be the subject of compensation.
2) October 1984	A methyl isocyanate leak at Middleport, New York, caused eye trouble to nine children, and an accidental pesticide leak at Linden, New Jersey, put 160 people in the hospital.
3) November 1984	Between 2 and 3 kg of bromine leaked in Geneva, Switzerland.
4) November 1984	29 people (local residents and employees) in Liverpool, U.K., were poisoned by a chlorine leak when two chemicals were mixed. Two months later, 16 were still receiving treatment. The accident was due to a labelling error. Civil proceedings are in hand and a fine of £3,600 has been imposed.
5) December 1984	A defective wagon carrying 80,000 litres of ethylene oxide at Little Rock, Arkansas, obliged the authorities to evacuate 2,500 people for a night.
6) December 1984	3,000 people were evacuated for 24 hours from Callao, Peru, following a tetraethyle pipeline break.
7) December 1984	At Matamoras, Mexico, 3,000 people had to be evacuated and 200 received hospital treatment when 35,000 litres of ammonia leaked at a fertilizer factory.
8) January 1985	42 people had to be hospitalized when chlorine leaked in a textile plant at Trichur, India, and four Gujarat villages were troubled by a gas leak from a chemical plant. At Javalpur, 100 people had eye and throat irritations after inhaling gas leaking from sodium hydrosulphate drums contaminated by water.
9) January 1985	At Karlskoga, Sweden, 30 tons of sulphuric acid vapor formed a 3 km2 cloud over the town. The accident, caused by cold weather in the Bofors-Nobel plant, involved evacuating 300 people and hospitalizing 20. The 35,000 residents were advised not to leave their homes and to keep doors and windows closed.

10) January 1985	15 tons of ammonia leaked at a national fertilizer plant at Cubatao, Brazil, resulting in the evacuation of 5,000 people and hospitalization of 300.
11) February 1985	A cloud of chlorine and hydrochloric acid put 25 people in the hospital in Westmalle, Belgium. The town center was closed off to traffic, and residents were advised to stay at home with doors and windows closed.
12) February 1985	An ammonia leak in a prawn-processing plant in North Sumatra injured 130 workers, some requiring hospital treatment.

Source: Adapted from Henri Smets, "Compensation for Exceptional Environmental Damage Caused by Industrial Activities" (paper prepared for Conference on Transportation, Storage, and Disposal of Hazardous Materials, Laxenburg, Austria, July 1-5, 1985).

West Virginia. The gas leak in Bhopal, which understandably caused panic among the people of that tortured city, occurred on March 28, 1985, when 100 tons of chlorine which had been lying in storage in the plant was being transferred to railway tank cars for sale elsewhere as the Carbide factory had been closed down after the December disaster.

Unthinkable as may be another gas leak at the Carbide plant in Bhopal, it is even more unthinkable—given the double standards followed by the company in spite of its protestations to the contrary—that an accident should occur at the Carbide plant in Institute. After all, that plant had been shut down for more than four months after the Bhopal disaster for extensive retrofitting and upgrading of its safety systems. Presumably all of the operating personnel at the plant had been instructed by the Carbide management to be *especially careful* that no accident occurred since, after Bhopal, the whole world (and especially the surrounding community) would be watching. But notwithstanding all of these circumstances an accident did occur—a leak of a toxic gas known as aldicarb oxyme on August 11, 1985.

The Cause of Disasters: Multiple Failures

The August 11 accident at Institute, which sent 135 persons to the hospital, was a classic case of multiple failures. There were operator errors. For example, plant operators pumping steam into the jacket surrounding the tank where the chemical was stored, thus heating it when it should have been cooled. This caused another runaway reaction as in Bhopal. When the accident was discovered, another operator punched the wrong chemical into the computer that is part of a recently installed computerized safety system.

There were also design failures as in Bhopal. A watering system near the tank intended to contain leaks was not strong enough to contain this one. A recently installed computerized safety system, known as Safer, had not been programmed for this particular chemical. And it appears that the pipe leading from the tank to the neutralizer and the flare was too small to handle the on-rush of the gas when the runaway reaction gathered momentum.

Nor is that the last chapter in the continuing record of *serious* gas leaks *since* Bhopal. In India and the United States alone, there have been three major ones after the August incident in Institute, each involving—as Perrow predicted—multiple failures. In September, chlorine gas leaked from a chemical plant in Bombay, causing one death and injuring more than 100 persons. This was followed on December 4, 1985—just a year and a day after Bhopal—with a much more serious leak of oleum from another chemical plant in Delhi, killing one person and sending 350 more to the hospital. Back in the U.S., still another incident occurred in early January 1986 at a uranium-processing plant in Oklahoma, killing one worker and injuring at least 30 others.

These accidents, like Bhopal, involved multiple failures in varying combinations—malfunctioning equipment, maintenance, personnel, and safety systems. Indeed, multiple failures are characteristic of serious industrial accidents everywhere as the appendix on major industrial disasters in the twentieth century makes abundantly clear. Consider these points, expressed in Perrow's own words at the Newark Conference:

•The "tea break" in the Union Carbide plant in Bhopal had its parallel in the decision of Seveso managers to leave a chemical, thought to be inert under the prevailing conditions, in a retort unattended over the weekend.
•Inoperative safety devices, such as the cooling system at Bhopal, are discovered endlessly in accident investigations; nothing is perfect so it is inevitable that they will be out of service from time to time. Few plants will pay for duplicates of all major safety devices to allow maintenance or changes. It would be like building two parallel dams, in case one develops cracks.

•Poorly trained personnel are legion in the nuclear power industry; it is only after an accident such as the one at Three Mile Island that we become aware of cheating on examinations, or grossly inadequate training. Chemical plants are better in this respect than nuclear plants, but the comments of chemical safety engineers at industry conferences indicate that the chemical industry does not provide enough reliable training in the U.S.

•One engineer said, ''The way it is now, we are in difficulties and I don't think anybody is sophisticated enough to operate the plant safely.'' An engineer at another plant, analyzing a major accident, observed, ''If a system is so complex and intricately meshed as to require super human operators to constrain the process within safe limits, then it needs some modifications. With new technologies and higher volumes, there will be catastrophes unless some help is given the plant operators.'' This suggests that even the best trained chemical plant operators will not be trained well enough.

•Accident reports in the industry routinely (and usually mistakenly) blame operators, suggesting the personnel is quite inadequate. At Bhopal, the experienced personnel had left for plants with more promising futures, leaving only inexperienced operators. But the condition is hardly unique to India; U.S. and British plants suffer from declining sales and loss of the best personnel, and yet continue to operate. Indeed, just such a problem contributed to the Flixborough disaster. No system with catastrophic potential can rely upon superhuman operators, or even the most highly trained; plants must be designed to be safe with the most marginal, barely adequate level of training and experience, even that which will accompany declining profits. Bhopal is not unique.

•Production pressures, endemic in capital-intensive industries, probably contributed to the Bhopal disaster. One report suggested that this was the reason for the large inventory of MIC. It noted that since MIC was so difficult to produce, the plant made large quantities of it when the process managed to work. Pressures to have large inventories to keep things running, to use ever more dangerous substances, to get back on-stream with shoddy and temporary setups are so common in the chemical plants and other systems as to hardly require comment.

•To quote just one accident report following a fire in an ammonia plant in Louisiana, ''As usual, following an unplanned shutdown, down time has to be kept to a minimum.'' So they started it up. The coils that had never met engineering specifications were not replaced, they were just patched. Other deficiencies were left until

a plant shutdown some months in the future. The baffling inter-
actions that were admittedly not understood by either the operators
or the engineers remained baffling. The irrelevant flow indicators
that were shut down because of their confusing signals were left
shut down and production went on. Meanwhile, the report blamed
the accident on operator error—a judgment that prevents any con-
demnation of either management or the system as a whole.

"Why have there not been more Bhopals?," asked Perrow in
Newark. The answer, he has concluded, is that for an accident to be
truly catastrophic as in Bhopal, several factors must coincide. He gives
seven. In combinations of four or five, they occur every few months
in the U.S., but rarely do we have all seven together.

1. There is a large unplanned release of some substance or energy
   from the plant.
2. The release contains highly toxic or explosive elements.
3. The release travels over heavily populated areas.
4. Weather conditions bring it down to the ground, it becomes
   concentrated, and/or it finds an ignition source if it is explosive.
5. People are in the area. For example, it is a weekday, or they are
   sleeping at night.
6. Warnings fail or are too late.
7. Plant personnel and the people in the area are not aware of the
   extreme toxicity of the substance being released.

All seven factors were present at Bhopal. Take away any one or
two of these, and the scale of the disaster will be greatly reduced.
Flixborough, as an example, happened—fortunately—on a weekend.
A cyclohexane plant in Florida released a cloud of explosive gas 2,000
feet long, 1,200 feet wide, and 100 feet high. But again, fortunately,
it found no ignition source and was finally dissipated. A vapor cloud
drifted over rural Illinois in 1972. After travelling two miles, it found
its spark and devastated five acres—but largely unpopulated ones.
There were a couple of hours of warning before the Teton Dam collapsed. It can almost always be said of a major accident: "We were
lucky it wasn't worse."

Close calls on the scale of the Bhopal disaster occur frequently
in the U.S., Perrow insisted, but we rarely hear about them. Now,
thanks to Bhopal, we are more likely to know about them from the
newspapers, at least for the next few months, because they are considered to be news. Take the *New York Times* story (March 15, 1985)

about an accident in a Union Carbide plant in Charleston, West Virginia. The scenario is so familiar as to be commonplace, and it certainly contradicts the remarks of Union Carbide Chairman Warren Anderson at the March 20 Carbide press conference a few days later where-Carbide's own report on the Bhopal disaster was released. There was excessive build-up of steam in a three-story column in the Charleston plant for unknown reasons. This led to a release of 5,700 pounds of a mixture that contained 100 pounds of poisonous mesityl oxide. The release continued for a 15-minute period and then drifted a half a mile to a shopping center where it left several shoppers semi-conscious. Doctors treating the victims at the shopping center did not know what the poison was. The plant was not even aware it was making the release. And Union Carbide denied for two subsequent days that it was the source before finally admitting it.

Even more to the point was the August 11 leak of the toxic gas, aldicarb oxyme, at the Union Carbide plant in Institute, West Virginia, mentioned above. This incident occurred five months after Perrow was speaking at the Newark Conference, but reflected many of the same characteristics of the March leak. Along with all of the operator and design failures already noted, there was a delay in notifying the surrounding community of 30 minutes or more, and first efforts to provide medical treatment for the victims were plauged by inadequate information on the toxic characteristics of the chemical.

Disasters such as Bhopal are likely to happen in what Perrow calls ''system accidents''—the unexpected and mysterious interaction of multiple failures in a system where the tight coupling of the system makes recovery difficult. They are, he argued, inevitable in systems which have these characteristics. Most such systems have catastrohpic potential—to take hundreds or even thousands of lives in one blow and to shorten and cripple the lives of hundreds or even thousands more. They are not frequent but they are only marginally more likely in Bhopal or the outskirts of Mexico City than they are in Institute, West Virginia, Flixborough, England, Seveso, Italy, and Texas City, Texas.

Paul Shrivastava, Associate Professor of Management at the Guaduate School of Business Administration of New York University and a resident of Bhopal for 25 years, addressed the question of whether more Bhopals can happen here in a somewhat different way. Like Perrow, he made the distinction between ''technical accidents''—major or minor—and tragedies. All technical accidents, obviously, do not lead to tragedies. But some do, and consequently, if technical accidents can occur in the U.S., tragedies like Bhopal can also happen.

Nobody designs plants, Shrivastava continued, to enhance the probability of disasters. When chemical engineers start working on the design of a chemical plant, they determine all the required specifications for safe operation and then multiply these specifications to insure that probabilities of a disaster are as close to zero as possible. "But accidents still do occur. Accidents defy probabilities. Even more, disasters defy probabilities."

Shrivastava argued that three basic myths surround the assertion that Bhopal-type disasters cannot happen here. The first myth is that we have better technology and better operators in the U.S. and therefore can prevent technical accidents, which lead to disasters, from occurring. But technical accidents happen all the time, as Perrow has pointed out, in high-risk industries in the United States and other industrialized countries.

The second myth, according to Shrivastava, is that we have superior risk management practices in the U.S. which prevent technical accidents from turning into runaway disasters that spill out of industrial plants into surrounding communities. This myth has led to a false sense of complacency in the public about the possibility of major tragedies like Bhopal because people think they are protected through the regulations and standards of remote federal agencies like the Environmental Protection Agency and the Occupational Safety and Health Administration. In fact, most communities at risk do not even know what kinds of hazardous technologies exist within their midst. Shrivastava estimated that there are some 6,000 hazardous industrial plants and over 10,000 hazardous waste dump sites in the U.S. today.

Consequently, there is a very real question of whether risk management, no matter how scientific it is, will ever be able to cope with such enormous and widespread exposure to risk. But the reality is that risk management, even though it may sound quite scientific, is a very new technology, hardly 15 years old. It therefore suffers from all of the deficiencies and shortcomings of a new professional activity as it strives to learn from its mistakes.

One of the major problems with risk management is that it is based on analyses that, more often than not, are confined primarily to technological sources of risk. Practitioners of risk management think that if they account for all the technological hazards embedded in a production system, they have actually managed to contain its riskiness. But production systems are operated by people who are products of different social and cultural environments. So the same technology might be much more risky in a place like Newark, New Jersey, and much less risky if located somewhere else.

As if this were not enough, risk profiles of industrial technologies keep on changing over time—with changes in the environment and even changes in the weather. We simply do not have, Shrivastava insisted, risk management systems which can monitor continuously changing risk profiles as they evolve over a period from the time a plant is designed and built to the time it becomes operational five to ten years later, let alone throughout its operational life of several decades.

Finally, in considering the effectiveness of risk management, we need to recognize that risk analysis is based on what Shrivastava calls pathetically limited data about the hazardousness and toxicity of different raw materials, intermediate substances, and industrial processes. For example, complete health hazard assessments exist for only ten per cent of pesticides and five per cent of food additives. Not only is there a paucity of data, but according to Shrivastava, we do not even know how to test most of the chemicals on the market. Of 664 toxicity tests evaluated in a recent study by the National Toxicology Program, only 27 per cent were judged acceptable.

The third myth, closely related to the second, is that we in this country have much greater capacity to cope with serious industrial accidents when they do happen. It is certainly true, Shrivastava conceded, that we do have more resources and infrastructure for dealing with disasters than many other countries, including government agencies like the Federal Emergency Management Agency, not to mention a variety of services and facilities at state and local levels. No doubt in this respect most communities in the U.S. are better off than Bhopal in India.

But the response time in emergencies of the kind that occurred in Bhopal is very short—usually no more than 15 to 45 minutes. Most of the damage in an accident with catastrophic potential has actually occurred within 45 minutes. The result is that, even if the facilities for coping with disasters are greater, there is not much which can be accomplished in such a short period of time. So having better resources for disaster management certainly does not provide us with any immunity—a point well illustrated by the August 11 leak at the Carbide plant in Institute, West Virginia.

Evacuation of people from adversely affected areas, Shrivastava points out, is often considered to be the single most important response to disasters. But for people living in heavily populated areas, it is simply not realistic to expect mass evacuation in a short period of time.

Indeed, recent Congressional hearings on the Bhopal disaster reveal that people living in areas in New Jersey with hundreds of chemical plants had no idea about the nature of the hazards surrounding them.

They could not tell the difference between a siren indicating the end of a work shift and an evacuation siren. Companies which regularly release chemicals into the environment typically do not have contingency plans with information on evacuation procedures, safety precautions, or medical treatment—or if they do, only a handful of persons in the plant know about these plans, and almost never, responsible officials and leaders in the surrounding community.

Little Bhopals as Daily Occurrences

Another response to the question, "Can it happen here?" was posed at the Newark Conference by Dr. Donald Luria from the Department of Preventative Medicine and Community Health of the New Jersey School of Medicine and Dentistry: "My own perception is that we have small Bhopals every day. After all, man is not infallible. Even if we ignore greed and venality, industrial accidents will continue to occur because of incompetence or just plain error." The accuracy of Dr. Luria's perception was underscored by the unpublished report to the EPA which surfaced six months after the Newark conference and recorded 6,928 toxic chemical accidents over five years—or *five accidents each day!*

Some people, especially in industry, think that we can reduce the margin of error by the burgeoning technology of automation—that is, computers and robots. Dr. Luria is skeptical. Computers and robots do make mistakes, he noted, because they are created and programmed by human beings who also make mistakes. The functioning of the computerized chemical safety information system known as Safer installed recently at the Carbide plant in Institute, West Virginia, illustrates his point. In the August 11 leak of aldicarb oxyme,we learned after the accident that the system had never been programmed for this particular chemical. Because it had not been, when the leak was first detected by one of the plant operators, he punched in another chemical which, because it has different characteristics, gave a different reading. This led plant supervisors to believe that the leak would be confined to the plant, and consequently they delayed sounding the public alarm to warn the surrounding community. (As it happens, the chemical the operator put into the computer system was methyl isocyanate!)

Now we are about to go a step further by infusing robots with the ability to draw inferences and make judgments—so-called artificial intelligence. We assume that somehow this will make them infallible in dealing with the problem of industrial safety. Dr. Luria argued on the contrary that robots will continue to make judgmental errors just as human beings do.

We are particularly disturbed about Bhopal because it involved tens of thousands of people. We often appear, Dr. Luria continued, much less concerned about small disasters—the little Bhopals—that involve only a few people, perhaps because they are happening all the time and it is hard to sustain the horror and outrage provoked by a massive disaster like Bhopal. But obviously to the individual worker or member of the surrounding community who is dead or maimed or incapacitated, it really does not make much difference whether he or she is one of ten victims or 100 or 10,000.

Little Bhopals occur not only when workers and persons from the surrounding community are actually killed or seriously injured. Far more important in terms of numbers are those who suffer from ''sub-acute effects'' or for whom serious symptoms appear only after a very long period of time. A good example of sub-acute effects comes from low-level exposure to mercury which produces more subtle results such as difficulties in thinking and motor functioning.Chronic, long-term abnormalities are well illustrated by repeated or continuing exposure to asbestos. Hundreds of thousands of people in this country, Dr. Luria pointed out, are exposed to these kinds of perils from the worksite and from hazardous wastes and products from the worksite in the community.

Coping with Bhopals, Large and Small

Other leading authorities in the field of occupational health and environmental protection readily agree with Dr. Luria that we experience little Bhopals all the time in the U.S. and that dealing with these hazards to human health and the physical environment is at least as important as coping with massive tragedies like Bhopal. Speaking at the Newark Conference, Dr. Barry Castleman, an environmental consultant and one of the pioneers in the 1970s in developing safeguards against hazardous substances like asbestos and vinylchloride, reinforced Dr. Luria's point by emphasizing how many thousands of people in this country died or were effectively disabled for life before even the most minimal first steps were taken to deal with such hazards.

Others like Dr. David Wegman, head of the Occupational Health Science Department at the University of California in Los Angeles and another Newark Conference speaker, pointed out how little we know about the toxic effects of chemicals like MIC, and when we do try to find out, it is usually after a major disaster like Bhopal rather than before. (The U.S. government has now embarked—after Bhopal, of course—on a toxicity testing program for MIC, costing perhaps $750,000. Why, Dr. Wegman asked rhetorically, could we not have spent this small sum of money—at least in relation to the stakes involved—*before* Bhopal in order to know how to treat the victims of that awful disaster?)

The melancholy reality according to Dr. Wegman is that we almost always respond to great tragedies after they have occurred, not to trying to prevent them before they happen. This led him to conclude, addressing the original question, ''Can it happen here?'':

> What is the probability of another Bhopal? It is 100 per cent.
> There is no question there will be another one. I do not know if
> the magnitude will be the same—or greater or less. But there will
> be another one. There will be many more. What we have to do
> is to do everything we can to try to prevent another Bhopal from
> happening. But sooner or later it will occur.

Will It Happen in New Jersey?

The Bhopal Conference was held in Newark, New Jersey, for good reason. New Jersey has one of the highest concentrations of chemical plants anywhere in the world. To many, New Jersey is a chemical time bomb—a Bhopal waiting to happen.

Few people who know the facts about hazardous industries and industrial wastes in New Jersey would deny this statement, according to Dr. Tom Livewright, Senior Public Health Physician in the New Jersey Department of Health. And if anyone should know, it is Dr. Livewright. For he and other state government officials concerned with protection of public health and the environment are like, in his words, ''a referee in a tag team wrestling match between a well-coached team of industrial heavyweights and an often uninstructed, uninformed group of unwitting workers and residents.'' As if this did not make the contest unequal enough, the industrial heavyweights take part only on condition that, if they do not like the way the match is going, they will pick up their marbles and go elsewhere—to other states or pollution-havens in the Third World where environmental and health regulations are less stringent and costly.

New Jersey has the unenviable distinction of being the state with the largest number of industrial waste sites on the Environmental Protection Agency's most critical list for priority clean-up. But almost everyone knowledgeable on the subject agrees that the EPA list is only the tip of the iceberg, certainly as far as New Jersey is concerned.

Beyond that, the state probably has the highest concentration of hazardous industries using high-risk technologies of any state in the country. Still worse, these industrial plants have distressing records of industrial accidents involving releases of toxic chemicals into the atmosphere, which is precisely, of course, what happened at Bhopal. From October of 1984 to March of 1985 there were at least 14 incidents of accidental release of chemicals into the air in the Newark to Woodbridge, New Jersey, region. Among the more serious which involved the Department of Health's Emergency Response Unit were at an American Cyanamid plant on October 6, 1984, a DuPont plant on November 27, and an American Cyanamid plant again on January 4 and 21, 1985. Of the 14 incidents, eight happened before Bhopal and six after.

The melancholy reality is that this rate of toxic release is about normal for the U.S. chemical industry as Raphael Moure, another Newark Conference participant, documents in an appendix to this book, "How Safe Are U.S. Chemical Plants—and the Communities around Them?". New Jersey's predicament is having such a high concentration of these plants in a small area within a small state.

The New Jersey Response

So New Jersey is in a very real sense Bhopal waiting to happen. What can a state and its citizens do in the face of such a predicament? There are no pat answers, needless to say, and there is no way, at least in the view of Dr. Livewright, of making New Jersey immune to a Bhopal-type disaster. Still some steps can be taken, and they are worth noting because New Jersey, being much more exposed to the risk of serious industrial accidents, often finds itself in the lead in trying to cope with such risk exposure.

Thus, the State Health Department set up four and a half years ago the Emergency Response Unit. The Unit is on call seven days a week, 24 hours a day, and is backed up by a team of physicians, toxicologists, and epidemiologists. Since the Unit was created, it has responded to 315 major incidents—an average of 72 each year.

Nearly half of these responses have been outside normal working hours and more than 60 per cent have involved fires, explosions, spills, leaks, or venting incidents. Over 25 per cent of the incidents have occurred in industrial plants. More than half resulted in serious health complaints, and almost 40 per cent involved persons requiring hospital emergency treatment or admission. In short, living with serious accidents, at least some of which are potential Bhopal-scale disasters, is a continuing fact of life in New Jersey.

In the state government's effort to cope with the continuing threat to its citizens from high-risk industries, the Department of Health is joined by the Department of Environmental Protection which has responsibility, among other things, for monitoring and regulation of air pollution. While the Department of Health reacts to an accident with the Emergency Response Unit (which is part of a larger state government emergency response team that also includes officials from the Department of Environmental Protection), DEP's Division of Environmental Quality responds with fines and orders to conduct evaluations of risk followed by appropriate remedial measures. These enforcement actions seek to reduce the frequency of chemical accidents, for, as Dr. William O'Sullivan,Chief of Engineering and Technology for the DEP Division of Environmental Quality pointed out to the Newark Conference, the most critical issue is the prevention of accidental releases of toxic chemicals. Because such accidents happen so quickly, any emergency response mechanism, no matter how sophisticated and finely tuned, can only do a limited amount to protect surrounding communities. It is rather like closing the barn door after the horse has been stolen.

After Bhopal, the Department undertook a search for toxic chemicals in New Jersey similar to MIC. It searched several data bases to which DEP has access, including the Air Pollution Enforcement Data System with the Department's Air Pollution Control Program, the Industrial Survey Data Base within DEP's Office of Science and Research, and the Hazardous Waste Manifest System within the DEP Division of Waste Management. Dr. O'Sullivan emphasized that while these data bases provide better information on industrial chemical use than are available in most other states, more and better data is needed. "Our task to evaluate the risk of chemical facilities," he observed, "would be much easier and more quickly accomplished if New Jersey's Right to Know legislation was now in effect for manufacturing operations."

While DEP discovered only limited use of MIC in small quantities in some laboratories in New Jersey, it did identify six chemicals which, while not considered as serious a risk as MIC, have some characteristics that might result in serious, if not catastrophic, accidents. Merely identifying these chemicals and where they are used does not, of course, assure that there will never be a major accident involving one of them.

Part of the problem is in monitoring a very large number of chemical plants located within the state on a continuing basis. While the New Jersey Department of Environmental Protection does regularly inspect these plants, it cannot be every place all the time. And there is no way it can prevent unsafe operation of plants using these chemicals, even if the safety systems pass muster at the time they are inspected. (At the Union Carbide plant in Bhopal, three major safety systems which should have been operational were not functioning for one reason or another at the time of the disaster, various monitoring devices were not working properly, and the public warning siren had been shut off. The picture at the Carbide plant in Institute, West Virginia, after the August 11 aldicarb oxyme leak, turned out not to be much better—a pipe too small to carry the massive volume of gas to the neutralizer and flare tower, a spray system likewise inadequate for the massive task of containing the runaway reaction, and a computerized information system not programmed for the chemical involved in the leak.)

New Jersey's Struggle for the Right to Know

New Jersey state government does have a variety of tools at its disposal in the continuing struggle to make industries operate more safely and minimize risk to their workers and the surrounding community, including fines against offending companies (which recently were sharply increased) and even the power to shut down an operation which is considered to be particularly hazardous. But perhaps most important in its arsenal of weapons is the recently enacted New Jersey Worker and Community Right to Know Law, for unless people know about the risks to which they are exposed, they cannot take action to protect themselves.

This Right to Know Law provides for a comprehensive system of disclosing and disseminating information about hazardous substances present in workplaces and capable of being released into the surrounding environment. This law is probably the most comprehensive of state Right to Know laws. It guarantees,according to Kathleen O'Leary, Chief of the Occupational Health Program in the New Jersey Department of Health, citizens of New Jersey access to the exact chemical identity of hazardous substances to which they may be exposed at their workplace or in their community. It also provides them with information concerning the short- and long-term effects of exposure to these hazardous substances. As it was originally enacted, the law covered 45,000 employers and approximately 1.3 million workers. The law also makes it possible for the Department of Environmental Protection and the Department of Health to establish a data base on the presence of hazardous substances throughout the state; such a data base will help both departments in carrying out their efforts to protect the environment and public health.

Unfortunately, this comprehensive and forward-looking law immediately invited counterattack. The first challenge came from the Reagan Administration in Washington. The federal government's Occupational Safety and Health Administration adopted in November of 1983 a regulation that places crucial regulatory decisions in the hands of the regulated parties and restricts coverage to manufacturing. Even worse, from New Jersey's point of view, this OSHA regulation preempts more stringent state laws on hazardous substances in the workplace.

Industry quickly joined in the counterattack, and the New Jersey law was involved in legal challenges on several fronts in both state and federal courts. The most significant litigation involved the U.S. District Court of New Jersey where a group of plaintiffs led by the New Jersey Chamber of Commerce and the U.S. Flavors and Fragrance Materials Association challenged the Right to Know Law in light of the OSHA regulation. In January 1985 the court enjoined the state from enforcing the Right to Know Law against manufacturing enterprises, a huge exclusion which covers most of the situations that might perpetrate a Bhopal-like disaster.

But the battle is not over. The state legislature, prompted by trade unions and environmental, consumer, and other public interest groups, is looking at fresh legislation that will get around the OSHA regulation by focusing on the Community Right to Know (under which workers, acting as members of the community, can also exercise their right to know). The state is also appealing the court decision, while new momentum is gathering behind a National Right to Know Law. In the meantime, however, O'Leary pointed out to the Newark Conference that "a citizen in New Jersey has a right to know what hazardous substances are present in his dentist's office or his local high school but does not know the names of chemicals in any large chemical plant that might be one block from his home."

To push for new legislation, a Right to Know Coalition has been formed in New Jersey. According to Bill Kane, the United Auto Workers' staff representative on the Coalition and another Newark Conference speaker, a new bill was introduced in April 1985. The bill requires manufacturing companies to label all containers with chemical names and with the chemical abstract service numbers of hazardous and non-hazardous substances. The bill also requires manufacturers to complete workplace environmental emergency service information surveys which will be made available to the public, to firefighters, and to state agencies. Hazardous substance fact sheets on these surveys will be supplied to firefighters, the public, and hospital emergency rooms. But to get a bill like this passed will take determined effort by a lot of organizations and concerned citizens—exactly the reason for forming the New Jersey Right to Know Coalition.

So the struggle to deal with hazardous substances continues, and New Jersey is one of the main battlegrounds. Notwithstanding all of the efforts that have been made in New Jersey, the fact remains that the lives and well-being of millions of New Jersey workers and citizens are still at risk, and New Jersey remains a chemical time bomb. The answer to the question, ''Will it happen in New Jersey?'', must remain: ''Yes, it could.''

Chapter 6

WHAT CAN WE DO TO PREVENT FUTURE BHOPALS?

There is much that citizens, including workers, can do to help prevent future Bhopals, even though, sooner or later, somewhere another Bhopal will occur, for all of the reasons that Charles Perrow of Yale has analyzed. But in addition to huge catastrophes like the Bhopal disaster, we must also be concerned about little Bhopals—the numerous small accidents that occur all the time in hazardous industries—and slow Bhopals—the kinds of exposure to hazardous substances that take their toll not in a flash but in a lifetime, like asbestiosis.

The magnitude of this mixture of risk exposure—slow Bhopals, little Bhopals, and big Bhopals—is very large. It has been estimated that over 100,000 workers every single year die in the United States of America because of some exposure to toxic chemicals—simply because they hit a time clock. And that does not include workers injured, sometimes seriously, nor people in surrounding communities who are injured or die from industrially polluted water, from chemical dumping, and from emissions in the atmosphere.

Even if we consider only workers and not people in surrounding communities, there is, as Mike Wright, Health and Safety Director of the United Steel Workers put it at the Newark Conference on Bhopal, a Bhopal every eight to 18 days, depending upon how many people you think died in Bhopal. So there are many Bhopals in just one year only in the U.S. If we had worldwide figures, they would certainly be several orders of magnitude greater.

It is crucial to look at differing combinations of and variations on Bhopal because, as Charles Levinson, General Secretary Emeritus of the International Chemical and Energy Workers Federation from Geneva, Switzerland, pointed out at the Newark Conference, Bhopal will never repeat itself in exactly the same configuration. It will repeat itself—inevitably in his view—in a catastrophe of comparable magnitude, but it is very unlikely ever to recur again in the same detail and pattern. This means that we must take a number of different steps and develop a variety of responses to prevent future industrial disasters.

The significance of this situation was underscored by Dr. Irving Selikoff, Director of the Mt. Sinai School of Environmental Medicine and one of the pioneers in the struggle to bring justice to the victims of hazardous industries. He told the Newark Conference that, within the last 40 or 50 years, the nature of our environment has changed in a fundamental way. We now live in a chemical world. At the end of 1984, the American Chemical Society had 6.9 million substances in its registry file—with about 50,000 in common use. Over 560,000 new substances were added to the registry in that year. Of these, perhaps 500-600 were added to the repertoire of chemicals produced commercially.

The task this poses for protecting the well-being of workers and communities is, Selikoff emphasized, enormous. In 1984, the American Chemical Society reported that it was registering new chemicals at the rate of 65 per hour! But it often takes years before the hazardous character of a particular chemical is discovered. Selikoff mentioned vinyl chloride as a good example. It was first produced in the U.S. in 1938, but it was not until 1974 that we learned just how destructive vinyl chloride could be.

If the costs and benefits of living in this chemical world were more equitably distributed, the problem of how to deal with future Bhopals would not be quite so serious. But the reality is different, whether it be the United States or India. For the overall pattern, as both Raphael Moure of the UAW and Mahesh Buch, the former government official and now environmental activist from Bhopal both pointed out in Newark, is that economic benefits—and particularly profits from industry—are privatized, while the social costs and overheads, ranging from damage to the environment and human health to infrastructure like roads and schools, are not. Everyone ends up paying for those. It is indeed quite possible that many chemical products, if all of those social costs and overheads were directly charged to them, would be so expensive that no one would buy them or that a company would not be able to make any profit.

The stakes in trying to prevent more Bhopals are, therefore, very large. In this chapter we shall look first at some of the issues involved and steps that are or should be taken to prevent future Bhopals in the United States before looking at the situation in the rest of the world. Many of the issues involved and the steps that need to be taken elsewhere in the world are, of course, similar to those in the U.S. We have drawn extensively from the presentations made at the Bhopal Conference in Newark in March 1985 in which some of the leading authorities in the U.S. and India on worker health, industrial safety, and environmental protection took part.

In the United States

The first thing to be said about the situation in the U.S. is we are not totally unprotected against hazardous chemicals like the one that spewed forth from the Union Carbide plant in Bhopal. There are some existing laws on the books like the Toxic Substances Control Act and state and local Right to Know Laws, and there are agencies concerned with protecting workers and the public such as the Occupational Safety and Health Administration and the Environmental Protection Agency. Mike Wright of the United Steel Workers put it this way in Newark:

> These laws and the regulations of those agencies help. Properly enforced, they decrease the chances for a major chemical disaster in the U.S. But it was especially ironic after Bhopal to listen to chemical executives and members of the Reagan Administration cite such laws as the reasons why Americans are safe. Chemical companies fought those laws every step of the way and are fighting against them today. Reagan's political appointees in the EPA, OSHA, and the Office of Management and Budget are doing their best to avoid enforcing the laws.
> If Americans are protected at all it is because the labor and environmental movement fought for strong laws and are fighting today to see that they are enforced. If we have learned anything from the long struggle for safer working conditions and a healthier environment it is that we cannot depend on companies to keep their operations safe without strong regulations. And we cannot depend on government to enforce those regulations without constant pressure from workers and concerned citizens.

A critical step in preventing future Bhopals, therefore, is to halt and reverse the trend toward weakening these laws and their enforce-

ment. Dr. Victor Sidel, President of the American Public Health Association and another pioneer in the struggle for worker and community
protection, observed just how bad the situation has become under the
Reagan Administration. A comparison of OSHA actions in fiscal years
1980 and 1982 reveals that serious violations were down 50 per cent,
repeat violations down 65 per cent, and willful violations down 91 per
cent. "Either U.S. industry has cleaned up its act in the most remarkable fashion between 1980 and 1982," Sidel asserted, "or this
is a studied disregard of the regulations and laws that exist in the
United States and willful neglect of regulatory responsibility."

This problem is well illustrated by the struggle to get a meaningful
Right to Know standard about industrial hazards adopted through
OSHA. That struggle began in 1974 and was fought every inch of the
way by the U.S. Chamber of Commerce, National Association of
Manufacturers, Chemical Manufacturers Association, and other major
industry groups. A good standard for hazard communication was finally
proposed late in the Carter Administration. But one of the very first
acts of the Reagan Administration was to withdraw that proposed
standard and start working on its own watered-down version. Bill Kane
of the UAW refers to it not as the Right to Know but the Right to
Snow.

Another critical problem in preventing future Bhopals is to address
the lack of preventive maintenance in hazardous industries. The prevailing posture all too often in the petro-chemical industry, according
to Victor Sidel, is to "run it till it breaks down." Many U.S. chemical
plants, especially in the Northeast and the Midwest, are old and de-
caying. Industry has learned it is more profitable to run these plants
without stopping, hoping to milk as much production out of them as
possible before they become irreparable or obsolete. As Bhopal clearly
demonstrates, this lack of preventive maintenance leads to toxic disasters occasionally and toxic accidents all the time.

In a perverse kind of way, Dr. David Wegman of the University
of California in Los Angeles observed in Newark, we seem to need
tragedies like Bhopal to make any progress at all in protecting workers
and the public from industrial hazards. They do help to get laws and
regulations passed. But the response is almost always reactive and
does not lead to meaningful efforts at preventing future accidents which
may be of equal severity but follow a different configuration. If we
really mean to prevent future Bhopals, Wegman argued, we will have
to change that and make a real effort at serious prevention. Victor
Sidel of the American Public Health Association summed it up this
way: "We need a national policy on preventive maintenance in haz-

ardous industries to make sure manufacturing plants and storage facilities are not allowed to deteriorate and that responsible kinds of
capital reinvestment are made in those facilities.''

Perhaps Dr. Wegman's complaint, while lamentable, is inevitable. Mike Wrightof the United Steel Workers pointed out the old saying
in union circles that ''all safety standards are written in blood.''

A good place to begin in trying to bring about better prevention
is with the kind of safety code for preventing chemical disasters that
is now being developed by the AFL-CIO through a small working
group with representation from different unions and environmental
groups. The code will include, according to Mike Wright, provisions
for all plants which manufacture, use, store, and transport highly toxic
or flammable materials in quantities sufficient to cause a disaster. A
company operating such a plant would have to prepare an engineering
safety analysis listing the chemicals, detailing the process and equipment in place, and explaining the various ways in which a release
might occur. That kind of analysis is perfectly feasible, he noted, and
responsible companies do it all the time.

Under the proposed code, the second thing a company would be
required to do would be to prepare a comprehensive emergency plan
with provisions for chemical containment, alarms, evacuation, and
medical services. Both the engineering safety analysis and the emergency plan would be available to workers, the union, community
residents, and public officials.

Most important in trying to prevent Bhopal-type disasters are
regulations in the code requiring the best possible controls for preventing catastrophic releases. For example, the process would have
to include back-up safety systems so that no single accident or failure
could trigger a disaster. To the extent possible, dangerous chemical
intermediates would be used immediately after they are generated so
that large quantities would not accumulate. This last point is crucial
in understanding the Bhopal disaster. The Indian engineers, as we have
noted, originally wanted to design the plant in Bhopal without MIC
storage so that it would immediately be used in manufacturing the
pesticide Sevin, but they were overruled by the parent corporation in
the U.S.

Yet another feature of the code being drafted by the AFL-CIO
working group is that the best possible piping and valve systems would
be required, along with automatic shut-down systems. As Raphael
Moure's appendix documenting leaky valves and other fittings in chemical plants clearly demonstrates, this is a very serious issue. The code
will also require comprehensive worker training and there will be

special provisions for the transport of highly dangerous chemicals. Many of the provisions of this code are also found in a recommendation of the Citizens Commission on Bhopal released on the first anniversary of the Bhopal disaster, "International Principles of Industrial Plant Safety."

No one, least of all those involved in drafting the code, are under any illusions that it will be an easy task to get that code adopted. But they are determined, first of all, to try to achieve basic agreement within the labor movement on what a proper set of practices by industry to prevent chemical disasters should include, and having agreed upon that, to begin the long and difficult struggle to get it accepted by industry and embedded as appropriate in government regulations.

It is abundantly clear that if we are going to make any serious progress in preventing future Bhopals, we must have much better information about hazardous substances. The National Academy of Sciences, according to Irving Selikoff, recently undertook a review of the adequacy of the information we have about the environemntal and health effects of chemicals. This review covered 65,000 of the most commonly used chemicals in the U.S.—pesticides, cosmetics, industrial chemicals, food additives, drugs, and so forth. The study concluded that for 90 per cent of these, we know very little or nothing—and this conclusion applies only to the most commonly used chemicals.

Rashid Shaikh, former Director of the Program in Environmental Health and Public Policy at the Harvard School of Public Health, now Staff Scientist at the Health Effects Institute in Cambridge, Massachusetts, and another Newark Conference speaker, emphasized the inadequacy of toxicity testing in the United States today with particular reference to pesticides. It was, after all, a chemical intermediate used in the manufacture of a pesticide that was the key substance involved in the Bhopal disaster. Pesticides by their very nature are harmful, at least to some living things, since they are supposed to control, if not kill, pests that attack agricultural crops and trees. Therefore, one would think that any meaningful program to test the toxicity of hazardous substances, even if it could not make much progress in covering the 65,000 chemicals generally in use in the United States today, at least be able to achieve some significant coverage of that particular category of chemicals.

Alas, Dr. Shaikh reports, this is not the case. On one-third of the pesticides examined in the National Academy study, there was absolutely no information available on their toxicology. On another third, a little information was available but there was no hazard evaluation. And of the remaining third, some evaluation had been undertaken but only in about ten per cent of the cases was anything approaching a comprenensive health hazard evaluation done.

So this is just how bad the situation is: only one out of every ten chemicals used as pesticides has a complete health hazard evaluation. And this for a catagory of hazardous substances for which there have been some legislation and regulation on the books for a period of time and which have been tested much more extensively than other chemicals.

Dr. Selikoff summed up the problem of lack of information on the toxicity of hazardous substances in these words: "We do not have enough information. If we have it, it is not disseminated where it is needed. And if it is disseminated, it is all too often not used." All three aspects of the problem are important, but we have to start with building a much more comprehensive information base on the toxicology of hazardous substances. For without the right information, we have nothing to disseminate, and if we do not disseminate information, it certainly cannot be used.

Closely related to the need for better information on the toxicology of hazardous substances is the need for proper epidemiological studies so that we can monitor systematically over time the health consequences of exposure to these substances in the workplace and in the growing number of toxic waste disposal sites throughout the U.S. These kinds of studies, to be meaningful, need to be conducted not for months or years but for decades. They therefore require very long-term funding and that is rarely available. In addition, Dr. Donald Luria of the New Jersey School of Medicine and Dentistry argued in Newark, we need to be able to provide low-cost targeted surveillance for individuals and communities exposed to contaminated food and water. In the case of the latter, it is not just drinking water with which we must be concerned; evidence accumulates that volatile substances may be absorbed through their presence in bath water. And although this may not be harmful to an adult worker if only small amounts are absorbed through the skin, it can be a major problem for young children or for pregnant women.

But perhaps the most immediate and obvious step which needs to be taken to prevent future Bhopals is the enactment of meaningful and effective Right to Know laws and regulations. They can and should be enacted by municipalities and states, as New Jersey did and is now tackling again, unless and until we get a national Right to Know law with real teeth in it. Virtually all of the experts in occupational and community health and environmental protection agree that the present OSHA Hazard Communication Standard is totally inadequate.

Right to Know laws are a critical step forward, because without accurate information about hazardous substances and processes, it is impossible to knowwhen to act. But as Bill Kane of the UAW stressed in Newark, ''We've got to start looking beyond the Right to Know. We've got to start looking for the Right to Act. If we get all the chemical information that we are asking for, so what. It's not going to do us any good unless we do something with it.''

Just what the Right to Act should include has not yet been spelled out in detail. Victor Sidel of the American Public Health Association argues for national legislation to empower workers to control the monitoring and maintenance of workplace hazards, pointing out that Sweden and Great Britain, among other countries, already have such laws on the books. Kane and other activists on these issues go beyond that in urging that workers and people in the surrounding community should have the power to force a corporation to clean up its act if it is posing a threat to human health and the environment, and if the industry will not comply, take the ultimate step of closing down the operation until it does. In a variation on the same theme, the Citizens Commission on Bhopal, in its recommendation on ''Worker and Community Involvement and Empowermemt in Industrial Plant Safety'' released on the first anniversary of the Bhopal tragedy, called for the deputization of at least one worker inspector and one community inspector in each workplace where hazardous substances are involved.

Bill Kane reflected the fears and frustrations of workers and people in surrounding communities whose well-being and even whose lives have been placed at risk by hazardous industries in their midst when he said at the Newark Conference: ''Citizens and workers should have the right to protect their own health, to protect their children's health, to protect their jobs, and to protect the economic health of their communities. Corporations have been running over us for too long and it is about time they stopped.''

Elsewhere in the World

Elsewhere in the world, and especially in the Third World, the place to begin in addressing the question, ''How can we prevent future Bhopals?'' is to ask whether the Union Carbide plant that produced the worst industrial disaster in history was needed in the first place. (Many would argue that we need also to address this prior question in the United States as well.)

The standard argument on behalf of hazardous industries that

produce chemical products like pesticides is that the products themselves help to improve the quality of living and may even save lives.
In the Third World generally and in India in particular, this argument
is focused on pesticides and their alleged impact on the production of
food crops. It is contended that hazardous industrial plants like the
Union Carbide installation in Bhopal, even if they do pose a risk to
workers and the surrounding community, produce much larger benefits
for the society as a whole by helping the country to grow more food
and, therefore, to prevent starvation and alleviate malnutrition.

But does this really happen? David Weir, Director of the Center
for Investigative Reporting in San Francisco, addressed this question
with co-author Mark Shapiro in their book, *Circle of Poison* (San
Francisco: Institute for Food and Development Policy, 1981). What
they discovered undermines this line of argument.

"We found," Weir observed in Newark, "that in case after case,
in region after region, and in crop after crop, 50 to 70 per cent of all
pesticides used in Third World countries were *not* used on local food
crops but were used on export crops—coffee, tea, sugar, tapioca,
winter fruits and vegetables, and non-food crops such as rubber and
cotton." (Sevin, the Union Carbide pesticide made in Bhopal, has
been extensively used on cotton.)

So it is by no means clear that hazardous industries using hazardous substances do contribute significantly to the well-being of the
local people, even though they may make a handsome contribution to
the balance sheets of the multinational corporations which operate these
plants. (Ironically, as we now know, the Carbide plant in Bhopal did
not even do that; being a money loser almost certainly aggravated the
neglect of proper maintenance and safety.) There is a further problem
caused by the momentum of advanced technology as it spreads inex-
orably out around the globe from the major industrialized countries
where it was developed in the first place. It tends to preclude serious
consideration, development, and use of alternative methods or products.

Dr. Nicholas Ashford, Director of the Center for Policy Alternatives at the Massachusetts Institute of Technology, argued at the
Newark Conference that in all countries, when looking at the question
of whether or not to set up industries using and making hazardous raw
materials and products, we need much more rigorous assessments of
the technology involved than generally occurs, if it occurs at all. This
assessment must give proper weight to the risks such technologies pose
to human health and the environment, not only in manufacturing but
also in use over time. An equally careful examination of alternatives

is also needed. Only now do we see in the United States that greater and greater use of pesticides, leaving aside the hazards involved in their manufacture, storage, and transportation, are slowly poisoning our soil and ground water. They are also becoming less and less effective as pests develop resistance to them, so that more and more need to be applied, a kind of vicious circle.

Similar awareness is beginning to emerge in some of the other industrialized countries, leading to the development of non-chemical alternatives such as integrated pest management. But this process, Ashford contended, has hardly begun in many parts of the Third World, where the risk to human health and the environment posed by indiscriminate use of pesticides is even greater than it is in the industrialized countries.

Technology assessment of the sort that Ashford called for must address another critical problem which applies not only to the Third World but industrialized countries as well—namely, the inadequacy of most cost-benefit analyses, which are typically part of a technology assessment exercise. Even when no serious effort at technology assessment is made, cost-benefit analyses are customarily undertaken as part of an investment decision in building a new plant or expanding an existing one, whether by a local company, a multinational corporation, a government planning department, or an international development agency like the World Bank.

The difficulty is that these kinds of analyses rarely take sufficiently into account the social costs of long-term damage to the environment and human health. Economists all too often dismiss these costs as "externalities" that cannot be meaningfully measured or monetized and, therefore, cannot be calculated along with other costs and benefits. These kinds of analyses also rarely look seriously at the question of alternatives, which may not produce as dramatic results in the short term but are much safer and involve much less risk in the long term.

Ashford pointed out that one vital function of meaningful standards and regulations for protection of public health and the environment is to help create a market for what he calls "responsible alternatives." Recognition of the existence of these alternatives is vital in addressing the prior question of whether pesticides like Sevin being made by Union Carbide in Bhopal are truly essential. He argued that we must not allow ourselves to be boxed in by those who insist that it all comes down to a trade-off between economic growth and industrial development on the one hand and protection of the environment and human health on the other. "We should be dealing not with such a trade-off but with the question of restructuring the nature of industrial production so that it is less polluting and hazardous. In our vehemence and anger about Bhopal and Union Carbide, we must remember that industry is not monolithic. There are technological opportunities to shift the balance toward safer and less risky products and processes, so that we can have our cake and eat it too, even though there may be different people making the cake.''

There are other compelling reasons for addressing the question of alternatives in considering how we can prevent future Bhopals elsewhere in the world. Not the least of these is the huge number of persons in the Third World who are poisoned every year by the use, let alone the manufacture, of pesticides. David Weir reported in Newark that the World Health Organization once calculated that 500,000 people are poisoned each year by pesticides, perhaps 5,000 of them fatally. Oxfam, the British relief and development organization, reanalyzed the WHO figures recently and came up with a number of 750,000 people a year, based on the same assumptions used by WHO. But the actual number may be much higher still. Weir recalled a conversation with the Minister of Agriculture in Thailand who estimates that in that country alone there are approximately one million cases of pesticide poisoning every year. So the problem of use—some would say more accurately, misuse—of pesticides in the Third World has a very serious and widespread impact on public health.

Nor is this poisonous onslaught confined to the Third World. In what is often called the ''boomerang effect,'' residues of pesticides banned or severely restricted in the United States are turning up on foodstuffs imported from the Third World. A good example is coffee. From 1974 to 1977, the U.S. Food and Drug Administration found that 35 out of 74 samples tested (47 per cent) were contaminated with such pesticides such as DDT, Lindane, Dieldrin, and Malathon.

Notwithstanding the size and global reach of the pesticide problem, the problem can be meaningfully addressed, if not absolutely controlled, with sufficient political will on the part of governments. Out of the 65,000 chemicals produced comercially, Weir reported in Newark that only 1,000 to 2,000 are made in sufficient quantity and have such hazardous properties that they need to be the object of major attention. That surely is a manageable number for regulatory agencies of national governments to cope with. But the reality is that most governments do not appear to be sufficiently motivated to act decisively, whether because of industry resistance or perceived lack of public concern.

While Weir may be right that in theory the problem of how to deal with hazardous chemicals worldwide is manageable, not only is political will lacking within many governments. At least as important, according to Charles Levinson of the International Chemical and Energy Workers Federation, is the fact that industries which have a high concentration of hazardous products and processes tend to be dominated by a handful of multinational companies. In the pharmaceutical industry there are ten companies which account for 60 to 70 per cent of world production. A similar pattern exists in other branches of the chemical industry such as petro-chemicals and agricultural chemicals.

The pesticide industry illustrates Levinson's point well. According to David Weir, some 30 MNCs control 90 per cent of the world market. Just five of them control over half of the market. Four of the five are European based, while one is American (Monsanto). Bayer, the West German company known mainly for aspirin, commands the largest share of the world pesticide market (partly because it sells not only its own products but those of other companies) while Monsanto is the world's largest pesticide producer. Union Carbide is one of the 30 MNCs, although not among the largest five.

By almost any standard, this is a highly concentrated industry in which a handful of large companies dominate a huge world market in pesticides. While this market appears to be reaching the saturation point in a number of industrialized countries as pests become more resistant to pesticides and environmental controls begin to have greater impact, it is growing by leaps and bounds in Third World countries. In Africa over the last decade, there has been a quintupling of pesticide sales and use. In Asia and Latin America, absolute increases are almost certainly much greater. Yet these poisonous substances are much more abused in the Third World than elsewhere. Developing countries account for only one-sixth of worldwide pesticide usage but roughly half of all the pesticides poisonings.

One of the consequences of this situation, Levinson argued in Newark, is that conventional controls and regulatory mechanisms at the national level rapidly lose their potency. While the U.S. government is certainly capable of forcing Union Carbide to respond to national laws and regulations on that part of the company's operations in the U.S., it has no authority over those parts of Union Carbide which are, in legal terms, corporate citizens of other soverign states. As an MNC like Carbide moves more and more of its operations offshore, the degree of control of that company by the U.S. correspondingly diminishes. "If governments can no longer exercise meaningful control over their own enterprises which have become increasingly multinational," Levinson asked rhetorically, "what are we going to use in place of the authority of national governments?"

There are no easy answers to this question, as Levinson readily conceded. The United Nations and other international intergovernmental organizations are all consensus bodies—that is, they reach decisions at the lowest common denominator of universal acceptance. The likelihood that such a decision-making mode will ever achieve meaningful standards for dealing with hazardous industries and products is remote.

The international trade union movement has been trying to develop a countervailing force through the creation of multinational company councils—that is, bodies that bring together trade unions representing workers in a single company on a worldwide basis. In Levinson's own union, this effort has advanced over the past three decades to the point where, in 1984, there were over 400 "solidarity actions" initiated by these councils against the multinational corporations with which they were concerned. But whatever the progress achieved, Levinson would be the first to recognize that the struggle is far from over and remains a highly unequal one. National unions, themselves composed typically of many different locals, are no match at the international level for the centralized, hierarchical decision-making structures that characterize most MNCs.

If the United Nations system and the international trade union movement, even though they may make some headway, are not likely in the foreseeable future to develop into effective means for regulating the behavior of multinational corporations worldwide on issues of industrial safety, worker health, and environmental protection, what else can be done? Strengthening the regulatory capabilities of developing countries is one obvious answer. And in fact that is occurring in some countries, albeit at a slow rate which may not be keeping pace with the predigious growth of hazardous industries in the last decades of the twentieth century. Effective regulation of hazardous products imported from industrialized countries into the Third World is difficult enough, as the number and volume of these products increases. Much harder is to deal with hazardous technologies used in manufacturing operations within the country, as the Bhopal disaster has so clearly revealed.

Barry Castleman, who is one of the leading authorities on exporting hazardous industries, gave some melancholy facts and figures to the Newark Conference to underscore this point. In Bolivia, the Chief of the National Institute for Occupational Safety and Health has a salary of about $50 a month. That is about twice as much as tin miners make in Bolivia, and many of them are contracting silicosis before they reach the age of 30. Meanwhile, MNCs that mine tin in

Bolivia are lobbying against legislative provisions that would allow tin workers to get compensation for silicosis before they are totally disabled from it.

In Madhya Pradesh, the state in India where Union Carbide's Bhopal plant is located, there are 15 inspectors to check 8,000 factories. These inspectors have no vehicles and have to plead with the very companies they are regulating for rides in order to get to the factories. They do not have laboratory facilities and sampling instruments to do the necessary testing to verify what hazards are present in many of these locations.

Similar tales could be produced from other Third World countries. But people in the U.S. should not be complacent. As we have shown elsewhere in this book, there has been a serious erosion in the capacity of U.S. government agencies like EPA and OSHA to maintain proper surveillance of U.S. industries using or manufacturing hazardous products, and there is a far larger number of such industrial facilities here.

So we come back to the inescapable proposition that we must have, where high-risk technologies are involved, effective international standards and the best means we can devise to make them enforceable. There should be no question of double standards where extreme risk to workers and the surrounding community is present, as in Bhopal.

Rashid Shaikh of the Health Effects Institute in Cambridge observed in Newark that while we are far from achieving a worldwide consensus on how to deal with these problems, we can see a convengence of opinion in the international community, aided and abetted by the Bhopal disaster. Shaikh described that converging opinion as insisting, as a basic minimum, that exporting countries should take the responsibility for providing information about hazardous substances and technologies to importing countries so that importing countries can make their own decisions more wisely— the principle of informed consent. Yet others would argue that this is no longer sufficient and we must raise our sights to include *enforceable* international standards where high-risk technologies as in Bhopal are involved.

To achieve that goal will not be easy. The best hope in the eyes of Mike Wright of the United Steel Workers is to build a worldwide labor and environmental movement. Indeed, as a first step in that direction, the safety code for preventing chemical disasters being drafted by the AFL-CIO will be shared with trade unions in other countries in an effort to develop acceptance of an international code—that is, one comprehensive trade union program for preventing chemical disasters worldwide.

Then the hard work really begins. Interaction with the world environmental movement to refine this code and make it even more effective will be necessary. After that will be the still more arduous task of seeing that it is implemented through every concerned international organization such as the ILO and the OECD where the commitment and determination of workers and environmentalists joined together has the hope of prevailing. "This is a terribly ambitious goal," Wright concluded. "Nobody has really ever done this before. But the situation demands nothing less."

Some would argue that this kind of goal can never be achieved, no matter how hard environmentalists and workers struggle. But others insist that we have no choice and that, if we can clearly fix the costs of not doing so, the task, while still difficult, will not be impossible.

Dr. Irving Selikoff of the Mt. Sinai School of Environmental Medicine noted that when a decision is made by a major chemical company to introduce a new chemical, on the face of it this appears to be a clearly private decision of the company concerned. But these private decisions, as we know all too well from Bhopal, have major public consequences.

This can be best illustrated with asbestos, in which Selikoff played a major role in producing scientific evidence of serious long-term health impacts. Up to the end of the last decade, one calculation estimates that asbestos poisoning has cost the U.S. taxpayers—through Medicare, Medicaid, and other government programs—$17 billion. But before this industrially induced health problem has run its course, it will cost the taxpayers over $300 billion. If these "externalities" were directly charged to the asbestos industry, that industry would no longer be economically viable and its products affordable by consumers.

Nor is a risk of this magnitude, Selikoff emphasized in Newark, insurable. Consequently, manufacturing companies would not be able to shift the burden of this kind of risk as they strive to do with other risks less cataclysmic in character. But however they seek to cope with such risk exposure, Selikoff argued that a more fundamental question remains.

> If we knowingly gamble with the lives of others, and if we fail, what should the penalties be? If you shoot crap and unfortunately you throw snake eyes or something similar, you lose your money. But here we're gambling with the lives of others. What should the penalties be? Now the insurance industry has learned to deal with some of the financial consequences—the financial penalties if they fail. We often talk of civil penalties. There is even in some jurisdictions in some countries an attitude now that if you kill

people, whether slowly or rapidly, there might even be criminal penalties.

Given the enormity of the problem and its awesome character, what can those of us concerned about the preservation of human health and dignity and proper accountability when that health and dignity is threatened or destroyed do?, Selikoff asked his Newark audience. His response to his own question: "We have no alternative, each and every one of us, but to get actively involved in the struggle that lies ahead."

Chapter 7

AN AGENDA FOR CITIZEN ACTION

The key issues or actions around which an agenda for citizen action should be shaped are at least five in number. The first is the double standard for protection of human life and well-being so starkly revealed in the Bhopal tragedy. All of the loss of life and terrible suffering caused by the gas leak at the Union Carbide plant in Bhopal will not have been completely in vain if it provides us with an opportunity to banish, for once and for all, the cultural chauvinism which surrounds the notion of having double standards. Human life is as precious in Bhopal, India, as it is in Institute, West Virginia.

The second is to bring about, finally and long after it should have been done, meaningful accountability for protection of human life and the environment by multinational corporations. They may continue to escape the tax collector in one country by shifting their operations or assets to another, but when it comes to such primordial questions as nurturing, rather than destroying, human life, they must face up to the same rigorous standard anywhere in the world.

Closely related is the third issue of assuring that, when export of high-risk technologies is undertaken by MNCs, responsibility for safety procedures and standards is clearly spelled out. MNCs should be required, as an integral part of any technology transfer agreement, to provide detailed data on safety systems and their experience with those systems in manufacturing plants in other countries, as well as information on the toxicology of hazardous substances and the results of maximum credible accident studies involving these substances. MNCs should then be held liable for any failure to meet their responsibilities under such agreements, as should government agencies and companies in the importing countries.

The fourth is the need to greatly increase public awareness of the relationship of hazardous industries to such critical problems as worker health and industrial safety, environmental and consumer protection, and alternative approaches to agriculture that diminish substantially dependence on chemical inputs.

Finally is the question of violations of human rights. Most fundamental is the right to life itself, so wantonly violated on that awful night in December, 1984, in Bhopal. There are also the rights to know and to participate in decisions which affect the well-being, and indeed survival, of workers and members of the community surrounding hazardous industries. Beyond that is the right to hold accountable the economically and politically powerful who cause injury or death to the innocent and powerless.

If these are the critical problems which citizen action and response to the Bhopal tragedy should address, what are the key steps needed to tackle these problems? Without exhausting all of the possibilities, here are a dozen grouped in five major categories:

A. *Action Research*: Independent research as a basis for action undertaken by citizen groups and worker organizations is necessary as a check on parallel research by government and industry. Such a research agenda should include:

1. The truth about what really happened in Bhopal, who was responsible, and what were the consequences. This will inevitably be the principal responsibility of groups in India, but their counterparts in the U.S. can play an important supporting role, especially in acquiring intelligence on the operations and practices of the parent of the Indian company in whose plant the accident occurred—namely, Union Carbide Corporation.

2. Use and abuse of pesticides and other environmentally harmful agricultural chemicals. Especially important is careful and systematic documentation of personal injuries from agricultural chemicals.

3. Exposure of workers to excessive or preventable risks in hazardous industries. Equally important here is careful documentation of personal injuries.

4. Alternatives to the use of pesticides and other chemical inputs in agriculture, and alternatives to extremely hazardous or highly toxic substances throughout industry.

5. Maximum credible accident studies, which should be prepared by every industrial plant using, storing, or making hazardous materials and monitored by community and worker groups.

6. Regulatory models for assuring safety of workers and surrounding communities from hazardous industries.

B. *Public Awareness*: Citizen groups have a major role to play in building public understanding through action campaigns and related initiatives such as the following:

1. Organizing a boycott of Union Carbide products and mass demonstrations at Carbide facilities if justice is not done to the Bhopal victims within a reasonable period of time.

2. Undertaking a "dirty dozen" campaign which would identify the most harmful or misused pesticides or other agricultural chemicals and encourage stoppage of their production and use of alternatives. Such a campaign was launched in June 1985 by the Pesticide Action Network (PAN), a worldwide coalition of consumer, environmental, church, and public health groups.

3. Initiating a campaign among farmers to inform them about and urge them to use alternative approaches which minimize dependence on environmentally damaging agricultural chemicals.

C. *Government Policies and Regulations*: If there was ever any question, Bhopal should have answered it once and for all. Self-regulation by industry in handling and use of hazardous substances is hopelessly inadequate. (Needless to say, industry efforts to improve industrial plant safety and make information about toxic substances more readily available to the public such as the Chemical Manufacturers Association's recently established National Chemical and Response Information Center are most welcome, but they are no substitute for effective government standards.)

Government policies and regulations to protect human beings and the environment are therefore essential, and environment, public health, consumer, worker, and other citizen organizations have an absolutely vital role to play in seeing that the right policies are formulated and that they are then vigorously implemented. Some key tasks are:

1. Participating in the prior decisions that lead to the creation of a hazardous manufacturing facility within a country or community such as industrial licensing in a country

like India or zoning and environmental impact decisions in many communities in the U.S. Here is the time to insist upon full disclosure of hazards and toxic effects and their treatment, the design of the facility to cope with such effects, and alternatives to the facility. It is axiomatic that the company seeking approval for a new facility will not present alternatives; citizen groups have a special responsibility to do so.

2. Beefing up to several times its present size the government program of toxicity testing, which is hopelessly insufficient. The costs are trivial in relation to the staggering loss of live and personal injury sustained in an industrial disaster like Bhopal.

3. Establishing a meaningful national policy on preventive maintenance in hazardous industries and then giving the regulatory agency or agencies assigned to monitor it sufficient muscle to do so.

4. Early passage of a strong national Right to Know Law that will supplement, but not supersede, state and local laws. This law must give workers and communities whose well-being, and indeed very survival, are being placed at risk by hazardous industries in their midst essential information about the risks to which they are exposed.

5. Establishing a worker and community Right to Act policy. The certainty that there will be, sooner or later, another big Bhopal, together with all of the little Bhopals and the slow Bhopals that go on all the time in the United States, means that the time has come to empower workers and communities to force industry compliance with the highest safety standards when extremely hazardous substances are being manufactured, stored, transported, and used. Sweden and Britain already have laws that give workers certain rights in this regard, and the chemical industries in those countries have not ceased to function. We can do no less in the U.S.

D. *Law*: Citizen organizations, including public interest law groups, need to address themselves to central legal questions posed by the Bhopal disaster. The character of the issues involved has been set forth in Chapters 3 and 4 on justice for the Bhopal victims and the tangled web of litigation.

1. Insuring that the consolidated legal action of the Bhopal victims now in the Federal District Court in New York

be effectively litigated. Premature settlement of this case is likely to be adverse to the interests of the Bhopal victims who should in any event be provided with interim relief while the litigation proceeds—just as Judge Keenan, in whose court the case is being tried, has now asked Union Carbide to do. Only if the case is litigated will key legal issues be settled. Equally important, only through litigation will we be able to establish, once and for all, what really happened at Bhopal and who is responsible. Self-serving statements to the press by principals in the Bhopal affair are no substitute for the facts of the matter as determined through the application of the rigorous rules of evidence that apply in a court of law.

2. Strengthening legal doctrines applicable to toxic torts through the various cases before Indian and U.S. Courts, both federal and state. Such legal doctrines when more fully explicated through case law (supplemented or reinforced, if necessary, by statute law), will fix, clearly and unequivocally, responsibility for safety and protection when known dangerous substances are being handled. Litigation building on existing law should lead to an enhancement of the role of law in the prevention and deterrence of such disasters in the form of a new post-Bhopal jurisprudence as set forth in the concluding section of Chapter 3.

E. *A New Approach*: Bhopal and all the public attention it has stimulated have made abundantly clear what activists and professionals in worker safety and public health fields have known for a long time—government regulations, even when they are well formulated and effectively implemented, are not enough to protect the lives and well-being of those exposed to risk from hazardous substances and industries, even though such regulations are essential. The Bhopal disaster has created an opportunity to formulate new strategies based upon much more active participation of workers and members of communities at risk. These "participative policing systems" would involve not only government agencies and industry representatives but also representatives of workers and the surrounding community. Citizen groups have a critical role to play in formulating such approaches and working for their actual initiation in specific industrial locations where very hazardous substances are being handled.

Yet another important issue in which community and worker organizations should join hands is the jobs of workers in hazardous industrial facilities. Workers and communities need some protection in the event a particularly risky operation is curtailed or shut down. One approach would be the creation of a national indemnity fund which could be based on a cess levied on companies handling or producing hazardous materials. This fund would provide for transitional support, retraining, and relocation if workers lose their jobs in such circumstances and would support alternative economic development strategies for surrounding communities. Failure to address this vital question will continue to make it possible for industry to drive a wedge between workers and citizens in surrounding communities—as has sadly occurred in the wake of Bhopal in Institute, West Virginia—when in fact they share a much larger common interest in safe operation of industrial facilities and in holding corporate management responsible for the risk exposure they both experience.

F. *International Standards*: The time has come to establish meaningful international standards for industries that pose severe risks to human health and the environment. There is no other way to deal with the problem when major industrial corporations have the capacity to move manufacturing operations involving hazardous substances to any corner of the globe. To be meaningful, such standards must be enforceable. The recent recommendation of the Citizens Commission on Bhopal regarding ''International Principles of Industrial Plant Safety'' encompass some of the key issues which these standards should cover.

Such a task will not be easy and will certainly never be achieved without strong pressure from workers and citizens and the organizations representing their concerns. U.S. groups need to team up with their counterparts in other countries in a coordinated effort to work toward:

1. Formulating international norms—drawn from ''best practice'' technical solutions—for design and operation of industrial plants handling or manufacturing highly toxic substances and for the storage, transportation, and use of such substances.

2. Drafting an international code on research and development on highly toxic substances which would require—as

a *quid pro quo* for permission to market the resulting product—an adequate level of effort in determining and making freely available the health and environmental effects of these substances and in seeking appropriate counter measures to minimize or contain these effects.

Making significant progress on such a large agenda is an enormous challenge to citizen groups. The challenge is all the greater because most such groups are chronically understaffed and underfinanced, unlike their adversaries in industry. (Alas, these groups sometimes find well-heeled adversaries in government too, even though in a political democracy government should be on the side of the people, in the struggle to protect human health and the environment.) The efforts of many individual organizations—local, state, and national—will be needed.

To coordinate these various efforts and to assure that they have maximum visibility and impact, a broad-based coalition of citizen groups is needed. The Citizens Commission on Bhopal, representing a wide spectrum of environmental, consumer and church organizations, trade unions and workers' groups, public health, legal, and scientific groups, has been established for this purpose. The Commission is striving to tackle as much of the foregoing agenda as it can, seeking the involvement of voluntary groups in India and other countries wherever appropriate and possible.

While the agenda set forth here is primarily directed toward U.S. citizen action, many of the issues are of concern to other countries, both industrialized and developing, and especially, of course, India. Citizen groups in each country will necessarily want to determine their own agendas for action, leading to parallel efforts in a number of countries.

Coalescence of such efforts in different countries should make possible meaningful action at the international level. The first step would be the initiation of a review of existing international mechanisms—e.g., the International Register of Potentially Toxic Chemicals in Geneva or the Consolidated List of Harmful Products at UN headquarters in New York—to strengthen the world's information base on toxic substances. An examination should also be made of the existing roles and activities of such international agencies as the World Health Organization, International Labour Organisation, United Nations Environment Programme, Food and Agriculture Organization, UNICEF, and other UN agencies like the Centre on Transnational Corporations in order to determine how their efforts might be made more effective and contribute more substantially to initiatives at the local, state, and national levels.

Other aspects of this international study phase would include exploration of the development of an international law doctrine based on the *Fletcher v. Rylands* principle regarding levels of responsibility for safety and protection when known dangerous substances are being handled—i.e., international legal norms for toxic torts. (Such law already exists in several common law countries but is at a very early stage of development.) Parallels in international law— e.g., airplane safety conventions—would also be examined, as would private international law/conflict-of-laws issues such as choice of judicial forum for legal action, determination of applicable jurisdiction, and enforcement of foreign decrees.

This international study and the efforts of citizen's commissions or study groups in different countries should culminate in an international conference at which the results of the work of the U.S. Citizens Commission on Bhopal and comparable groups in other countries and the international study would be brought together. The international conference would address itself to the steps which need to be taken at the international level to establish meaningful norms and standards based on "best practice" procedures already in place, to share information more widely, and to develop appropriate codes or guidelines for performance by those involved in the manufacture, distribution, and use of highly toxic substances.

EPILOGUE: THE MEANING OF BHOPAL

The Response of Union Carbide, the Government of India, and the Media

One of the most striking aspects of the Bhopal disaster has been the nature of the response that it has evoked from three of the principal parties involved: the government of India, Union Carbide, and the media. While all three have reacted very differently, in a certain sense they share much in common. Expressed simply, everybody has been at pains to emphasize that, although the events in Bhopal were catastrophic in every sense of the word, the episode is, for all practical purposes, over. To listen to their representatives hold forth, one is left with the impression that the administrative response has been more than adequate, that the damage has been far less serious than was originally feared, and that all which remains is a quick resolution of the legal issues arising from the accident.

Union Carbide has sought to reassure its shareholders and creditors that the worst is over and that the events at Bhopal will have no impact of any consequence on the future of the company. In a show of bravado—arrogance, some would call it—the Carbide management declared the same dividend as in the previous year and concluded, in its 1984 annual report, that coping with the Bhopal disaster does not require any special financial provision by the company. Investors responded by bidding the price of Carbide stock well above its pre-Bhopal level—aided and abetted by an ultimately failed takeover bid by another chemical company, the GAF Corporation.

Bhopal has likewise lost the attention of much of the media. Their concerns today reflect little more than those of either the government

131

of India or Union Carbide—that is, a quick resolution of the issue of compensation. While the case before Judge Keenan still draws considerable notice, it has become rather like a classic melodrama in their eyes. The corporation beseiged, the greedy personal injury lawyers, the large amounts of money that are at stake, these are what the media considers important or at least newsworthy. For the rest of us, there are only the "lessons of Bhopal" to be learned, the moral issues to be addressed, and thus, the rationalization of the episode to complete.

What explains this urgency to wind up the affair? Union Carbide certainly has an interest in seeing the whole sordid business wrapped up as quickly as possible. After all, their principal objective is making money, and this is best done outside the glare of public attention, especially the kind that Bhopal has generated.

Union Carbide's performance in the Bhopal affair is a manifestation of characteristic corporate schizophrenia—and, as more facts emerge about the company's seamy past, vintage Carbide as well. On the one hand, Carbide's principal officials, led by Warren Anderson, the Chairman, mouth expressions of sympathy for the victims and a desire to alleviate their plight. On the other, their legal counsel in both India and the U.S. fight every challenge tooth and nail, conceding not one iota of responsibility for the worst industrial disaster in history. Simultaneously, a public relations campaign of extraordinary magnitude is launched to distort the cause of the accident while minimizing its impact on its victims. How else can we explain how the fanciful "sabotage" theory being touted by Carbide keeps popping up, here or there, in the world's press?

On the one hand, Union Carbide strives to project an image of "Mr. Clean" within the chemical industry. On the other, as the Society for Participatory Research in Asia/Highlander Center publication, *No Place to Run: Local Realities and Global Issues of the Bhopal Disaster* has painstakingly documented, Carbide has a sordid record of disregard for worker safety and community health at its installations, not only in such places as India, Indonesia, and Puerto Rico but also at its plants in such U.S. locations as West Virginia, Tennessee, and Texas.

Carbide's efforts to supress and distort adverse information about the health and environmental impacts of its operations bear striking resemblance to a 50-year effort to cover up and evade responsibility for the health effects of asbestos examined in rich detail by Paul Brodeur in a meticulously documented four-part series in *The New Yorker*, "The Asbestos Industry on Trial" (June 10, 17, 24, and July 1, 1985). The time spans are, of course, quite different. The asbestos tragedy has played itself out over five decades or more, while Bhopal has been history only for a little more than a year. But the tactics are the same—supression of data, deception, legal stonewalling, refusal to admit responsibility unless compelled by the courts, and even then, to offer the most niggardly compensation for grievous wrongs, including the ultimate one of death.

But the government of India and the media cannot be presumed to share Union Carbide's concern with containment and speedy disposition. After all, where a tragedy of such enormity has occurred, it is surely newsworthy and any government could reasonably be expected to seek full justice on behalf of the victims who are its citizens. This it would do by determining the extent of the injustice done and by conveying this to the public in order to seek their support for its actions. But while the government of India has gone through all the motions of pursuing the case against Carbide, it has thus far given the impression of not being entirely serious in its efforts to secure full compensation for the victims.

How else would one explain the fact that in the first critical year after the tragedy, the government failed to publish even a preliminary report on the causes and the true magnitude of the disaster. Or the fact that the size of the compensation reportedly being sought bears so little relation to the true cost of bringing justice to the victims. One suspects that, more than anything else, the government is embarrassed by what happened at Bhopal. The most pro-business government in independent India's history finds itself in the unenviable position of having to confront a multinational coporation. After all, there is a much larger issue involved—the need to open up the economy to foreign investment in order to accelerate the pace of industrial development. So what if thousands of people, who in any case have little to do with this development, should die in the course of its pursuit?

The Grotesque Debate over Costs and Benefits

The government of India certainly understands the cost/benefit dimension of the issue. Those who determine its policies rest comfortably in the knowledge that they stand to benefit from the existence of such industries, while not necessarily bearing its costs. In fact, all the parties to the case seem implicitly to endorse such an argument.

As the *Wall Street Journal* has editorialized, what does it matter if a few people die in the course of development? Had it not been for pesticide manufacture, so the specious argument runs, many more would have died from starvation. A more cynical proposition would be hard to find. By seeking to include mass murder within the realm of acceptable risks associated with industrial development, this contorted assertion extends cost/benefit analysis to cover all exigencies.

In fact, cost/benefit analysis in dealing with the risks of modern society has not only been carried to grotesque limits but generated a whole new mythology called risk assessment. Charles Perrow of Yale in his book *Normal Accidents* (p. 12) captures the essence of this new mythology in these words:

> The new risks have produced a new breed of shamans, called risk assessors. As with the shamans and physicians of old, it might be more dangerous to go to them for advice than to suffer unattended [because of] the dangers of this new alchemy where body counting replaces social and cultural values and excludes us from participating in decisions about risks that a few have decided the many cannot do without. *The issue is not risk but power*. [Emphasis supplied.]

It is one thing to say that a worker who *knowingly* accepts a job in a plant manufacturing toxic substances is implicitly accepting the risks of being exposed or contaminated—but even in such a case, the law provides for compensation if it can be proved that such exposure was on account of the management's negligence. (There is little evidence that the Carbide workers in fact knew just how dangerous the stuff they were handling really was.) But to extend the argument to rationalize the events at Bhopal is something else. The people who were exposed to the gas were quite innocent of its manufacture. They had absolutely nothing to do with the decisions that enabled the plant to be constructed in the first place and even less to do with its design or operation. To contend that they indirectly benefited from its operation is highly debatable and possibly erroneous, but anyway quite beside the point.

Catastrophes and Voiceless Victims

Social catastrophes on the scale of Bhopal cannot be construed as acceptable risks attendant upon normal industrial activity. Bhopal is a manifestation of the grossest social irresponsibility of our time and those who are guilty must be held accountable for their actions, and not allowed to take refuge behind such specious propositions. While it may be true that chemical manufacture is by its very nature hazardous, such an observation does not constitute a justification for what happened at Bhopal. Yet the fact that this proposition is actually advanced is itself revealing. For it demonstrates the arrogance of these corporations which would blame the victims for their failures as much as the utter contempt in which they hold all meaningful considerations of public safety.

The government of India can afford to go along with such a proposition only because of who the victims are: the poor, the destitute, people who lack effective voices and therefore power. One wonders what the government's—and the world's—reaction would have been if the victims had been of middle-class origin, if the plant had been located further south within the city of Bhopal so that affluent neighborhoods were exposed to concentrations of the gas that swamped the shanty towns in the northern end of the city.

Had the victims mostly consisted of professionals, bureaucrats, executives, and their families, it is almost certain that the attitude of the authorities would have been different: a lot more indignant for certain, more strenuous in their efforts to determine accurately the scale of damage, firmer in their resolve to prosecute Union Carbide and secure justice for the victims—and a lot more information made available to the public on the nature of this mass-poisoning and its likely long-term effects. There is in fact a contemporaneous incident which should remove any uncertainty about the validity of the foregoing proposition. As Claude Alvares reminds us in an angry (but carefully researched) piece in *The Illustrated Weekly of India* on the first anniversary of Bhopal ("The Greater Bhopal Tragedy," December 1, 1985), the relatives of all the 300-odd middle-class victims of the June 23, 1984, Air India crash off the coast of Ireland were speedily provided with compensation of nearly Rs.1 million (some $85,000) each.

Perhaps even the media's coverage would have been significantly different. What is most incongruous about the present situation is that, even when fresh information is becoming available on the health problems that Bhopal's survivors today face, against which the accident and its immediate impact almost pale into insignificance, the media chooses to treat the subject as a thing of the past. Yet the fact remains that the accident and the events of the days that immediately followed constitute little more than a curtain-raiser to a mass disaster, the implications of which are only now being fully grasped and the consequences of which will almost certainly extend into the next century.

Liability, Negligence, and Social Responsibility

Society imposes a duty on everyone to avoid acts which are in their very nature dangerous to the lives of others. There are certain situations where the duty of care is higher because the risk of harming another is so much greater. The rule defining such a duty of care was first enunciated in 1868 in a British court, in the landmark case of *Fletcher v. Rylands* (1864 Law Reports, 3HL-330) which established the doctrine of strict liability. In that case, Mr. Justice Blackburn stated the opinion of the Court of Exchequer Chamber in these words:

> We think that the true rule of law is that the person who, for his own purposes brings on his land and collects and keeps there anything likely to cause mischief if it escapes, must keep it at his peril and if he does not do so, he is *prima facie* answerable for all the damage which is the material consequence of its escape.

If we were to apply this principle to the events at Bhopal, it is clear that Union Carbide would be held directly responsible for the catastrophe that struck this city and held liable to compensate all those who have had to bear the consequences of its negligence.

But Union Carbide does not think so. Carbide officials, faced with the prospect of financial ruin in consequence of suits being filed against the company, have sought to distance themselves from their Indian subsidiary. They have suggested that it was only the lack of competence on the part of local management that caused the accident. Some believers in multinational enterprise as Third World salvation, no doubt including at least a few Carbide officials, go still further and seek to let the company off the hook by advancing the fallacious argument that, since the government of India was unable to regulate safety standards in the plant, Carbide cannot be blamed for its admittedly shoddy standards.

While it is indisputable that the government of India shares some responsibility for what happened at Bhopal, this does not detract from Union Carbide's own liability. For such an argument assumes that safety standards are something on which a company can compromise within a regulatory framework, and presumably ignore, in the absence of one. Is lack of enforcement an excuse for failure to comply with regulatory standards? And what if there are no standards? Is liability, or more broadly social responsibility, only limited to relevant regulation? Suppose UCC were to dump nuclear waste upon a community which had no laws governing waste disposal, and the lives of its members were thereby jeopardized? Could Union Carbide disclaim all responsibility?

Broadly speaking, there are two ways to ensure that companies maintain high safety standards. One relies exclusively on legislation and regulations which carry penal consequences in the event of breach.

The alternative approach would instead rely on litigation and the imposition of heavy damages to discipline the company. Most countries employ a mixture of the two approaches: some legislation prescribing standards, but also encouragement of victims of industrial negligence to litigate against the offender. In the final analysis,it is the possibility of litigation and the consequent prospect of paying substantial compensation to the victims, together with adverse publicity and effective unions working to protect the health and lives of their members that combine to insure that industry maintains high safety standards. If we can add to the mix the active involvement of surrounding communities at risk, we will have an even stronger combination.

All too often the imposition of punitive damages on an offending company is perceived by the public as a form of retribution. There are few clearer cases in history than Bhopal where, on the basis of evidence thus far available, what certainly appears to have been gross negligence has caused such enormous damage in terms of human life and suffering. On these grounds, Union Carbide should certainly be punished. But punitive damages are also a form of deterrent, preventing such disasters from happening again. The fact that Carbide could be forced to liquidate some of its assets to compensate the people of Bhopal should send a powerful message to other companies using high-risk technologies and deter them from maintaining criminally lax safety standards and disregarding public safety. If the Bhopal tragedy were ultimately to result in the establishment of new standards of corporate behavior enforceable throughout the world, those who died or whose health was irreparably damaged in the Bhopal tragedy would not have suffered in vain.

But, of course, a very different outcome of the Bhopal disaster may occur. Some who call themselves political realists suggest it is much more likely. Union Carbide and the government of India may come to terms for an amount of money that will neither do justice to the Bhopal victims nor act as an effective deterrent of the kind of behavior and industrial practices that made it possible for Bhopal to happen. Should that occur, the resolution of the Bhopal disaster will be following the apparent course of other toxic tragedies such as asbestos.This will raise a fundamental question about the meaning of Bhopal similar to asbestos—namely, the capacity of contemporary societies to survive their own destructive propensities.

In his conclusion to the series on asbestos litigation in *The New Yorker*, which offers many parallels to the Bhopal disaster, Paul Brodeur addresses the possibility that Congress, by passing legislation that will protect companies that inflict grievous injuries on workers and consumers through their products and practices, may let companies off the hook. Such legislation, coupled with the perversion of the bankruptcy code by companies overwhelmed by the visitation of their past sins through the court system, will not only deny victims the opportunity to secure justice for the wrongs done them by these companies but have the net effect of institutionalizing the production of hazardous products and the development of high-risk technologies. The result, which would apply equally if Carbide were to get off the hook after having perpetrated the worst industrial disaster in history, is that, in his somber words:

> [We] bid fair to repeat an ironic disaster of history—the one that is said to have overtaken the latter-day Romans who continued to use lead vessels in the making of wine even after they had been warned that they might be poisioning themselves by doing so. In our case, it seems, we are being asked not only to ignore the warnings we have received about occupational and environmental cancer and other [industrial hazards]...We are being solicited by the private-enterprise system, as it is now constituted, to deny just compensation to tens upon tens of thousands of its victims...and to become its accomplices in the destruction of public health and therefore of our own.

The Bhopal tragedy poses yet another fundamental question, along with the propensity of contemporary societies for self-destruction. We are beginning to understand who decided that the city of Bhopal should be exposed to such cataclysmic risk. But who should have made that choice and on what criteria? In a word, who controls technology in the modern world? How do we achieve meaningful participation of those whose lives are so intimately affected in decisions about risks that, as Charles Perrow so forcefully states, "a few have decided the many cannot do without." That is the ultimate challenge of the Bhopal tragedy.

NOTES ON SOURCES

Chapter 1: What Happened at Bhopal

The single most authoritative investigation of what happened in Bhopal is that being undertaken by the Central Bureau of Investigation, the Indian equivalent of the FBI. A comprehensive report on the CBI investigation has not been released, but an account based in part on the investigation up to that point appeared in the Indian news magazine, *Sunday*, 7-13 April, 1985.

Another significant government of India-related investigation is that by Dr. S. Varadarajan, the Director General of the Council for Scientific and Industrial Research, a government-supported chain of research laboratories and institutes. Shortly after the first anniversary of the disaster, the government finally released the 81-page Varadarajan report, in part to refute Union Carbide's claim that sabotage caused the disastrous gas leak.

A very large number of journalistic accounts about the disaster have appeared. Among the more substantial efforts at investigative journalism are articles by Arun Subramaniam and colleagues in *BusinessIndia*, notably one by him and Bharat Bhushan, "Bhopal: What Really Happened?," February 25-March 10, 1985, and the first anniversary cover story by him, Javed Gaya, and Rusi Engineer, "Towards Corporate Responsibility: Why the Guilty Must Be Punished," December 2-15, 1985. Also noteworthy is the series by Stuart Diamond and colleagues at the *New York Times*, particularly his "The Bhopal Disaster: How It Happened" (January 28, 1985). It was the Subramaniam/Bhushan article which first reported the design modification of the jumper line as providing the most likely route for the water to get into the methyl isocyanate tank, resulting in the runaway reaction which caused the disaster. Important as well are rebuttals of the Union Carbide "sabotage" theory as the cause of the disaster by Radhika Ramaseshan in the *Sunday*

Observer, Kannan Srinivasan in the *Indian Express*, and Ivan Fera in the *Illustrated Weekly of India* ("Not Sabotage," September 1, 1985).

A useful collection of articles from a variety of sources, mostly Indian, on what happened at Bhopal is found in Lawrence Surendra, comp., *Bhopal: Industrial Genocide?*, Hong Kong: Asian Regional Exchange for New Alternatives (ARENA), 1985. A careful account of the accident itself and the currently available evidence regarding it has been presented by Vijay Shankar Varma, a faculty member of the Department of Physics at the University of Delhi, in "Bhopal: The Unfolding of a Tragedy," *Alternatives* (Vol. XI, No. 1, 1986).

The Union Carbide Corporation issued its own account of the tragic event (*Bhopal Methyl Isocyanate Investigation Team Report*, Danbury, Connecticut: The Corporation, March 1985). There is some discussion about the actual event in one of the first books on Bhopal published—*A Cloud Over Bhopal* by Alfred deGrazia, Bombay: Kalos Foundation, 1985.

In July 1985, a trade union delegation from Europe and North America issued its report on the Bhopal tragedy, based on extensive interviews with Carbide workers as well as other sources. The *Trade Union Report on Bhopal* (Geneva and Brussels: International Confederation of Free Trade Unions and International Federation of Chemical, Energy, and General Workers' Unions, July 1985) confirms the jumper line explanation first reported in *Business-India*. Also important in explaining what happened is a report by the Bombay-based Union Research Group, *The Role of Management Practices in the Bhopal Gas Leak Disaster* (June 1985).

Some of the best coverage in terms of what happened at Bhopal and its implications for the chemical industry has appeared in various articles in the *Chemical and Engineering News* that have appeared from time to time since the gas leak occurred. Particularly noteworthy are "A C&EN Special Issue: Bhopal, the Continuing Story" (February 11, 1985) and the first anniversary cover story by Wil Lepkowski, "Bhopal: Indian City Begins to Heal But Conflicts Remain" (December 2, 1985).

Other important sources include Union Carbide's own documentation, among the most important of which are these:

> Union Carbide India, Ltd., Agricultural Products Division, *Operating Manual: Methyl Isocyanate Unit* (written by V.K. Behl, S.P. Choudhary, C.R. Iyer, S. Khanna; reviewed by K.D. Ballal), Bhopal, India: UCIL, October 1978. (This manual was significantly revised in 1984, making permissible some of the lapses in safety and maintenance that triggered the Bhopal disaster.)
> L.A. Kail, J.M. Poulson, and C.S. Tyson, *Operational Safety Survey: CO/MIC/Sevin Units*, Union Carbide India, Ltd., Bhopal Plant, May 1982
> Union Carbide Corporation, *Material Safety Data Sheet*, New York: The Corporation, n.d. (E-43458A).

Also important on the issue of plant design and safety is Occupational

Health and Safety Administration, *OSHA's Response to Methyl Isocyanate (MIC) Concerns*, Washington: OSHA, 1985.

Chapter 2: The Impact of Bhopal

A body of literature, more or less scientific in character, is beginning to emerge on health and environmental impacts of the Bhopal disaster. Much of this literature is cited in Appendix 4 in this book. Also useful in summarizing a number of medical studies and investigations underway is a mimeographed report from the Indian Council of Medical Research, *The Health Effects of Inhalation of Toxic Gas at Bhopal*, New Delhi: ICMR, n.d. [?—July 1985]. Important as well is the government of India Air Pollution Control Board report on the Union Carbide plant in Bhopal, *Gas Leak Episode at Bhopal*, n.d. [?—April 1985].

A whole spate of accounts of the health and environmental impacts of the gas leak have been appearing in recent months, among them the following:

> Praful Bidwai, "Bhopal in Retrospect-I: Story of an Unended Disaster," *Times of India*, December 3, 1985, and "Bhopal in Retrospect-II: Health Damage Severe, Persistent," *Times of India*, December 4, 1985.
> Madhya Pradesh Vigyan Sabha (in collaboration with Delhi Science Forum, Kerala Sasatra Sahitya Parishad, and Janvadi Lekakh Sang/ M.P.), *Bhopal Genocide and Its Aftermath*, Bhopal: MPVS, December 1985.
> Centre for Science and Environment, *The State of India's Environment, 1984-85: The Second Citizens' Report*, New Delhi: CSE, 1985, especially the chapter on "Health," which includes a long and generally authoritative discussion of the Bhopal disaster (pp. 205-232).
> Delhi Science Forum, *Bhopal Gas Tragedy*, New Delhi: DSF, January 1985.
> Claude Alvares, "The Greater Bhopal Tragedy," *Illustrated Weekly of India*, December 1, 1985.

Government data on relief efforts are contained in Madhya Pradesh Government, *Bhopal Gas Tragedy*: *Relief and Rehabilitation —Current Status*, Bhopal: The Government, August 1985. Some of the numbers in this report were updated as of November 1985 in a public relations handout prepared for the first anniversary of the gas leak by the Directorate of Information and Publicity for the Madhya Pradesh government, *We Shall Overcome*. A critical account, based on a field visit in June 1985, has been prepared by Paul Shrivastava, *The Politics of Misery in Bhopal*, New York: Industrial Crisis Institute, July 1985.

The problems of voluntary agencies and social activists in Bhopal have been widely reported in the Indian press. See especially the documentation report of the Washington Research Institute, Vivek Pinto and Steven D.

O'Leary, eds., *Reprints of Selected Documents on the December 1984 Union Carbide Chemical Incident*, San Francisco: WRI, June 1985. Also useful on voluntary agencies in Bhopal are two additional reports and one article from the voluntary agency sector:

> Delhi Committee on Bhopal Gas Tragedy, *Repression and Apathy in Bhopal*, Delhi: Lokayan, August 1985.
> Eklavya, *Bhopal: A Peoples' View of Death, Their Right to Know and Live*, Bhopal: Eklavya, 1985.
> Shiv Visvanathan, "Bhopal: The 'Imagination' of a Disaster," *Alternatives*, Vol. XI, No. 1 (1986).

The complex chemistry of the Bhopal gas leak was first reported by M. Arun Subramaniam in *BusinessIndia* ("The Dangers of Diagnostic Delay," August 12-15, 1985). Further discussion of the probable nature of the chemistry involved is provided by Dr. A. Karim Ahmed, Research Scientist at the Natural Resources Defense Council, in Appendix 4 of this book

Chapter 3: Justice for the Bhopal Victims

A background paper on this subject was prepared for the Citizens Commission on Bhopal and released on the first anniversary of the Bhopal tragedy, December 2, 1985. The compensation question and related issues are discussed by Alfred deGrazia in his book mentioned above, *A Cloud Over Bhopal*, as well as by Rob Hagar in *BusinessIndia* ("Taking Carbide to Court," March 25-April 7, 1985). The parallels between the struggle for justice for the Bhopal victims and the victims of asbestos poisoning are numerous and illuminating; on the latter subject see Paul Brodeur, "The Asbestos Industry on Trial," *The New Yorker*, June 10, 17, and 24 and July 1, 1985.

Chapter 4: The Tangled Web of Litigation

The sources mentioned for Chapter 3 deal as well with issues discussed in Chapter 4. Other significant sources include Steven J. Adler, "Bhopal Journal: The Voiceless Victims," *The American Lawyer*, April 1985 (which is said to have been read by Judge Keenan and helped to make him aware of the plight of the victims, triggering his demand at the first pre-trial hearing that Union Carbide provide interim relief), and a second article by Adler, "Carbide Plays Hardball," *The American Lawyer*, November 1985. Also useful is M. Arun Subramaniam, "Union Carbide: A Law unto Itself?," *BusinessIndia*, August 12-25, 1985 (which first reported Union Carbide's contradictory behavior in arguing *forum non conveniens* in both Indian and U.S. courts).

On criminalization, see the first anniversary cover story in *BusinessIndia* by Subramaniam and others, "Toward Corporate Responsibility: Why the Guilty Must Be Punished," (December 2-15, 1985) and a special issue of the *Multinational Monitor* dealing with the legal issues posed by the Bhopal disaster (July 31, 1985).

Chapter 5: Can It Happen Here?

The major source for this chapter is the transcript of the Workers' Policy Project Conference on Bhopal held in Newark on March 20-21, 1985, "After Bhopal: Implications for Developed and Developing Nations." Other useful sources include Charles Perrow, *Normal Accidents,* New York: Basic Books, 1984, Henri Smets, "Compensation for Exceptional Environmental Damage Caused by Industrial Activities" (paper prepared for Conference on Transportation, Storage and Disposal of Hazardous Materials, Laxenburg, Austria, 1-5 July 1985), and a forthcoming book by Paul Shrivastava on the management implications of industrial catastrophes, Boston: Ballinger, 1986.

On the frequency of accidents in U.S. chemical plants, see Appendix 3 in this book by Raphael Moure and Stuart Diamond's account of an unpublished report for the Environmental Protection Agency, "U.S. Toxic Mishaps in Chemicals Put at 6,928 in 5 Years," *New York Times*, October 3, 1985.

Chapter 6: What Can We Do to Prevent Future Bhopals?

The major source for this chapter is the Workers' Policy Project Conference on Bhopal mentioned above. Also useful is the Trade Union Report on Bhopal mentioned previously. A good summary of efforts within the United Nations System by the UN Environmental Programme, International Labour Organisation, Food and Agriculture Organization, etc. is given in the overview paper for the Informal Seminar to Further International Cooperation for Environmental Management of Industrial Process Safety and Hazards (Geneva, 2-5 December 1985), New York: UN Centre on Transnational Corporations and UN Environmental Programme. Various guidelines and codes being developed within the UN System are reproduced in Martin Abraham, *The Lessons of Bhopal: A Community Action Resource Manual on Hazardous Technologies*, Penang, Malaysia: International Organisation of Consumers Unions, September 1985.

Chapter 7: An Agenda for Citizen Action

Helpful ideas on citizen responses and initiatives related to Bhopal are given in the International Organisation of Consumers Union's *Manual* mentioned above. Also useful is Anil Agarwal, Juliet Merrifield, and Rajesh Tandon, *No Place to Run*: *Local Realities and Global Issues of the Bhopal Disaster*, New Market, Tennessee and New Delhi, India: Highlander Education and Research Center and Society for Participatory Research in Asia (PRIA), n.d. [?—May 1985]. The Highlander Center-PRIA report also includes background information on Union Carbide's environmental and safety record.

The Citizens Commission on Bhopal is issuing a series of background reports (of which this book is one) and recommendations on different aspects of the Bhopal tragedy. The address of the Commission is given in the front of the book.

Books and Other Sources on the Bhopal Tragedy

An historic event such as the Bhopal tragedy merits its own literature, and Bhopal is beginning to accumulate some. A number of books and more extensive examinations of different aspects of Bhopal have been published, the more significant of which have been mentioned in the notes on sources for various chapters of this book. Several others are reportedly in preparation, including those by David Weir of the Center for Investigative Reporting in San Francisco (and co-author of *The Circle of Poison*), who is working on a book for the International Organisation of Consumer Unions; Stuart Diamond, correspondent for the *New York Times* who has been covering the Bhopal story; Larry Everest, *Behind the Poison Cloud: Union Carbide's Bhopal Massacre*, New York: Banner Press, 1986; and Robert Engler of New York University and author of a long article in *The Nation* on "Many Bhopals: Technology Out of Control," *The Nation*, April 27, 1985.

Appendix 1

Who's Who in the Bhopal Story

Union Carbide Corporation (Corporate Headquarters: Danbury, Connecticut)

Warren M. Anderson, Chairman and Chief Executive Officer
Alec Flamm, President and Chief Operating Officer
J.M. Rehfied, Executive Vice President (also on the Board of Carbide's Indian subsidiary)
Robert Oldfield, President, Agricultural Chemicals Division (resigned after Bhopal incident)
Jackson B. Browning, Vice President for Health, Safety and Environmental Affairs
Ron Van Mynen, Corporate Director of Health and Safety (headed team of Union Carbide scientists and engineers sent to Bhopal to investigate the disaster)
Dr. Bipin Avashia, Medical Director of Carbide plant in Charleston, West Virginia (sent telex, later disavowed, to Bhopal regarding treatment of victims for cyanide poisoning with sodium thiosulphate)
Shurburn Hart, Head, Public Affairs Department
Hank Karawan, Manager, Carbide's plant in Institute, West Virginia (the "sister plant" to the one in Bhopal, where methyl isocyanate is also manufactured)
Bud G. Holman, Chief Outside Counsel in Bhopal litigation (partner, Kelley, Drye and Warren, New York)

Union Carbide India, Limited (Corporate Headquarters: Calcutta)

Keshub Mahindra, Chairman
V.P. Gokale, Managing Director
K.S. Kamdar, Vice President, Agricultural Products Division
Chandra Prakash Lal, Vice President and Secretary
Dr. Arya Loya, Medical Officer
Edward A. Munoz, former Managing Director of UCIL (and Vice President of Union Carbide Corporation, now retired; claims in sworn affidavit that the parent corporation made the decision to store MIC in large quantities at the Carbide Bhopal plant)
Jaganath Mukund, Works Manager, Bhopal Plant
P.S. Roychaudhury, Assistant Works Manager, Bhopal Plant
S.P. Choudhary, MIC Production Manager, Bhopal Plant
K.B. Shetty, MIC Supervisor, Bhopal Plant
K. Moses, Water Supply Officer, Bhopal Plant
R.N. Nagu, Chief of Security Services, Bhopal Plant
Vijay Kumar Gupta, Chief Outside Counsel in Bhopal

Government Officials in India

National or Central Government

Rajiv Gandhi, Prime Minister
Asoke K. Sen, Indian Law Minister (top legal official)
H.R. Bharadwaj, Minister of State for Law and Justice
K. Parasaran, Attorney General
B.S. Sekhon, Law Secretary, India
Vasant Sathe, Indian Minister of Chemicals and Fertilizer
Dr. S. Varadarajan, Government of India Chief Scientist and Director-General Council for Scientific and Industrial Research

State and Local Government

Arjun Singh, Chief Minister of Madhya Pradesh State at the time of the Bhopal disaster (the equivalent to governor of a U.S. state)
Motilal Vohra, present Chief Minister of Madhya Pradesh
A.O. Qureshi, Law Secretary, Madhya Pradesh State Government
Dr. Ishwar Dass, Additional Chief Secretary and Relief Commissioner, Madhya Pradesh State Government

Dr. M.N. Nagu, Director of Health Services, Madhya Pradesh State Government

Dr. R.K. Bisarya, Mayor of Bhopal (at the time of the disaster)

Justice N.K. Singh, Chairman, Bhopal Poisonous Gas Leakage (1984) Enquiry Commission

Physicians and Other Medical Personnel

Dr. Bipin Avashia, Indian physician who is Medical Director at the Union Carbide plant in Charleston, West Virginia

Dr. N.R. Bandhari, Superintendent of Hamidia Hospital, Bhopal

Dr. Heeresh Chandra, Head of Forensic Medicine, Gandhi Medical College, Bhopal

Dr. Max Daunderer, Clinical Toxicologist from West Germany who brought 50,000 doses of sodium thiosulphate to treat victims of cyanide poisoning

Dr. Ramana Dhara, a doctor from Hyderabad active in the Medico Friends Circle (who conducted a study on behalf of that group on the medical situation in Bhopal with Dr. Abhay Bang, Dr. Shyama Narang, and Dr. Mira Sadgobal)

Dr. Peter Halberg, an eye specialist from New York sent to Bhopal by the Union Carbide Corporation

Dr. S.R. Kamat, of Seth Medical College and KEM Hospital, Bombay who conducted a study of victims of the Bhopal disaster with several colleagues in Bombay

Dr. Arya Loya, Medical Officer at Union Carbide's Bhopal Plant

Dr. N.P. Misra, Head of the Department of Medicine, Hamidia Hospital, Bhopal

Dr. M.N. Nagu, Director of Health Services, Madhya Pradesh State Government

Dr. Thomas Pettit, a lung specialist from the University of Colorado Medical School sent to Bhopal by the Union Carbide Corporation

Dr. V. Ramalingaswami, Director General, Indian Council of Medical Research, New Delhi

Dr. Mira Sadgopal, author (with Dr. Rani Bang) of "Effects of the Bhopal Disaster on Women's Health"

Dr. Hans Weil, a lung specialist from the Tulane Medical School sent to Bhopal by the Union Carbide Corporation

Lawyers and Other Personnel Involved in Bhopal Disaster Litigation

Judge John F. Keenan, Federal District Court, Southern District of New York (before whom various law suits on behalf of victims of the Bhopal disaster in U.S. federal courts have been consolidated)

Bud G. Holman, partner, Kelley, Drye and Warren (representing Union Carbide Corporation)

Michael V. Ciresi, partner, Robins, Zelle, Larson and Kaplan, Minneapolis (lead counsel for the government of India and member of three-person executive committee appointed by Judge Keenan to represent the plaintiffs' lawyers)

Stanley Chesley, partner, Waite, Schneider, Bayless and Chesley, Cincinnati (member of the three-person executive committee appointed by Judge Keenan to represent plaintiffs' lawyers)

F. Lee Bailey, partner, Bailey and Broder, Boston and New York (member of the three-person executive committee appointed by Judge Keenan to represent plaintiffs' lawyers)

Jack S. Hoffinger, New York (appointed by Judge Keenan as the Liaison Counsel between the court and the executive committee of plaintiffs' lawyers)

Kevan Cleary, New York (public interest lawyer representing clients from Bhopal *pro bono*; recently appointed U.S. Attorney in Brooklyn, his place in the Bhopal case being taken by Robert C. Cheasty, Berkeley, California)

Rob Hager, Director, Legal Division, Christic Institute, and attorney for the Citizens Commission on Bhopal (in filing the *amicus* brief with Judge Keenan on *forum non conveniens*).

Vijay Kumar Gupta, Union Carbide Counsel in the Bhopal District Court

Voluntary Agency Personnel and Social Activists in Bhopal

Mrs. Rukmini Bhargava, Self-Employed Women's Association (SEWA)

Tapan Bose, Nagrik Rahat auṛ Punarvas Samiti (Citizens Committee for Preservation and Rehabilitation)

Mahesh Buch, National Centre for Human Settlements and Environment

Denis Carneiro, Action for Gas Affected People (AGAPE)

Vinod Raina, EKLAVYA

Anil Sadgopal, Zahreeli Gas Kand Sangarsh Samiti Morcha (Poisonous Gas Disaster Struggle Movement)

(See also contact persons in other parts of India and other countries throughout the world concerned with the Bhopal disaster in Appendix 2.)

Appendix 2

Citizen Groups around the World Working on Responses to Bhopal

AGAPE (Action for Gas Affected People)
c/o Church of St. Francis (Opposite Pachsheel Cinema)
Jehangiribad
Bhopal 462 008 M.P.
INDIA

Contact: Fr. Denis Carneiro

All India Drug Action Network
C-14 Community Centre
Safdarjang Development Area
New Delhi 110 016
INDIA

Contact: Mira Shiva

Asia-Pacific Peoples Environment Network
c/o Sahabat Alam Malaysia (SAM)
   (Friends of the Earth Malaysia)
37 Lorong Birch
Penang
MALAYSIA

Contact: D. Rajendran

Asian Regional Exchange for New Alternatives (ARENA)
A4,2/F, G-Block, Hung Hom Bay Centre
104-108 Baker Street, Hung Hom, Kowloon
HONG KONG

Contact: D. Lawrence Surendra

Australian Consumers Association
57 Carrington Road
Marrickville, NSW 2204
New South Wales
AUSTRALIA

Contact: John Braithwaite

Bhopal Cyanate Relief Fund, Inc.
13847 E. 14th Street, Suite 118
San Leandro, CA 94578
USA

Contact: Dr. Vin Sawhney

Bhopal Disaster Monitoring Group
c/o Peoples Research Institute on Environment and Energy
3F Baptist Kaikan
7-26-24 Shinjuku
Shinjuku-ku, Tokyo 160
JAPAN

Contact: Nobuo Matsuoka

Bhopal Trade Union Solidarity Group
c/o Transnational Information Centre/London (TICL)
54 Ayres Street
London SE1 1EU
UNITED KINGDOM

Contact: Barbara Dinham

Bhopal Victims Support Committee
c/o Southall Monitoring Group
Top Floor, 50-52 King Street
Southall
Middlesex UB2 4PB
UNITED KINGDOM

Contact: Suresh Grover

Cadre of Media Resources and Action
(CAMERA)
19 Harimal Somani Marg
Bombay 400 001
INDIA

Contact: Philip Padachira

Center for Investigative Reporting, Inc.
54 Mint Street, Fourth Floor
San Francisco, CA 94103
USA

Contact: David Weir

Centre for Education and Documentation
3 Suleman Chamber
4 Battery Street
(Behind Regal Cinema)
Bombay 400 039
INDIA

Contact: Arjun Rajabali

Centre for Science and Environment
807 Vishal Bhawan
95 Nehru Place
New Delhi 110 019

INDIA

Contact: Anil Agarwal

Centre for Social Medicine and Community Health
Jawaharlal Nehru University (JNU)
New Delhi 110 067
INDIA

Contact: D. Banerji

Christic Institute
1324 N. Capitol Street
Washington, DC 20002
USA

Contact: Rob Hager

Citizens Commission on Bhopal
45th Floor
122 East 42nd Street
New York, NY 10168
USA

Contact: Karim Ahmed/Shelley Hearns

Citizen's Committee for Relief and Rehabilitation
(Nagrik Rahat aur Punarvas Samiti)
34 Asiana, Kolefiza
Bhopal 462 001
INDIA

Contact: J.P. Diwan

Consumer Council of Zimbabwe
P.O. Box UA 582
Union Avenue
Harare
ZIMBABWE

Contact: Sheila Bassoppo-Moyo

Consumer Education Centre
4 Sesha Vilas
3-6-293 First Floor
Hyderguda
Hyderabad 500 029
INDIA

Contact: V.K. Parigi

Consumer Education and Research Centre
Thakorebhai Desai Smarak Bhavan
Near Law College
Ellisbridge
Ahmedabad 380 006
INDIA

Contact: Manubhai Shah

Consumer Guidance Society of India
Hutmet-J, Mahapalika Marg
Opp. Cama Hospital
Bombay 400 001
INDIA

Contact: Pushpa Motwani

Consumers Union of U.S., Inc.
256 Washington Street
Mount Vernon, NY 10553
USA

Contact: Rhoda Karpatkin/Jean Halloran

Council on International and Public Affairs
777 United Nations Plaza, Suite 9A
New York, NY 10017
USA

Contact: Ward Morehouse/David Dembo

Delhi Committee on Bhopal Gas Tragedy
c/o Lokayan
13 Alipur Road
New Delhi 110 054
INDIA

Contact: Smitu Kothari

Delhi Science Forum
B-1 2nd Floor
J-Block, Saket
New Delhi 110 017
INDIA

Contact: Dinesh Abarol

EKLAVYA
E1/208, Arera Colony
Bhopal 462 016
INDIA

Employees Union Research Group
Union Carbide India, Ltd.
17 Dalvi Building
Poibavdi, Parel
Bombay 400 012
INDIA

Environment Liason Centre
P.O. Box 72461
Nairobi
KENYA

Contact: Simon Muchiru/David Bull

Friends of the Earth International
1045 Sansome Street
San Francisco, CA 94111

USA

Contact: David Chatfield

Gandhi Peace Foundation
221 3 Deen Dayal Upadhyaya Marg
New Delhi 110 002
INDIA

Contact: Sri Anupam Mishra

Grun Alternative Liste Rathaus
Zimmer 170.2000,
Hamburg 1
FEDERAL REPUBLIC OF GERMANY

Contact: Erwin Jurtschitsch

Highlander Centre
Route 3, Box 370
New Market, TN 37820
USA

Contact: Juliet Merrifield/John Gaventa

India/America Committee for Bhopal Victims
c/o Kevan Cleary
31 East 31st Street
New York, NY 10016

India Council of Medical Research
Ansari Nagar, Post Box 4508
New Delhi 110 019
INDIA

Contact: Dr. V. Ramalingasurmi, Director General

Indian Social Institute
Lodi Road

New Delhi 110 005
INDIA

Industrial Crisis Institute
100 Bleeker Street, Suite 2B
New York, NY 10012
USA

Contact: Paul Shrivastava

International Center for Law in Development
777 United Nations Plaza, Suite 9A
New York, NY 10017
USA

Contact: Clarence Dias

International Coalition of Activists Against
Environmental Damage Caused by Bayer
Hofstr. 27A
5650 Solingen 11
FEDERAL REPUBLIC OF GERMANY

Contact: Germute von Muller

International Federation of Plantation, Agricultural
and Allied Workers (IFPAAW)
17 Rue Necker
CH-1201 Geneva
SWITZERLAND

Contact: Jose Vargas

International Organisation of Consumers Unions
Working Group on Hazardous Technology
P.O. Box 1045
Penang
MALAYSIA

Contact: Martin Abraham/Anwar Fazal

International Youth Federation
Klostermolle, Klostermollevej 48
Voerladegard
8660 Skanderberg
DENMARK

Contact: Mohan Mathews

Kalos Foundation for a New World Order
55 Mamta-A
Appasaheb Marathe Marg
Prabhadevi
Bombay 400 025
INDIA

Contact: Alfred deGrazia

Kerala Sastra Sahitya Parishad
(Kerala Peoples Science Movement)
Parishad Bhavan, Trivandrum 695 001
Kerala
INDIA

Contact: Professor B. Ekbal

Labor Institute
853 Broadway
New York, NY 10003

Contact: Les Leopold

Lokayan
13 Alipur Road
New Delhi 110 054
INDIA

Contact: Smitu Kothari

Medico Friends Circle
326, V Main, I Block
Koramangala
Bangalore 560 034
INDIA

Contact: Dr. Ravi Narayan

Medico Friends Circle
c/o Gandhi Bhavan
Bhopal
INDIA

Contact: Dr. Mira Sadgopal

Movement for Environmental Protection
54 Johnny John Khan Road
Royapettah
Madras 600 014
INDIA

Nagrik Rahat aur Punarvas Committee
c/o J.P. Diwan
34 Asiana Kolefiga
Bhopal 462 001 M.P.
INDIA

National Bhopal Disaster Relief Fund
Miami, FL
USA

National Council of Churches in India
Nagpur
INDIA

National Wildlife Federation
1412 16th Street, NW
Washington, DC 20036
USA

Contact: Barbara Bramble

Natural Resources Defense Council
122 East 42nd Street
New York, NY 10168
USA

Contact: Karim Ahmed

No More Bhopals Network
IOCU
P.O. Box 1045
Penang
MALAYSIA

Contact: Anwar Fazal

Parisar
c/o ''Yamuna''
I.C.S. Colony
Ganeshkhind Road
Pune 411 007
INDIA

Contact: Ravindra Bhagwat/Vijay Paranjpye/Vasant Palshikar

Parisara
7 Balaji Layout
Bangalore 560 084
Karnataka
INDIA

Peoples United No More Bhopals Movement
for a Safe Environment
19 June Blossom Society
60A Pali Road, Bandra East
Bombay 400 050
INDIA

Contact: Padma Prakash

Pesticides Working Group
c/o Legal/Health and Safety Section
Agricultural and Allied Workers
National Trade Group of the Transport
and General Workers Union
Headland House, 308 Grays Inn Road
London WC1 8DS
UNITED KINGDOM

Contact: Reg Green/David Gee

Rashtriya Abhiyan Samiti
(National Campaign Committee)
c/o Vibuthi Jha, Advocate
49 Shyamala Road
Bhopal 462 002
INDIA

Rural Coalition
20001 N Capitol Street
Washington, DC 20002
USA

Contact: George Coling

Society for Participatory Research in Asia (PRIA)
45, Sainik Farm
Khanpur
New Delhi 110 062
INDIA

Contact: Rajesh Tandon

Trade Unions International of
Chemical, Oil and Allied Workers (ICPS)
45 Benezur Utca
1068 Budapest
HUNGARY

Contact: The Secretary General

Urban Development Institute
38-F Maker Tower
Cuffe Parade
Bombay 400 005
INDIA

Contact: Rashmi Mayur

Urban Environment Conference, Inc.
c/o United Steel Workers of America
815 16th Street, NW
Washington, DC 20006
USA

Voluntary Health Association of India
C14 Community Centre
Safdarjang Development Area
New Delhi 110 016
INDIA

Contact: Dr. Mira Shiva

Wahana Lingkungan Hidup Indonesia
(Indonesian Environmental Forum)
Jalan Suryopranoto, No. 8
Jakarta Pusat
INDONESIA

Contact: Erna Witoelar

Workers' Policy Project
853 Broadway, Room 2014
New York, NY 10003
USA

Contact: Tony Mazzocchi

World Environment Center
605 Third Avenue, 17th Floor
New York, NY 10158
USA

Contact: Libby Bassett

Zahreeli Gas Kand Sangarsh Samiti Morcha
c/o R.K. Sharma
EWS-87, Dhobi Ghat
Behind Char Bungalows
Bhopal 462 002
INDIA

Contact: Anil Sadgopal

Source: Adapted from Martin Abraham, *The Lessons of Bhopal: A Community Action Resource Manual on Hazardous Technologies*, Penang, Malaysia: International Organisation of Consumers Unions, 1985.

Appendix 3

How Safe Are U.S. Chemical Plants—and the Communities around Them?

Dr. Rafael Moure
United Auto Workers

Communities at Risk

How many U.S. communities are at risk? In 1980, the EPA studied the products and locations of Synthetic Organic Chemicals Manufacturing (SOCM) plants in the U.S. Although other chemical plants (inorganic chemicals production) are also of concern, this discussion is limited to SOCM plants in the U.S. The last complete census of SOCM conducted by EPA in 1978 identified 1,270 plants of this type in the U.S.

The distribution of SOCM plants in the U.S. is shown in Table 1. The SOCM plants in these eight states represent 57.4 + of the synthetic organic chemical capacity of the U.S. Some of these plants are very old and leak-prone and are built within metropolitan areas. The City of Newark, for example, has 37 chemical companies within the urban perimeter.

Governmental Efforts at Prevention

The chemical industry has always claimed that the potentially serious problems to the communities where chemical plants are located are minimal.

163

They have created an illusion of fail-safe operations. This myth was examined in 1978 by the U.S. Environmental Protection Agency and found to be false.

The EPA initiated a complex study to develop background information on the SOCM industry to serve as a basis for a performance standard for Fugitive Emissions in SOCM plants of volatile organic chemicals.

The EPA surveyed a substantial number of SOCM plants to identify sources of leaks. A total of 33 chemical plants were surveyed, as well as 17 petroleum refineries. The rationale was that identifying specific pieces of equipment as sources of leaks will determine which equipment requires special care and what engineering controls would control such leaks. Leaks were defined as any volatile release greater than 10,000 parts per million.

Obviously, the control of a 10,000 ppm leak would prevent a major release that could seriously threaten communities in the vicinity of the chemical plant.

The first group evaluated were six organic chemical plants from the Monsanto Company. Frequency of leaks was examined in more than 6,000 pieces of equipment. The results appear in Table 2.

A substantially larger survey was conducted in 24 plants. The results appear in Table 3.

The evaluation of leaks in 13 refineries appear in Table 4. Two DuPont and one Exxon petro-chemical plants were also evaluated. The results appear in Tables 5 and 6.

A summary of the results show that from 5+ to 50+ of tens of thousands of equipment units evaluated in the SOCMI are expected to leak in "normal" operations. Information from Bhopal suggests that the tragedy took place when a "normal" leak from a safety valve was let go until after the tea break. It is logical to conclude that a systematic approach to prevent and control these leaks in the identified leak-prone equipment would go a long way to prevent an uncontrolled risk situation.

The EPA Performance Standard for Equipment Leaks on Valves, Open-end Lines, Pump Seals, Compressor Seals, Control Valves, Pressure Relief Valves, Flanges and Drains (EPA-Ct 60.480-October 1983) was published, finally, after seven agonizing years in limbo. The Standard calls for:

    (a) Visual monitoring of leaks on a weekly basis (soap solution);

    (b) Quantitative monitoring if usually positive;

    (c) Equipment modification to control leaks;

    (d) Re-monitor to check success or failure of modification. This applies to 359 organic chemicals—methyl isocyanate is not one of them.

Is it possible to control these leaks? The EPA evaluation of control modifications proves that, in most cases, well-known equipment modifications in the reach of any maintenance department do control leaks by and large 100+ of the time. Results of the EPA effectiveness control analysis appear in Table 7.

In addition, EPA promulgated regulations for emissions and controls of processing vessels and underground storage tanks in 1984. Are these regulations effective? The answer is no. Unfortunately, these regulations have only the value of the paper they are written on. Enforcement of these regulations are left to the states, and the only states that take seriously the release of toxic substances to communities are California and, recently, New Jersey. The rest of the country is only prepared to react to catastrophes—not to prevent them.

However, the worst loophole in the implementation of these basic precautions to prevent high risk situations is the stipulation in EPA CFR 60.480—that it only applies to *NEW SOURCES*. We all know that no significant new chemical plant construction has taken place since the 1981-82 economic recession.

The impact of this regulation in the 1,270 SOCM plants is minimal. Only if process changes or reconstruction takes place will this regulation apply to the old leak-prone chemical plants in the U.S.

Source for Tables 1-7 which follow: Environmental Protection Agency. *VOC Fugitive Emissions on Synthetic Organic Chemicals Manufacturing Industry - Bargaining Information for Proposed Standards Office of Air Quality Planning and Standard*, Washington, DC: EPA (450/3-80-033a-November 1980).

Table 1

Geographic Distribution of SOCM Plants in the United States

State	Number of SOCM Plants	% of Total
1. New Jersey	131	10.3
2. Texas	126	10.0
3. California	120	9.4
4. Ohio	88	7.0
5. Illinois	85	6.6
6. Pennsylvania	75	5.9
7. Louisiana	54	4.2
8. North Carolina	50	3.9

Table 2

Frequency of Leaks from Fugitive Emission Sources in Synthetic Organic Chemical Units (Six Unit Study)

Equipment Type	Unit A Chloromethanes		Unit B Ethylene		Unit C Chloromethanes		Unit D Ethylene		Unit E BTX Recovery		Unit F Toluene HDA	
	Number of sources tested	% with screening values 10,000 ppmv	Number of sources tested	% with screening values 10,000 ppmv	Number of sources tested	% with screening values 10,000 ppmv	Number of sources tested	% with screening values 10,000 ppmv	Number of sources tested	% with screening values 10,000 ppmv	Number of sources tested	% with screening values 10,000 ppmv
Valves	600	1	2301	19	658	0.1	862	14	715	1.1	427	7.0
Open-ended lines	52	2	386	11	(a)		90	13	33	0.0	28	11.0
Pump seals	47	15	51	21	39	3	63	33	33(b)	3.0	30	10.0
Compressor seals	(a)		42	59	3	33	17	6	(a)		(a)	
Control valves	52	6	128	20	25	0	25	44	53	4.0	44	11.0
Pressure relief valves	7	0	(a)		(a)		(a)		(a)		(a)	
Flanges	30	3	(a)		(a)		(a)		(a)		(a)	
Drains	(a)		(a)		(a)		39	10	(a)		(a)	

(a) No Data

(b) Pump seals in benzene service have double mechanical seals

Table 3

Summary of SOCMI Process Unit Fugitive Emissions
(Twenty-four Unit Study)

Source Type	Service	(1) Number Screened	(2) % Not Screened	(3) % of Screened Sources with Screening Values 10,000 ppmv	(4) 95% Confidence Interval for Percentage of Sources 10,000 ppmv
Flanges	Gas	1,443	4.6	4.6	(3.6, 5.8)
	Light liquid	2,897	2.6	1.2	(0.9, 1.8)
	Heavy liquid	607	2.4	0.0	(0.0, 0.6)
Process Drains	Gas	83	23.1	2.4	(0.3, 8.4)
	Light liquid	527	1.9	3.8	(2.3, 5.8)
	Heavy liquid	28	0.0	7.1	(0.9, 23.5)
Open-End Lines	Gas	923	17.5	5.8	(4.4, 7.5)
	Light liquid	3,603	10.4	3.9	(3.3, 4.6)
	Heavy liquid	477	21.5	1.3	(0.5, 2.8)
Agitator Seals	Gas	7	46.1	14.3	(0.4, 57.9)
	Light liquid	8	11.1	0.0	(0.0, 36.9)
	Heavy liquid	1	66.7	0.0	(0.0, 97.5)
Relief Valves	Gas	85	72.7	3.5	(0.7, 10.0)
	Light liquid	69	40.5	2.9	(0.3, 10.1)
	Heavy liquid	3	66.7	0.0	(0.0, 70.8)
Valves	Gas	9,668	17.5	11.4	(10.8, 12.1)
	Light liquid	18,294	12.2	6.4	(6.1, 6.8)
	Heavy liquid	3,632	9.9	0.4	(0.2, 0.7)
Pumps	Light liquid	647	4.3	8.8	(6.6, 11.1)
	Heavy liquid	97	40.5	2.1	(0.3, 7.3)
Compressors	Gas	29	9.4	6.9	(0.9, 22.8)
Other (a)	Gas	19	9.5	21.0	(6.0, 45.6)
	Light liquid	33	19.5	6.1	(0.7, 20.2)
	Heavy liquid	2	33.3	0.0	(0.0, 84.2)

(a) Includes filters, vacuum breakers, expansion joints, rupture disks, sight glass seals, etc.

Table 4

Leak Frequencies and Emission Factors from
Fugitive Sources in Petroleum Refineries

Equipment Type	Percent of Sources Having Screening Values ⟩10,000 ppmv *TLV-Hexane*	Estimated Emission Factor for Refinery Sources, *kg/hr-Source*
Valves	n/a	n/a
Gas service	10	0.021
Light liquid service	12	0.010
Heavy liquid service	0	0.0003
Pump seals	n/a	n/a
Light liquid service	23	0.12
Heavy liquid service	2	0.02
Compressor seals (hydrocarbon service)	33	0.44
Pressure relief valves	8	0.086
Gas service		0.16
Light liquid service		0.006
Heavy liquid service		0.009
Flanges	0	0.0003
Open-ended lines	n/a	n/a
Gas service		0.025
Light liquid service		0.014
Heavy liquid service		0.003

Table 5
*Frequency of Leaks(a) from Fugitive
Emission Sources in Two DuPont Plants*

Equipment Type	No. of Leakers	No. of Non-Leakers	Percent Leakers
Valves	48	741	6.1
Gas	35	120	23.1
Light liquid	11	143	7.1
Heavy liquid	14	478	0.2
Pumps	1	36	2.7
Light liquid	1	6	14.3
Heavy liquid	0	29	0

(a) Leak defined as 10,000 ppm or greater.

Table 6
*Frequency of Leaks(a) from Fugitive Emission
Sources in Exxon's Cyclohexane Unit*

Equipment Source	Total in Unit	Screened and Sampled	Percent Leaking	Emission factor(kg/hr)	99.8% Confidence Interval (kg/hr)
Valves					
Gas	136	136	36	0.017	0.008 - 0.035
Light liquid	201	100	15	0.008	0.003 - 0.007
Safety valves	15	15	87	0.064	0.013 - 0.5
Pump seals(b)	8	8	83	0.255	0.082 - 0.818
Compressor seals	n/a	n/a	100	0.264	0.068 - 1.045

n/a Not available
(a) Leak defined as 10,000 ppm or greater.
(b) Double mechanical seal pumps and compressors were found to have negligible leaks.

Table 7

Effectiveness of Equipment Modifications

Source Type/ Equipment Modification	Control Efficiency (%)
Pumps	
Sealless pumps	100
Double mechanical seals/closed vent system	100(a)
Closed vent system on seal area	100(a)
Compressors	
Double mechanical seals/closed vent system	100(a)
Closed vent system on seal area	100(a)
Safety/relief valves	
Closed vent system	60(b)
Rupture disks	100
Open-ended lines	
Caps, plugs, blinds, second valves	100(c)
Sampling connections	
Closed loop sampling	100
In-line valves	
Diaphragm valves	100
Bellows-sealed valves	100

(a) Although a control efficiency is not attained in all cases, it is achieveable in some cases.

(b) This control effectiveness reflects the fact that a closed system is normally sized for emergency relief.

(c) This control efficiency reflects the use of these devices downstream of an initial valve with VOC on one side and atmosphere on the other.

Appendix 4

The Health Effects of Methyl Isocyanate, Cyanide, and Monomethylamine Exposure

by

**Shelley Hearne, Katrina Cary,
Emily Barnett, and A. Karim Ahmed, Ph.D.,
Natural Resources Defense Council**

Observed Health Effects in Bhopal

The health effects from toxic chemical exposure vary among the Bhopal victims depending on numerous factors, including proximity to the site, age, and general physiological well-being. Besides the immediate deaths of thousands of residents and the widespread acute effects, it appears that many of the victims are suffering from severe long-term effects. A description of the acute and chronic symptoms follow below.

A.   Acute Effects[1]

Based on interviews with medical aid teams working in the affected areas and hospitals after the gas release, these were the general symptoms observed:
   —severe chest congestion

171

—vomiting
—foreign-body sensation in eyes
—diarrhea
—whiteness in the eye
—swelling of legs
—frothing at the mouth
—palpitation
—headache and giddiness
—vomiting of blood
—sore throat
—weakness of tongue and limbs
—pain and burning sensation in the chest
—paralysis
—coughing and breathlessness
—stupor
—chills
—coma
—cold/clammy skin
—fever

Severe chest congestion, along with chest pain, cough, and breathlessness were present in almost all cases. Eye problems were noted in approximately 90 per cent of the cases. In addition, headaches, giddiness and vomiting were commonly observed. Abdominal pain was not that frequent and some ten per cent of the victims experienced diarrhea.

B. Chronic Effects

In contrast to original claims, that "there is no reason to believe that there will be any long-term effects,"[2] Bhopal victims are suffering from delayed and long-term effects from exposure to the toxic gas release. Doctors at the King Edward Medical Hospital (K.E.M.), Bombay, who surveyed the localities affected by gas have found Bhopal residents with levels of thio-cyanate in the blood three times higher than Bombay citizens.[3] A medical survey conducted by the Citizens Committee for Relief and Rehabilitation examined 740 patients and found that injury persisted in almost all cases despite treatment.[4] In fact, problems still continue with occular, pulmonary, and neurological systems.

The K.E.M. study was conducted on 113 gas-affected people, most from the middle class who lived further from the plant and who were better fed. Some four months after the accidents, those victims still had the following symptoms, according to the report:[5]

—breathlessness or choking (85% on exertion)
—respiratory alkalosis (90%)
—chest pain (68%)
—"altered consciousness" (28%)

—bronchoalvola lavage
—central airway obstruction
—vomiting (42%)
—muscular weakness (22%)
—impaired O_2 uptake (88%)
—low vital capacity (27%)
—fibrosis in lung biopsies

Occular damage has been significant. Corneal ulcers developed a few days after the accident and there is the possibility of permanent damage or impaired vision.[6] Of the 74 patients treated at the K.E.M. Hospital, 22 suffered from occular damage.[7]

Delayed symptoms of central nervous system (CNS) disorders began appearing several days after the toxic gas release.[8] Several cases of cerebral paralysis have been documented at Hamidia Hospital, Bhopal.[9] Three children in their pediatric ward died of failure of the CNS with intense convulsions and coma. Serious motor disabilities and paralysis of the lower limbs have also been noted.[10] Other neurological disorders such as disorientation, irritability, depression, loss of concentration and coordination are apparent and widespread.[11]

Primary damage occurred in the lungs of most victims. The Bhopal survivors will probably suffer increased incidence of pulmonary fibrosis, emphysema, and chronic bronchitis.[12] Many victims have also complained of easy fatigability and exhaustion that inhibit their ability to function or work normally. Tests by K.E.M. Hospital's cardio-vascular and thoracic department have revealed that some patients have lost as much as 80% of their lung function. Doctors also indicated there are significant cases of interstitial pneumonitis and extensive fibrosis of the lung tissue.[13] It appears that much of this damage may be irreversible. Many of the Bhopal victims also appear to be especially susceptible to secondary infections of the lungs and respiratory tract.[14]

The toxic gas release has also been linked with severe gynecological disorders in women. One preliminary survey of 198 women located within eight kilometers of the Union Carbide plant found 100 with gynecological symptoms.[15] Another study performed on gas-affected women—with a control group of women from similar socio-economic status, occupation and environment—yielded significant findings. The clinical diagnosis is outlined below in Table I.[16]

Evidence of reproductive and fetotoxic effects of MIC are just being established. The Indian Council of Medical Research (ICMR) determined that 36 spontaneous abortions, 27 stillborns and six deformaties could be linked to the MIC leak.[17] In addition, a statistically significant increase in the rates of abortions was noted for women in the gas affected areas as compared to the control population. Private groups claim these numbers to be larger.

Table 1
Clinical Diagnosis of Gas-Affected Women
Compared with a Control Group

	Gas Affected Group	Control Group
Total women studied	114	104
Pelvic examination done	72	52
Leucorrhoea	65/72 (90%)	14/52 (27%)
Pelvic Inflammatory disease (P.I.D)	54/72 (79%)	14/52 (27%)
Cervical erosion and/ or endocervicities	54/72 (75%)	23/52 (44%)
Excessive menstrual bleeding since gas exposure	27/87 (31%)	1/81 (1.2%)
Supression of lactation	16/27 (59%)	2/16 (12%)

C.   Autopsies[18]

Autopsies performed with associates of the Indian Council of Medical Research on 20 post-mortems revealed distinct characteristics. The blood was a cherry-red color and had thickened. The lungs also displayed a red coloring and were two to three times heavier in weight. The respiratory tract showed tracheitis, bronchitis, pulmonary edema, and bronchopneumonic changes in the later stages. The brain, kidney, and liver had been affected in a smaller proportion of the cases.

There were cases of brain edema, neurological damage, degeneration of the liver, and tubular damage of the kidneys. ICMR classified most of these changes as secondary in nature arising out of primary damage to the lungs. Out of the 20 ICMR cases, four had brain damage.

Toxicological Effects of Methyl Isocyanate

Most information available on human health effects from exposure to methyl isocyanate relate to low-dose occupational exposure values. By most reports, MIC is considered an irritant to the eye, nose, and throat with no long-lasting effects.

Very little information is available on chronic effects of MIC or its mode of action within the body.

A.   Available Human Information

Union Carbide, as cited by International Registry of Potentially Toxic Chemicals (IRPTC), states that pulmonary irritations to MIC can include the following symptoms: bronchospasm, asthma-like breathing, chest pain, coughing, choking, and pulmonary edema.[19] The NIOSH/OSHA Health Guidelines for Chemical Hazards warns that exposure to methyl isocyanate may cause a person to become allergic to it so that extremely low levels of exposure may cause asthmatic attack.[20] MIC is a highly toxic chemical, and death can occur in humans from sufficient inhalation.[21]

One case of worker exposure to high levels of MIC has been documented, resulting in an effect on the central nervous system.[22] In this case, a man accidentally took a ''whiff'' of a bottle containing MIC which led to lipo-thymic syndrome with convulsions. In this instance, there was a quick recovery.

B.   Animal Studies

Like the available human data, animal studies on methyl isocyanate focus on short-term effects from acute exposure. These studies include, LC50s,* occular exposure effects, and sensitization tests. Unfortunately, studies have not been performed, as of yet, to determine what possible delayed or chronic effects may occur from exposure to MIC.

* LC50 is an abbreviation for Lethal Concentration for 50% of the tested animal population studied. It, along with LD50 (Lethal Dose under oral ingestion), are measures of acute toxicity; they provide a relative scale for comparing toxicity under conditions of short-term exposure to a chemical agent.

1.   Acute Toxicity Studies (LC50s). A variety of mammalian species were subjected to acute toxicity studies. The most comprehensive studies were conducted with rats, and LC50s values for them are given below.

Table 2

LC50 For Rats by Inhalation 23/

Dose (Milligrams Per Cubic Meter)	Time Period (Minutes)
42.2	240
66.1	120
99.7	60
184.8	30
521.2	15
1,305.4	7.5

2. *Pulmonary Effects*. Several laboratory animal studies were performed which demonstrate the pathogenic effects of MIC exposure.

One rat inhalation study[24] documented the effects of MIC on pulmonary functions. At doses of 36.7 and 97.1 milligrams per cubic meter over a four-hour period, rats displayed signs of dyspnea (difficult or labored breathing), mouth breathing, abdominal breathing, and tachypnea (rapid breathing).

Rats that had been exposed to 150.8 milligrams per cubic meter of MIC for a four-hour period died within 24-48 hours.[25] Autopsies revealed 60-90 per cent hemorrhage with clear fluid present in the pleural cavity.

Other animal studies show pulmonary irritations from MIC to include bronchospasm, and asthma-like breathing, chest pain, coughing, choking, and pulmonary edema.[26]

3. *Central Nervous System*. Animal studies for MIC have generally not been designed to test for delayed neurological effects. In one case, though, rats exposed to 36.7 milligrams per cubic meter and up for a four-hour period showed decreased locomotor activity.[27]

Toxicological Effects of Hydrogen Cyanide

The toxicity of cyanide components, such as hydrogen cyanide, sodium cyanide, etc., rests on its ability to form complexes with metal ions. One set of enzyme complexes which are particularly susceptible are heme-porphyrin complexes. Of those available in the human body, the most important in cyanide poisoning is cytochrome oxidase, an enzyme that simultaneously catalyzes the oxidation of ferrous iron of one cytochrome and the reduction of molecular oxygen. Blockage of this pathway, though irreversible, serves to block the electron-transport system which is essential to cellular respiration.[28]

Therapy for cyanide poisoning is based on provision of substances which will compete with existing exzymes for the cyanide ion (CN-), and enhancement of the body's own detoxification mechanisms.[29] Cyanide combines with sulfur to form thiocyanate (SCN) in what is thought to be an irreversible[30] reaction catalyzed "sluggishly"[31] by an enzyme known as rhodanese (or transulfurase) that is found in many tissues, with its greatest activity in the liver.[32] The preferred sulfur source for this reaction, supplied exogenously, appears to be thiosulfate. (Endogenous sulfur sources have not yet been elucidated.)[33] Relatively non-toxic to the body, thiocyanate accumulates in the extracellular fluid and is excreted by the kidneys "irregularly."[34] One study suggests that eight to 12 mg. per 100 ml is a safe level.[35]

Methemoglobin, an oxidised form of hemoglobin containing ferric ion, combines with high affinity to cyanide to form cyanmethemoglobin, preemptively binding cyanide that would otherwise inactivate cytochrome oxidase.[36] In fact, *in vitro* studies show that "cyanmethemoglobin can reverse CN inhibition of cytochrome- oxidase activity."[37] Conversion of hemoglobin to methemoglobin can n can be induced by amyl nitrite, sodium nitrite or ami-nophenols.[38] Upon dissociation, methemoglobin will spontaneously return to hemoglobin by intraerythrocytic enzymes.[39]

A third substance, vitamin B-12 or hydroxycobalamin, combines with cyanide and is converted to vitamin B12 (cyanocobalamin).[40] However, be-cause of its poor solubility, vitamin B-12 is not suited to use for inactivation of multiple lethal doses.[41]

Due to the rapid absorption of cyanide through alveolar mucosa and skin, cyanide poisoning occurs by inhalation and absorption as well as ingestion.[42] Neither the liquid nor the vapor is an irritant to the skin or the respiratory tract.[43] The average lethal dose for humans, absorbed by tissue, is 0.5-1.5 mg/kg,[44] expressed as HCN. Blood content for a fatal dose due to inhalation of HCN gas is 0.1 mg% or more.[45] According to one source, continual inhalation of cyanide can be tolerated up to 30 ppm due to the body's de-toxification mechanisms, while the OSHA exposure limit is ten ppm (eight-hour time weighted average).[46] The lethal dose by inhalation is approximately 130 ppm.[47] For details see the table below:

Table 3
Relation of HCN in Air and Symptoms in Humans[48]

HCN (ppm)	Symptoms in Humans
1-5	Threshold of odor
20	Maximum safe limit for prolonged exposure
50-60	Maximum tolerable for one-half to one hour
100-150	Dangerous after one-half to one hour
300	May be lethal in a few minues
3,000	Rapidly lethal

A. Acute Symptoms

Acute sumptoms are characterized by unsteadiness, nausea, vomiting, syncope, then coma. Respiration is rapíd, then slow and gasping. The pulse is weak and often fast. Then convulsions, dilated pupils, involuntary urination, and defecation occur.[49] The action of a lethal dose initially causes stimulation of breathing due to anoxia at a cellular level, leading to a receptor cell response to the decrease in oxygen tension.[50] Death results from paralysis of the res-piratory center of the brain.[51] Because oxygen cannot be utilized, venous blood returns a bright red color of oxyhemoglobin,[52] often noted in autopsy findings.

Autopsies to determine cyanide poisoning have the potential to be misdiagnosed. According to one report, cyanide has been shown to be generated spontaneously in bacteriologically sterile blood in the brain, liver, kidney, uterous, and stomach, thereby risking being interpreted as CN poisoning. This phenomenon is explained by two possible mechanisms. Cyanide ions could result from the conversion of other cyanide containing substances present in the blood by blood enzymes, or by the action of cyanide producing bacteria such as *Pseudomonas pyocyaneus*.[53]

B. Chronic Cyanide Poisoning

Cases of workers exposed to cyanide in the workplace form the basis of our picture of chronic cyanide poisoning. Symptoms most often reported include headache, dizziness, nausea, weakness, or easy fatigue.[54] Slightly less often were almond or bitter taste (or "change in taste"), rash, increased sweating, dyspnea, nervousness, weight loss, and increased irritability. Other symptoms mentioned at least once include abdominal colic, irritation of the throat, lacrimation, psychosis, precordial pain, disturbances of accomodation, salivation,[55] eye irritation, nose bleed, cough, sore throat, chest pain, altered sense of smell, disturbed sleep, hemoptysis (spitting of blood from pulmonary hemorrhage), nasal congestion, wheezing, nightsweats, paresthesias of the extremities, syncope (fainting), palpitations, scalp pain,[56] poor vision, slurred speech, body tremor, tachycardia (rapid beating of the heart), muscular cramps, coughing, and sneezing.[57]

In one study of 36 workers, after a median time lapse of 9.5 months since exposure, 44 per cent of the symptoms experienced during active engagement remained.[58] Those residual symptoms which exhibited a significant exposure trend are a rash, a bitter almond taste, and headache.[59]

Studies of the toxic effects of patients treated for hypertension with thiocyanate drugs reveal that these patients experience a strikingly similar set of symptoms. In addition, a number of cases of enlarged thyroid have occurred in both groups, and in animal studies on thiocyanate poisoning. For these reasons it has been suggested that chronic cyanide poisoning may be identical to thiocyanate intoxication.[60]

Thyroid enlargement resulting from cyanide poisoning is due to the interference of several steps of iodine metabolism by thiocyanate or cyanide,[61] leading to lowered concentration of thyroid hormone, increased thyroid-stimulating hormones and subsequent thyroid enlargement.[62] In a study of 36 workers exposed to cyanide, 56 per cent had thyroid enlargements.[63] Goiter has also been reported to occur.[64] Because the thyroid plays a role in pregnancy, it has been postulated that thyroid dysfunction would have repercussions on fetal development.[65] The liver may also undergo certain changes with the depletion of protein bound cobalamin.[66]

Reported neurotoxic symptoms of cyanide containing substances point to a variety of effects. One epidemiological study of a population ingesting cassava, a plant containing cyanogenic glycoside, shows an association with tropical ataxic neuropathy.[67] One case of KCN poisoning in man shows the symptoms of acute anterior poliomyelitis,[68] while KCN studies on rabbits exhibit lesions on the anterior horn cells and myelin degeneration in peripheral nerves.[69] Other KCN studies show partial or complete demyelination of the brain and spinal cord.[70]

Most review papers postulate that neurological damage is most likely because of the secondary effects of CN poisoning, i.e., hypoxia.[71] However, it is not clear whether lesions occur after a single or perhaps after multiple doses of CN.[72] In addition, remyelination can occur, but it is often slow and incomplete.[73] Irreversible brain damage to the cortex occurs after 5-10 minutes of anoxia, and the medulla is impaired after 20-30 minutes.[74]

C. Sodium Thiosulfate (NTS) Therapy

There is no precedent for NTS therapy for chronic cyanide poisoning reviewed in the literature. However, several aspects of cyanide's behavior in the body contribute to our understanding of *how* cyanide could continue to be harbored in the bodies of Bhopal victims, and can help to explain how treatment with NTS might be plausible, even six months later.

According to the literature, "thiocyanate and cyanide are said to exist in an equilibrium through separate metabolic pathways in each direction."[75] Addition of NTS would push this equilibrium toward production of thiocyanate. In addition, and perhaps more importantly, it would provide an exogenous sulfur source which may be critical to a person who has a protein or sulfur deficient diet, or is otherwise malnourished. Liver damage observed at Bhopal may have reduced available stores of the detoxifying enzyme rhodanese and thus retarded thiocyanate production. Foodstuffs that are reported to contain cyanide, like cabbage, mustard, cassava,[76] even contaiminated food, may also contribute to an individual's cyanide pool. Thiocyanate elimination in one study of workers exposed to cyanide averaged 6-13 mg/litre.[77] Data on thiocyanate blood and urine levels before NTS treatment of Bhopal victims would be useful information to fill out the clinical picture.

Toxicological Properties of Monomethylamine (MMA)

A. Physical-Chemical Properties

Monomethylamine ($CH_3 NH_2$) falls into a class of aliphatic amines, derivatives of ammonia in which one or more of the hydrogen atoms are replaced by an alkyl radical. It is a strongly alkaline substance, having a stronger base strength than ammonia, with a dissociation constant, K at 25 degrees = 4.42 x 10^{78} (or pKa = 10.64).[79] The molecular weight of monomethylamine is 31.06, its vapor density is 1.07, slightly denser than air. Its boiling point is -6.5 degrees C and its melting point is -92.5 degrees C.[80] It is a flammable gas at ordinary temperatures and pressure (flashpoint = 0 degrees C), colorless with an ammonia-like odor at high concentrations and a fishy odor at low concentrations. At less than 10 ppm the odor is faint but readily detectable, from 20-100 ppm it becomes strong, and from 100-500 ppm, it is intolerably ammoniacal.[81]

B. Toxicity

Monomethylamine is a severe irritant of the eyes, mucous membranes, and skin. The recorded effects in man are largely limited to the local action of monomethylamine, including irritation of the eyes and respiratory system, coughs, burns, dermatitis, and conjunctivitis.[82] Its routes of entry include inhalation, ingestion, skin absorption, eye, and skin contact. "Exposure to the vapors of the volatile amines produces eye irritation with lacrimation [excessive secretion of tears], conjunctivitis, and corneal edema, resulting in 'halos' around lights.[83] Inhalation causes irritation of the mucous membranes of the nose, throat and lung irritation with respiratory distress and cough."[84]

In animals, "single exposures to near lethal concentrations and repeated exposures to sublethal concentrations result in tracheitis, bronchitis, pneumonitis, and pulmonary edema."[85] The toxicity data for animals, as summarized by Hartung, appear in Table 4.[86]

Table 4

Toxicity of Methylamines for Rabbits

Amine	Dose	Route	Response
Monomethylamine	0.3-0.4 g.	Intravenous	Not fatal
	2 g.	Subcutaneous	Not fatal
Dimethylamine	0.6 g. (salt)		Fatal
	4 g.	Oral	Fatal
Trimethylamine	6 g.	Subcutaneous	Minimum lethal dose
	0.4 g./kg.	Intravenous	Minimum lethal dose
	0.8 g./kg.	Subcutaneous	Minimum lethal dose

Data on the oral and percutaneous toxicity of monomethylamine appear in Table 5.[87] A single skin application will cause necrosis and a drop of monomethylamine solution (40%) applied to a rabbit's eye results in corneal damage.

Table 5
Monomethylamine - Acute Animal Toxicity

Amine	Acute Oral Toxicity LD50, rats (g./kg.)	Skin Irritation, Guinea Pig	Eye Effect, Rabbit
Monomethylamine	0.1 - 0.2 (10% solution)	40% solution, 0.1 ml., necrosis	40% solution, corneal damage

Based on a time weighted average for a 40-hour work week, the threshold limit value (TLV) for monomethylamine was determined to be 10 ppm.[88] Brief exposures to 20-100 ppm produce transient eye, nose, and throat irritation.[89] For mammals, the LC50 for acute inhalation is 2,400 milligrams per cubic meter, (approx. 2,000 ppm).[90] Union Carbide's *Unit Safety Procedures Manual* states that "exposure to 500-5,000 ppm for prolonged period may be fatal."[91]

Reaction and Thermal Decomposition Products of Methyl Isocyanate—A Short Note

Methyl isocyanate (MIC) is a highly reactive, volatile liquid with a low boiling point of 39.1 degrees C (102.4 degrees F) and a freezing point of below -80 degrees C.[92] It reacts strongly with a number of chemical agents such as water, acids, and alkalis. It can also polymerize at a rapid rate in the presence of metallic substances such as iron, tin, copper, and its alloy.[93] The Union Carbide *Material Safety Data Sheet* states that MIC "can undergo a 'runaway' reaction if contaminated" and that the thermal decomposition of MIC "may produce hydrogen cyanide, nitrogen oxides, carbon monoxide and/or carbon dioxide."[94]

It has been postulated that the massive MIC leak that occurred at the UCIL plant in Bhopal on December 2/3, 1984, was caused by water entering a storage tank containing approximately 90,000 lbs. of MIC.[95] It is well established that MIC is readily hydrolyzed by water to form monomethylamine (MMA) in a highly exothermic (heat forming) reaction:[96]

$$CH_3 NCO + H_2O \longrightarrow CH_3 NH_2 + CO_2$$

The monomethylamine formed in the above reaction can undergo further reaction with MIC to form 1,3-dimethylurea (DMU) and 1,3,5-trimethylbiuret (TMB). However, according to the two core residue samples analyzed by

Union Carbide in the MIC storage tank (obtained on December 20, 1984—over two weeks after the accident), only minor amounts of both MMA and TMB (1 to 8%) were found. Moreover, no linear polymers of MIC were present in the core samples, indicating that the formation of the above initial chain reaction products may not be an important route of chemical converstion of MIC.[97]

On the other hand, the predominant chemical substance present in the core samples was a cyclic MIC trimer (40-55%) and another cyclic compound, 1,3-dimethylisocyanurate (DMI) (13 to 20%).[98] The cyclic MIC trimer can be formed directly in an iron-catalyzed reaction of MIC, in the absence of water. Thus, cyclic MIC trimer accounts for up to 5,500 lbs. of the approximately 10,000 lbs. of the residue material left in the MIC storage tank. Of the remainder, another 2,000 lbs. of the residue could consist of DMI, the formation of which requires the presence of isocyanic acid (HNCO) as an intermediate product, formed in another set of complex side reactions of MIC.[99]

It is important to note that of the estimated 90,000 lbs. of MIC present in the storage tank, the Union Carbide Investigation Team Report postulated that 54,000 lbs. (or 60+) of the MIC could have been released into the atmosphere in its unreacted form. This release would have resulted from the high heat and pressure formed in a series of exothermic reaction of MIC, water and chloroform (present as a contaminant). However, based upon the simulated laboratory chemical reaction studies on MIC carried out by Union Carbide, 26,000 lbs. of MIC reaction and thermal decomposition products could not be accounted for.[100] Thus, as mentioned above, the core residue contained only an estimated 10,000 lbs. of reaction products. The Investigation Team Report speculates that much of the remaining unaccounted solid and liquid substances escaped through the safety valves during forming of the reaction mass.[101]

Another possibility of an unaccounted reaction product, not mentioned in the Union Carbide report, is the formation of HCN gas from the thermal decomposition of MIC at elevated temperatures. Blake and Ijadi-Maghsoodi have clearly shown that when MIC is pyrolyzed in the gas phase in the temperature range of 427-548 degrees C, HCN, CO_2 and H_2 gases are formed as major reaction products.[102]

There is strong circumstantial evidence, based on the observation that the cement casing of the stainless steel storage tank cracked during the accident, indicating that temperatures in excess of 400 degrees C may have been achieved in the MIC storage tanks.[103] It is, therefore, highly probably that a significant amount of HCN gas was released during the gas leak at the plant.

In addition to the unreacted MIC and HCN gases being released to the atmosphere, another gasous compound, monomethylamine (MMA) may also have been formed or released. The formation of MMA could have occurred in the first-step reaction of MIC with water, which then escaped in the early phases of the gas leak from the plant. More likely, however, is the formation of MMA after the release of unreacted MIC, where MIC could readily react with atmospheric water vapor to form high levels of airborne MMA.

In summary, while the series of events that caused the catastrophic release of MIC and its reaction products on December 2/3, 1984 in Bhopal cannot be fully ascertained at this time, the most likely scenario indicates that contamination of MIC with water led to a rise in temperature and pressure in the storage tank containing large quantities of MIC. Unreacted MIC, HCN, MMA, and other unknown gases and liquids escaped into the night as a mixture of a highly toxic gas cloud, causing unprecedented death and illness among the citizens of Bhopal.

Notes

1. "Bhopal Gas Tragedy," Delhi Science Forum Report, New Delhi, India, 1985.
2. Srinivasan, K., "Carbide Misled Doctors," *Express News Service*, Bombay, India, January 25, 1985.
3. "Toxicity of MIC Persists in Victims," *The Times of India*, Tuesday, May 14, 1985.
4. *Ibid.*
5. "Health Damage Alarming," *The Times of India*, March 25, 1985.
6. Srinivasan, *supra*, n. 2.
7. *Ibid.*
8. Fera, I., "The Day After," *The Illustrated Weekly of India*, Bombay, India, December 30, 1984—January 5, 1985.
9. *Ibid.*
10. Srinivasan, *supra*, n. 2.
11. Srinivasan, *supra*, n. 2.
12. Bhopal Gas Tragedy, *supra*, n. 1.
13. Fera, I., *supra*, n. 8.
14. Bhopal Gas Tragedy, *supra*, n. 1.
15. "Toxicity of MIC...", *supra*, n. 3.
16. "Effects of the Bhopal Disaster on the Women's Health: An Epidemic of Gynecological Diseases," Rani Bang, M.D., M.P.H., Gopuri, Wardha, India.
17. "6 Deformed Babies in India Linked to Bhopal Gas Leak," *The New York Times*, July 15, 1985.
18. "Thiocyanate in Some Gas Victims Urine," *Express News Service*, New Delhi, India, January 31, 1985.
19. "Methyl Isocyanate," Union Carbide Corporation, F41443A, 17-27, 1976.
20. NIOSH/OSHA, "Occupational Health Guidelines for Chemical Hazards," 1, 1978.
21. "Methyl Isocyanate," *supra*, n. 19.
22. Morel, C. *et al.*, Fiches Toxicologiques (Dans Les Cahiers de Notes Documentaires) 162:452, 1981.
23. Pozzani, U.C. and Kinkead, E.R.., "Animal and Human Response to Methyl Isocyanate," 1, 1966.
24. Fait, I.W. and Dodd, D.E., UNIC1, 43-121, 11, 1981.

25. UNIC2, 26-75, 2, 1963.
26. a. Kimerle, G. and Eben, A., *Archiv Fuer Toxikologie* 20:235, 1964. b. "Methyl Isocyanate," *supra*, n. 19.
27. Fait and Dodd, *supra*, n. 24.
28. Wolfsie, J.W. and Shaffer, C.B.: Hydrogen Cyanide: Hazards, Toxicology, Prevention, and Management of Poisoning, *Journal of Occupational Medicine* 1: 283, 1959.
29. Wolfsie *et al.*, *supra*, n. 28, p. 283.
30. *Ibid.*
31. "Cyanide" book of origin unknown, p.106. [Note re: "slugglishly": cross-referenced from Clemedson *et al.*, 1955]
32. *Ibid.*
33. Wolfsie *et al.*, *supra*, n. 1., p. 283.
34. Hardy, H.L., Jeffries, W.M., Wasserman, M.M., Waddell, W.R.: Thiocyanate Effect Following Industrial Cyanide Exposure, *The New England Journal of Medicine*, p. 968, June 22,1950.
35. *Ibid.*, p. 972.
36. Wolfsie *et al.*, *supra*, n. 28, p. 284.
37. *Ibid.*
38. "Cyanide," *supra*, n. 31, p. 107.
39. *Ibid.*
40. *Ibid.*
41. *Ibid.*
42. Wolfsie *et al.*, *supra*, n. 28, p. 282.
43. *Ibid.*
44. *Ibid.*, p. 283.
45. Niyogi, S.K.: "Drug Levels in Case of Poisoning," *Forensic Science 2*: pp. 67-98, 1973.
46. Wolfsie *et al.*, *supra*, n. 28, p. 283.
47. Blanc, P., Hogan, M., Mallin, K., Hryhorczuk, D., Hessi, S., Bernard, B. "Cyanide Intoxication Among Silver Reclaiming Workers," *Journal of the American Medical Association* 253, n. 3, p. 368, January 18, 1985.
48. *Ibid.*, p. 368.
49. Wolfsie *et al.*, *supra*, n. 28, p. 282 and p. 283.
50. *Ibid.*, p. 284.
51. *Ibid.*, p. 283.
52. *Ibid.*, p. 284.
53. The Production of Cyanide in Post-Mortem Material, *Acta Pharmol. Toxicol* 25: 339-344, 1967.
54. Found in four articles: Elghawabi, S.H., Gaafar, M.A., El-Saharti, A.A., Ahmed, S.H., Malash, K.K., Fares, R.: "Chronic Cyanide Exposure: A Clinical Radioisotope and Laboratory Study," *British Journal of Industrial Medicine* 32, p. 18, 1975; Blanc *et al.*, *supra*, n. 47; Wolfsie, *et al.*, *supra*, n. 28; Hardy *et al.*, *supra*, n. 34.
55. Elghawabi *et al.*, *supra*, n. 54, p. 216.
56. Blanc *et al.*, *supra*, n. 47, p. 369.
57. Hardy *et al.*, *supra*, n. 34, pp. 968-972.
58. Calculated from chart from Blanc *et al.*, *supra*, n. 47, p. 369.
59. *Ibid.*, p. 370.

60. Wolfsie *et al.*, *supra*, n. 28, p. 286.
61. Blanc *et al.*, *supra*, n. 47, p. 368.
62. Elghawabi, *et al*, *supra*, n. 54, p. 218.
63. *Ibid.*, p. 217.
64. "Cyanide," *supra*, n. 31, p. 108.
65. This speculation has been made in articles about Bhopal.
66. Blanc *et al.*, *supra*, n. 47, p. 371.
67. *Ibid.*, p. 368.
68. Hardy *et al.*, *supra*, n. 34, p. 970.
69. *Ibid.*, p. 970.
70. *Ibid.*, p. 971.
71. "Cyanide," *supra*, n. 31, p. 108.
72. *Ibid.*
73. *Ibid.*
74. Wolfsie *et al.*, *supra*, n. 28, p. 286.
75. Blanc *et al.*, *supra*, n. 47, p. 368.
76. Hardy *et al.*, *supra*, n. 34, p. 969.
77. *Ibid.*
78. *The Merck Index: An Encyclopedia of Chemicals and Drugs*, 8th Edition, Merck & Co., Inc., Rahway, NJ, 1968.
79. Sutton, W.L., "Aliphatic and Alicyclic Amines" in Patty, F.A. (ed.), *Industrial Hygeine and Toxicology* 2, ed. 2, New York: Interscience, 1963. p. 2040.
80. *Ibid.* p. 2038.
81. *Ibid.* p. 2052.
82. Sittig, Marshall, *Hazardous and Toxic Effects of Industrial Chemicals*, Noyes Data Corporation, New Jersey, 1979. p. 437.
83. Hanzlik, P.J., *J. Pharmacol. Exptl. Therap.*, 20:435 (1923); Bourne, L.B., *et al*, Brit. *J. Ind. Med.* 16:81 (1959); A.J. Amor, *Mjg. Chemist* 20:540 (1949); cited in Sutton, W.L., *supra*, n. 79, p. 2049.
84. Sutton, W.L., *supra*, n. 79, p. 2049.
85. *Ibid.* p. 2043.86. Hartung, W.H., *Chem. Revs.* 9: 389 (1931) cited in Sutton, W.L., *supra*, p. 2052.
87. Sutton, W.L., *supra*, n. 79, p. 2044 (abridged version of original chart).
88. OSHA Standard, *Federal Register* (U.S. Government Printing Office, Superintendent of Documents, Washington, DC 20402), Vol. 39, p. 23540, 1974; cited in RTECS, Tatken *et al.* (eds.), 1981-1982, NIOSH, U.S. Department of Health and Human Services, p. 711.
89. Sutton, W.L., *supra*, n. 79, p. 2052.
90. Toksikologiya Novykh Promyshlennykh Khimichesckikh Veshehestv. Toxicology of New Industrial Chemical Sciences. (Akademiya Meditsinskikh Nauk S.S.R., Moscow, n. 88, U.S.S.R.) Vol. 14, p. 80, 1975. Cited in *RTECS*, *supra*, n. 88, p. 711.
91. Union Carbide, *Unit Safety Procedures Manual*, cited in Subramaniam, Arun, "Bhopal: The Dangers of Diagnostic Delay", *BusinessIndia*, August 12-25, 1985, p. 133.
92. *Material Safety Data Sheet—Methyl Isocyanate*, Union Carbide Corporation, Danbury, CT.
93. *Ibid.*
94. *Ibid.*

95. *Bhopal Methyl Isocyanate Incident, Investigation Team Report*, Union Carbide Corporation, Danbury, CT, March 1985.
96. *Ibid.*, p.17.
97. *Ibid.*
98. *Ibid.*, p. 14.
99. *Ibid.*, p. 18.
100. *Ibid.*, p. 24.
101. *Ibid.*
102. Blake, P.G. and S. Ljadi-Maghsoodi, "Kinetics and Mechanism of the Thermal Decomposition of Methyl Isocyanate," *International Journal of Chemical Kinetics 14*: 945-952 (1982).
103. Bhushan, B., and A. Subramaniam, "Bhopal: What Really Happened?", Special Report #1, *BusinessIndia*, February 25-March 10, 1985, p. 105.

Appendix 5

The Worst But Not the First: Major Industrial Disasters In This Century

•*Institute, West Virginia* (August 1985): Toxic gases leaked from a Union Carbide pesticide plant that had been retrofitted with new safety systems in the wake of the Bhopal tragedy. No loss of life but some 135 people, including six workers at the plant, required hospitalization.

•*Cubatao, Brazil* (January 1985): A pipeline burst at a government-owned fertilizer manufacturing plant and spewed out 15 tons of liquid ammonia. No one was killed, but over 400 local residents were administered oxygen at first aid posts and some 5,000 others evacuated.

•*Koratty, Kerala, India* (January 1985): Toxic fumes of chlorine leaked from the dyeing section of a large privately owned textile mill. Although no lives were lost, some 40 workers had to be hospitalized.

•*Bhopal, India* (December 1984): Runaway reaction of methyl isocyanate in Union Carbide pesticides plant, killing from 2,500 to 10,000 and injuring 200,000 persons.

•*Mexico City* (November 1984): Explosion of liquified gas tanks belonging to Pemex, the Mexican government oil company, killing at least 452 nearby slum dwellers (the official estimate) and injuring 4,248 in Mexico's largest industrial disaster; more than 1,000 additional persons still listed as missing.

•*Cubatao, Brazil* (February 1984): Gasoline leaking from a pipeline exploded, setting off fires in a shanty-town in the Brazilian state of Sao Paulo. At least 500 people were killed, and several others seriously injured.

•*Denver, Colorado* (April 1983)": The puncturing of a railroad car, during switching operations, released 20,000 gallons of nitric acid. None dead, but at least 43 people were injured and 2,000 others evacuated.

187

•*Livingston, Louisiana* (September 1982): The derailment of 43 railroad cars carrying styrene, toulene, diisocyanate, vinyl chloride, and other chemicals, resulted in spills, explosions, and fires lasting seven days. Although no lives were lost, over 2,800 people were evacuated.

•*Belle, West Virginia* (April 1982): A pipeline carrying chlorine gas burst, releasing 29 tons of the chemical. None dead, but 13 people were injured and 1,700 others evacuated.

•*Montana, Mexico* (August 1981): A train derailment resulted in the rupture of two railroad cars carrying chlorine, releasing 90 tons of the chemical. At least 29 people were killed, over 1,000 injured and 5,000 evacuated.

•*San Juan, Puerto Rico* (May 1981): A valve failure at a chemical plant released two tons of chlorine. None killed, but 200 injured and 2,000 people were evacuated.

•*Newark, New Jersey* (July 1980): A railroad car ruptured and caught fire, releasing 26,000 gallons of ethylene oxide. None dead, but 4,000 workers had to be evacuated, along with people within a half-mile radius of the site of the accident.

•*Muldraugh, Kentucky* (July 1980): The derailment of 18 railroad cars caused two railroad cars carrying vinyl chloride to rupture and go up in flames. No lives lost, but 4 people were injured and 6,500 others evacuated.

•*Garland, Texas* (June 1980): Nine railroad cars derailed and ruptured, spilling 5,000 gallons of styrene. None killed, but five people were injured and 8,600 others evacuated.

•*Port Kelang, Malaysia* (June 1980): A fire resulted in the explosion of cylinders containing ammonia and osyacetylene. The explosion, heard 15 miles away, caused extensive damage, and the port had to be closed for six weeks. Three lives were lost, 200 injured and over 3,000 people were evacuated.

•*Somerville, Massachusetts* (April 1980): A railroad car carrying phosphorous trichloride collided with a locomotive and spilled 6,000 gallons of the chemical. None dead, but 418 people were injured and 23,000 others had to be evacuated.

•*Mississauga, Ontario, Canada* (November 1979): A total of 21 railroad cars carrying caustic soda, chlorine, propane, styrene, and toluene derailed. Three of the railroad cars carrying propane and toluene exploded and caught fire while a fourth railroad car carrying chlorine ruptured and a fire ravaged its contents without exploding. No loss of lives, but eight fire-fighters were injured and 250,000 people were evacuated.

•*Crestview, Florida* (April 1979): Seventeen railroad cars carrying acetone, anhydrous ammonia, carbolic acide, chlorine, and methanol derailed. The chemicals released by the ruptured railroad cars triggered fires and explosions. No one was killed, but 1,000 people were injured and 4,500 others had to be evacuated.

•*Three Mile Island, Pennsylvania* (March 1979): Radiation leak from General Public Utilities nuclear power plant, forcing the evacuation of some 60,000 people from surrounding areas.

•*San Carlos de la Rapita, Spain* (July 1978): An overloaded 38-ton truck carrying 1,518 cu. ft. of combustible propylene gas skidded around a bend and slammed into a wall, sending 100-ft. high flames into a campsite where 780 tourists were eating, sunbathing, and swimming. Some 215 lives were lost and several others injured.

•*Seveso, Italy* (July 1976): An uncontrolled exothermic reaction in a reactor at the Hoffman-LaRoche Givaudan chemical plant caused a terrific explosion. The ensuing release of some 10-22 lbs. of toxic tetrachlorodibenzo-p-dioxin contaminated soil and vegetation over 4,450 acres of land, and killed over 100,000 grazing animals. Although there were no immediate injuries or loss of human life, over 1,000 residents were forced to flee, and many children subsequently developed a disfiguring rash called chloracne.

•*Flixborough, England* (June 1974): A railroad car carrying cyclohexane at a NYPRO, Ltd. plant ruptured, resulting in the escape of about 400 metric tons of the chemical. The cyclohexane cloud exploded, setting off a fire over 20 acres of land. The blast killed 28 people, injured 89 and 3,000 others had to be evacuated; it also levelled every building on the 60-acre plant site.

•*Cali, Columbia* (August 1956): Seven trucks loaded with dynamite exploded in the center of Cali, destroying over 200 buildings, and leaving a crater 85 feet deep and 200 feet wide. Some 1,100 lives were lost.

•*Ludwigshafen, Germany* (July 1948): A railway car transporting dimethy-lether, used in the manufacture of acetic acid and dimethylsulfate, to the I.G. Farben chemical plant exploded inside the factory gates. The blast and re-sulting fire killed 207 people and injured 4,000 others.

•*Texas City, Texas* (April 1947): A freighter, carrying 1,400 tons of ammo-nium nitrate fertilizer, exploded after fire broke out on board, setting off a series of secondary explosions that destroyed much of Texas City. The blast rattled windows 150 miles away and the leaping flames also destroyed a nearby Monsanto factory producing a combustible ingredient of synthetic rubber, i.e., styrene. The next day another freighter, also loaded with nitrates, exploded in the same harbor. Some 576 people were killed and 2,000 others seriously injured.

•*Cleveland, Ohio* (October 1944): A poorly designed liquefied natural gas tank belonging to the East Ohio Gas Company developed structural weakness which led to a massive explosion. The resulting blast and fire claimed some 131 lives.

•*Oppau, Germany* (September 1921): The biggest chemical explosion in Ger-man history occurred at a nitrate manufacturing plant about 50 miles south of Frankfurt. The blast destroyed the plant, a warehouse, and levelled houses four miles away in the nearby village of Oppau. At least 561 lives were lost and some 1,500 people were injured.

•*Halifax, Nova Scotia, Canada* (December 1917): A French ship carrying about 1,000 tons of ammunition collided with a Belgian steamship, setting off explosions that destroyed a two-square-mile area of Halifax. Some 1,650 people were killed.

•*New York* (March 1911): Triangle Shirtwaist Company fire, killing 146 sweat-shop workers and leading to the New York State Factory Investigating Commission, which sparked reform of working conditions for industrial labor. The Commission spawned 56 new laws that set the basic standards for industrial safety and conditions for employing men, women, and children which we take for granted today.

Source: Martin Abraham, *The Lessons of Bhopal: A Community Action Resource Manual on Hazardous Technologies*, Penang, Malaysia: International Organisation of Consumers Unions, 1985, with additional events and details added by the authors.